The Good Ships of Newport News

Tug *Sparrows Point* of the Curtis Bay Towing Company backing down to get a towline aboard the James River Reserve Fleet ship *Santa Clara Victory*, February 24, 1971. (*See* Chapter 19.)

THE GOOD SHIPS
OF NEWPORT NEWS

An Informal Account of Ships, Shipping and
Shipbuilding in the Lower Chesapeake Bay
Region Together with the Story of the
Last Terrible Voyage of the *Yarmouth Castle*

By ALEXANDER CROSBY BROWN

TIDEWATER PUBLISHERS/*Cambridge, Maryland*/1976

Library of Congress Cataloging in Publication Data

Brown, Alexander Crosby, 1905-
  The good ships of Newport News.

  Includes index.
  1. Ship-building--Newport News, Va.--History.
2. Ships--History.   3. Steam-navigation--
Chesapeake Bay--History.   I. Title.
VM25.N45B76   623.82'009755'416   76-12100
ISBN 0—87033—220-1

Bay steamer drawing, courtesy Steamship Historical Society of America.

Title page designed by G. William Kirschenhofer; printed and bound in the United
States of America by Universal Lithographers, Inc., Cockeysville, Maryland and
Optic Bindery, Glen Burnie, Maryland.

Contents

Dedicated to

ELIAS SHIRLEY (BIG RED) BAYSDEN
1891–1974
A great shipbuilder
And a fine father-in-law
And to the many others who devoted their lives
to building Good Ships
"At a profit if we can—at a loss if we must"
for Newport News

Other Books by Alexander Crosby Brown

LONGBOAT TO HAWAII: An Account of the Voyage of the Clipper Ship *Hornet* (Assembled and Edited, 1974)

CHESAPEAKE LANDFALLS (1974)

CROSSES OF TEARS: The Miracle of the Fairy Stones (Children's Operetta, with Harold Chapman, 1971)

THE DISMAL SWAMP CANAL (1946; Revised and Enlarged, 1967 and 1970)

FOR HIS DEAR SAKE: A History of St. Andrew's Parish (1969)

DINGLE DINOSAUR'S GOOD DEED (With Shirley Hogge, 1967)

LIFE WITH GROVER: A Chesapeake Bay Retriever Who Thought He Was a Person (1962)

STEAM PACKETS ON THE CHESAPEAKE: A History of the Old Bay Line Since 1840 (1961)

WOMEN AND CHILDREN LAST: The Loss of the Steamship *Arctic* (1961)

MR. HARDY LEE: His Yacht (Edited, 1950)

THE MARINERS MUSEUM: A History and Guide, 1930-1950 (1950)

NEWPORT NEWS' 325 YEARS (Edited, 1946)

THE OLD BAY LINE, 1840-1940 (1940)

TWIN SHIPS: Notes on the Use of Multiple Hulled Vessels (1939)

HORIZON'S RIM: 'Round-the-World Voyage of the Schooner *Chance* (1935)

Preface

The twenty-one stories which comprise this book originally appeared in a variety of newspapers and magazines over the past twenty-one years, but mostly in the Sunday *New Dominion* Magazine Section of the Daily Press, Inc., of which I was then Literary Editor. All have to do with ships and in all but two, these are vessels identified in some capacity with Chesapeake Bay—specifically with Newport News or the adjacent waters of the James River and Hampton Roads. But chiefly they concern products of the great Newport News Shipbuilding and Dry Dock Company. For well over three-quarters of a century, this shipyard has established an enviable reputation for its products on all the Seven Seas.

Each article here has been given a new introduction, telling when, where and how it happened to have been written in the first place, as well as providing information to bring it up to date in the light of later events. I make no claims for literary perfection, but can confess to deriving a lot of pleasure from writing the stories—particularly those that took me afield, to watch the liner *United States* arrive at New York and the *Queen Elizabeth* sail away forever, as well as photographing excursions in the more immediate neighborhood. All illustrations not specifically credited to others were taken by me.

I am grateful to the editors of *The American Neptune*, the *Daily Press*, the Baltimore *Sunday Sun*, the United States Naval Institute *Proceedings*, *The Commonwealth: The Magazine of Virginia*, and *The State* (North Carolina) for permission to reprint material from their pages. I also thank a host of friends and associates who have helped along the way—particularly Will Molineux, Ruth Taylor, Howard E. Lee and Robert B. Smith of the Daily Press, Inc.; Board Chairman William McL. Ferguson, John L. Lochhead, Robert H. Burgess and William T. Radcliffe of The Mariners Museum; Phyllis Kyle Stephenson and Carl Cannon of Newport News Shipbuilding; Dr. Francis J. Braceland, my brother-in-law, for his memoir of the *Morro Castle* disaster; not to mention the hospitality of Frank O. Braynard, then Public Relations Director of the Moran Towing and Transportation Company, and to the knowledgeable custodians of the United States Maritime Administration's James River Reserve Fleet. And I particularly appreciate the kindness of The Mariners Museum, of Newport News, Virginia, and the Newport News Daily Press, Inc., in granting permission to use many of their valuable photographs reproduced here. My own prints were carefully processed for me by the Daily Press Photography Department under the direction of Bill Bonsor and Bea Kopp. To all, many thanks.

But since so much of the material covers the careers of Good Ships built at Newport News, my particular pleasure is to cite here the names of some of the veteran Shipyard people I have known who made them possible.

George Abernathy	Frank Harvey	Carl Penny
Ralph Angell	Eddie Heard	Pete Peterson
Al Ankers	Ned Hewins	Doug Petty
John Bader	Johnny Hogge	Jim Plummer
C.F. Bailey	Don Holden	Penny Plummer
Smokey Baker	Wythe Holt	John Pruden
Red Baysden	Joe Holzbach	Jack Reilly
Harold Bent	Bob Hopkins	Mark Ritger
Sumner Besse	Eddie Huffman	Lem Robertson
Bill Blewett	Andrew Hull	Ed Robeson
Lem Branch	Don Hyatt	E.G. Rogers
Alvin Butterworth	Mark Ireland	Shag Rutter
John Campbell	Gene Jaeger	Graham Scott
John P. Comstock	Cargill Johnson	Ran Scott
Alvin Cox	Jack Kane	E.O. Smith
Ralph Cyrus	Kemper Kellogg	Tilly Smith
Charles Dart	Karl Koontz	Ernest Sniffen
Fred Davis	Tom Lanier	L.R. Sorenson
Bob Fee	Frank Larkin	Charlie Soter
Homer Ferguson	Charlie Macdonald	Miss N.M. Tilley
M.M. Fitzhugh	J.A. Maclay	Tommy Tompkins
Bob Fletcher	W.S. McMahon	Bruce Vanderboegh
Otto Folkmann	George Mason	Guy Via, Jr.
William Gatewood	Bill Metts	Guy Via, Sr.
Donald Gay	Dwight Moorhead	Syd Vincent
W.W. Geggie	Harold F. Norton	Mike Ward
Herp Giese	Charley Palen	Monk White
E.P. Griffith	George Parker	Roger Williams
P.F. Halsey	Ken Peebles	Paul Wilson
Clifford Hancock	Joe Pendleton	Brock Woodward
Cas Hardaway		

Newport News, Virginia   A.C.B.

The Good Ships of Newport News

CHAPTER 1

(1893)

The Jaunty *Pocahontas,*
Pride of the James River

Tidewater Virginia was "peopled and planted" by ship. The confluence of many rivers at the lower end of Chesapeake Bay made it simpler for the pioneer colonists to use water, rather than attempt overland routes, as they gradually occupied territory wrested from the Indians. Soon every plantation had its river- or branch-side wharf, and boats propelled by sail or oar shuttled back and forth across the bays, estuaries and streams that comprised this "well-watered" land. Shipwrights were in great demand as the earliest settlers began to improve on the dugout canoes that the Indians used, thus creating a wide variety of colonial sailing craft for fishing and transport.

By the 18th century, well-established routes had been set up with numerous ferry crossings and lines branching out in all directions, with Norfolk—still the only lower Bay settlement qualifying as a city—at the center. Sailing packets crossed to Eastern Shore ports, served Mobjack Bay and adjacent waters and navigated the James to Richmond. When, early in the 19th century, the steamboat was invented to provide quick and more dependable transportation, Tidewater Virginia received it with open arms.

By the time the stories covered in this book occurred, a wide variety of steamboat lines were in regular operation, connecting all points in the lower Chesapeake by sailing out of Norfolk. Bay steamers also sailed up to Baltimore to join the vast network of craft radiating from there, as is well chronicled in Robert H. Burgess' and H. Graham Wood's splendid *Steamboats Out of Baltimore,* published by Tidewater Publishers in 1968.

Until the 1880s, when railroad magnate Collis P. Huntington acquired the Chesapeake and Ohio and extended its line down the peninsula from Richmond, Newport News was merely a hamlet of farmhouses and fishing shacks with a pier or two sticking out into deep water at Newport News Point, often called Point Breeze. George B. West recorded that people wanting to catch the steamboat between Norfolk and Richmond would wave a white flag on a stick at the end of West's Pier as the boat hove in sight, and the yawl would be sent in to pick them up.

Newport News proved to be a boom town. Huntington built a complex of coal-dumping piers and merchandise wharves and, in 1886, his Chesapeake Dry Dock and Construction Company was incorporated to handle repairs needed by vessels that called at the port in increasing numbers. But four years later, when plans were made to build a new iron-hull steam tug, the *Dorothy,* the company name was altered to reflect its new purpose as the Newport News Shipbuilding and Dry Dock Company. Founder Collis died in 1900, but the shipyard remained in the Huntington family as a private

1

corporation until 1940 at which time it was sold and shares offered to the public on the New York Stock Exchange. The existing management and policy continued, however, until 1968 when Tenneco, Inc., acquired control of the company.

The *Dorothy*, incidentally, is still in existence. Launched on December 17, 1890, the 90-foot, 180-ton tug was named for a daughter of William C. Whitney, an officer of the New York and Northern Railroad Company, for whom the vessel was built for use in towing in New York Harbor and the East River. She performed several years' service there and returned to Hampton Roads where, with a new diesel engine and the new name, *J. Alvah Clark*, she continued to ply her trade in local waters beginning in 1912.

Eventually the venerable towboat was acquired by Captain Raymond K. Davis of Newport News, who in 1923 at the age of 14, had served on board her as a deckhand. Davis used the *Dorothy* in his towing business until need of a new engine required putting her out to pasture at a dock in Newport

The 1890-built steam tug *Dorothy*, Hull No. 1 of the Newport News Shipbuilding and Dry Dock Company, is shown in this drawing as she will appear when reconditioned and displayed in front of the company's headquarters on Washington Avenue as a permanent monument to the organization's growth and history during the Bicentennial year.
Courtesy Newport News Shipbuilding.

News' Municipal Small Boat Harbor. Davis' firm merged with Allied Towing Company of Norfolk in the late 1960s and the long-neglected but still floating craft was towed over to Allied's facilities on the Eastern Branch of the Elizabeth River. No one paid her much attention and subsequently she filled with rainwater and quietly settled in the mud.

In the autumn of 1974, however, Allied, now needing the space the hulk occupied, pumped out the *Dorothy* and announced that they proposed to sell her for scrap. At this point I joined two Newport News Shipbuilding officials who had been watching the old boat for some time and we journeyed to Elizabeth River to look her over. We were agreeably surprised how well she looked, for her mud-streaked and battered appearance failed to hide the sweet lines and graceful sheer of the 83-year-old vessel. Determining that in the main her hull was still sound, upon our return we strongly recommended to the company that the *Dorothy* be purchased at her declared scrap value and be preserved.

Recognizing that not many manufacturing concerns could boast of showing off their very first product, shipyard president John P. Diesel then decided that the *Dorothy* should be spared the indignity of the ship wrecker. Accordingly, the vessel was purchased, small holes in her hull were temporarily plugged and the *Dorothy*, in tow of her younger sister tug, *Huntington*, was proudly returned across Hampton Roads to her birthplace.

President Diesel has announced that the *Dorothy*, plucked from her natural element by a giant shipyard crane and now cleaned and painted on the outside, will be returned to her former jaunty appearance and be permanently displayed. We applaud his vision in providing this proud shipbuilding community tangible proof of founder Huntington's much quoted dictum: "We shall build good ships. . . ."

Iron-hull paddle-wheel steamboat, *Ariel* at a James River landing. She began service on the James in 1878 and served until replaced by the new *Pocahontas* in 1893. She was scrapped in 1902. *From a photograph by Cook, Richmond, courtesy of The Mariners Museum.*

Approaching the turn of the century, the city of Newport News continued to grow and prosper, thus becoming a center of ship lines with local vessels serving Norfolk, Old Point Comfort, Hampton, Smithfield and James River landings. Their calls were made at Pier "A," which projected out into the river at the foot of 25th Street. Oceangoing craft stopping at the Chesapeake and Ohio Railway Company piers plied the Atlantic Seaboard and also served transoceanic ports.

One of the first Richmond boats which made regular stops at Newport News was a side-wheeler, the *Ariel*. In 1893 she was replaced on the day-long run by the new and elegant paddle steamer, *Pocahontas*, the subject of the following story. I have always been intrigued by the smart and saucy-seeming

"A Moonlight Excursion to Old Point Comfort, Va." The James River steamboat *Pocahontas* plied the river from 1893 to 1919 on daylight service between Norfolk, Newport News and Richmond. *From an 1893 lithograph in the collection of The Mariners Museum.*

little *Pocahontas*—like her Indian namesake—as she jauntily cut the wave
with her excessively tall black smokestack emitting a rich and pungent plume
of soft coal smoke—presently anathema to the environmentalists. I first attempted to reconstruct the boat's life story and began collecting pictures for
an article on her which appeared in the July, 1942, issue of *The American
Neptune*, the maritime historical quarterly.

The ensuing account, written in a more popular vein, appeared in the
Daily Press Sunday feature section of August 23, 1959, as one of a series of
articles on the "Good Old Days of Steamboating in Newport News Waters."

Subsequently, Virginia historian Parke Rouse, Jr., writing in the November 17, 1974, issue of the Norfolk *Virginian-Pilot*, discovered rocking on his
front porch in Charles City County, one Eddie Newsome, a 76-year-old
former fireman of the *Pocahontas* who proudly reported that his erstwhile
ship "could beat almost anything on the river," concluding that "Cap'n
Graves was the best skipper of them all."

––––––––––––

A favorite indoor sport of Virginia Peninsula old-timers—for that matter
of old-timers anywhere—is looking backwards to regret the passing of the
"good old days."

Certainly, in several respects, recent advances in technology and the increase in tempo of modern life have contrived to leave by the wayside many
of the more leisurely and pleasant activities of yesteryear. This is particularly
apparent in the field of transportation. The present jet-propelled generation
has witnessed first the decline, and now the extinction, of one of the most
enjoyable modes of travel—the once commonplace steamboat which finally
found itself no longer able to compete with swifter automobiles, buses and
aircraft.

One of the local casualties most to be bemoaned—since it afforded an
incomparably pleasant day-long diversion—was the steamboat line plying the
James River. Some Peninsula residents probably recall with nostalgic pangs
the enjoyment of a trip on the swift steamboat *Pocahontas* from Newport
News to Richmond in those selfsame "good old days." It cost only $1.50 to
make the journey then and the round-trip fare was but $2.50.

The *Pocahontas*, proud "palace steamer" of the Virginia Navigation Company, was built in 1893 and commanded for many years by Captain Charles
C. Graves, described by a former shipmate as "the best man on the river."
She plied the James for a full quarter century before being relegated to a
distant run in New Jersey waters, then eventually retired. This craft provided
the only outside link for many Virginia riverside dwellers. She zigzagged
from riverbank to riverbank transporting passengers, mail and varied freight,
on her 125-mile voyages up- and downstream.

The steamer's arrival at a way landing was always a matter of considerable
moment. Country folk along the route gravitated down to the wharf about
the time the boat was due and there was bustle and excitement as preparations were made for her to stop. First a flag was raised at the end of the pier
to signify that freight was there to be picked up. Then, rounding a river
bend, she hove in sight and headed in for a landing, backing down on the
paddles as the roustabouts caught and secured the mooring lines. Oftentimes
an unwilling cow had to be urged on board by kicks and tail-twisting. The
stops were never long, though, for the *Pocahontas* took pride in keeping to

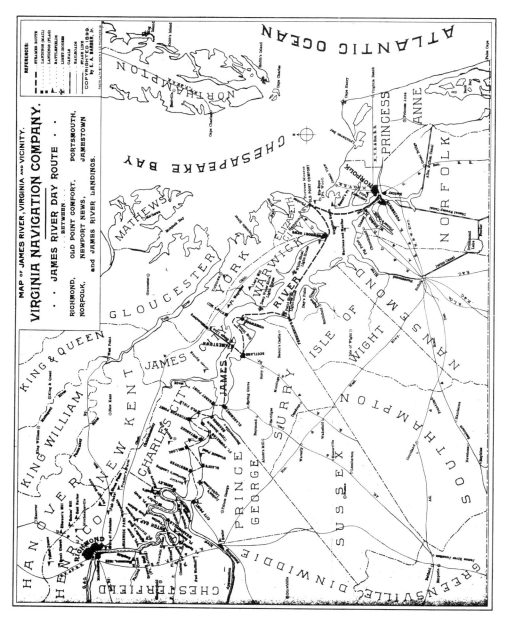

A map of the James River published in 1899 by the Virginia Navigation Company showing the route of the *Pocahontas* from Norfolk to Old Point Comfort, Newport News and James River landings to Richmond. *Courtesy of The Mariners Museum.*

6

her schedule. So, in a matter of moments, the boat gave an imperious toot on her steam whistle, the gangway was hauled ashore and she was on her way once more.

A map of the *Pocahontas'* route appeared in a Virginia Navigation Company leaflet, indicating the course she took by dotted line. It also showed the various scheduled stops and briefly described the sights afforded "Gay Nineties" travelers along the way.

The leaflet also gave the following description of the boat itself, then a new replacement for a still earlier side-wheel steamer, the *Ariel*, which had been in service on the river route from the days when Newport News was still a collection of fishing shacks and farmhouses.

"The Steamer *Pocahontas:* A Beautiful Stranger upon the James," the company leaflet was headed, going on to say that:

This recently completed vessel was built at Wilmington, Del., and is the handsomest craft ever employed in Southern waters. She is admirably designed for both first-class passenger and freight service. The hull is constructed of steel; length 205 feet; width, over guards, 57 feet; depth of hold, 11 feet. The main deck is fitted aft with roomy cabins for ladies, colored servants, and passengers, a broad social hall, barber shop, purser's office, mail-agent's room, smoking and bar-serving room, and card rooms.

The promenade deck is planned to afford abundant space fore and aft for outlook. A series of family state-rooms are ranged along each side amidships. The hurricane deck is arranged for the use of passengers. The finish is white and gold, with silk hangings and rich velvet carpetings. The chandeliers are in wrought iron and bronze. Steam heat and electric lighting are used throughout.

A novel feature is the electric orchestrion, giving the musical effects of a full band, which graces the promenade saloon.

A powerful searchlight is operated at night from the inside of the pilothouse.

The engine is of the most approved type, having an indicated horsepower of 2,100.

As the steamer runs throughout the year, a fine sun parlor encloses a portion of the forward deck in the inclement season. The dining-room is equipped with unusual care and taste and the service ranks with the best hotels. . . .

Leaving Norfolk at six o'clock in the morning, the swift *Pocahontas* first steamed over to Old Point Comfort before heading westward. At Newport News she docked at old Pier "A" at the end of 25th Street, a bustling communication center with steamboats coming and going for Smithfield and other points and fishing and trading vessels unloading all sorts of produce—vast quantities of watermelons in season—at the foot of the busy city.

Citing the Chesapeake and Ohio Railway's grain elevator as providing Newport News' then most conspicuous feature, the leaflet went on to state:

During the war [the Civil War, naturally!] this place was a great military camp, well fortified, and immediately in front occurred the sinking of the frigate, *Cumberland*, and the destruction by fire of the *Congress* by the Confederate ram, *Merrimack*, or, as she was called in the South, the *Virginia*, and the subsequent famous fight between the latter and the *Monitor*.

In addition to the great terminal wharves and buildings of the Chesapeake and Ohio Railway, the Newport News Shipbuilding and Dry Dock Company has in operation here one of the most costly plants in the United States, having attracted a population now numbering several thousands.

Leaving Newport News, the *Pocahontas'* next stop was at Fergusson's Landing in Burwell Bay, Isle of Wight County, not far from the present anchorage of the James River Reserve Fleet. This was a busy fishing point. A few miles farther along on the same side of the river, but in Surry County, she tied up at Homewood on Hog Island. Homewood, the leaflet advised, was "the pretty name bestowed by its late owner, Mr. Edward E. Barney,"

The jaunty river steamer *Pocahontas* leaving the Old Dominion Line pier at Norfolk, around 1910. *From an H.C. Mann photograph, courtesy of The Mariners Museum.*

on one of the finest plantations along the river. Directly opposite was King's Mill Wharf, originally the mail landing and stage route for Williamsburg.

Next stop was Scotland, an important lumber shipping point where the *Pocahontas* made connections with the now long-defunct Surry, Sussex and Southampton Railroad, one of Virginia's few narrow gauge lines. Opposite Scotland lies Jamestown. The leaflet devoted a lengthy paragraph to the history of this famous spot, mentioning parenthetically that, "from this historic place the steamer is supplied with pure drinking water from flowing artesian wells, and also many table delicacies."

It also stated that Mrs. Edward E. Barney, then the island's owner, had presented some land in the neighborhood of Jamestown's old ruined church tower—the only above-ground relic of early colonial days—to the Association for the Preservation of Virginia Antiquities. It was, of course, the A.P.V.A. who was initially responsible for proper recognition being given to Jamestown as a national shrine, thus making possible the Tercentenary Exposition

A circa-1910 view of the Newport News' Pier "A" at the foot of 25th Street. The steamboats moored to the pier are the *Pocahontas* (left) and the *Smithfield*. Under way and steaming by anchored vessels off Newport News' Casino Grounds is the *Accomack*.
Library of Congress photograph, courtesy of The Mariners Museum.

in 1907, the recent 350th anniversary observances and the now permanent Jamestown Festival Park.

Thereafter, stops made by the *Pocahontas* on her upstream course read like the focal points on a contemporary Garden Week tour—Claremont, "long regarded as the finest estate in Virginia"; Brandon, "a splendid old estate and still in the hands of the original family of Harrisons"; Upper Brandon; Weyanoke; Westover; Berkeley; Bermuda Hundred. But travelers recalled that unless flagged down by someone waving a white cloth, the boat did not stop.

After Bermuda Hundred the river narrows with the Appomattox branching off from it at City Point. Then comes Shirley, Malvern Hill,

Curle's Neck, Deep Bottom, Meadowville, Varina, Fort Darling, Warwick Park, and finally journey's end at Rocketts Landing just below Richmond in front of Libby Hill. If the steamboat had not been delayed by more than ordinary amounts of freight, the time would be 5:30 p.m.

Possibly that evening, if it were summertime and the moon was right, the *Pocahontas* would steam a few miles back down the river to Warwick Park for an evening excursion. But the next morning would see her ready to retrace her course for Norfolk once more. Mondays, Wednesdays and Fridays, the *Pocahontas* headed downstream. Tuesdays, Thursdays and Saturdays she went up. Sunday, appropriately, was her day of rest.

A few derelictions could be noted in her long career—the *Pocahontas* occasionally ran aground and had to wait for the tide to be refloated. Once in a while she banged into the wharves too hard and on one occasion she perilously came all too close to turning over when a deckload of excursionists all hurried across to one side of the vessel to look at something extraordinary going by. However, Captain Graves promptly spun the wheel and, as the *Pocahontas* came into a sharp turn, he thus set up a counter list until the boat could be brought back to proper trim once more.

But the worst thing that happened to her was a disastrous fire on the night of April 30, 1904. Fortunately she had completed her day's run and was tied up—with only a skeleton crew on board—to her dock at Rocketts when a watchman discovered flames. The Richmond Fire Department was called out to fight its first shipboard conflagration. But there was no stopping it. Gingerbread decorations and wicker furniture "burned like tinder" said the *Times-Dispatch*, and made a "striking picture."

Ultimately, enough water was pumped into the *Pocahontas* to sink her and the fire went out. Destruction was first thought to be total, but when the charred ruins cooled and the hull was refloated, it was discovered that the boat was still sufficiently sound to make rebuilding worthwhile. This was done and, a year later, she had been completely restored according to her original plans.

The Old Dominion Line took over the Virginia Navigation Company in 1906, but the *Pocahontas* continued the same tri-weekly daylight sailings up and down the river. Her later career may be briefly related. After World War I, the Old Dominion Line gave up its short line services including those of the *Pocahontas*' nocturnal running mates—the sister ships, *Berkeley* and *Brandon*, propeller steamers which alternated on overnight trips between Norfolk and Richmond. In 1920, then, the *Pocahontas* was sold to the Keansburg (New Jersey) Steamboat Company. For another 15 years the venerable little vessel plied across lower New York Bay between Keansburg and the tip of Manhattan Island. Finally, too ancient for further use even as a spare boat, she was allowed to rest on the mud at Keyport, New Jersey, and was broken up in November, 1939. One relic of the old vessel has come back to this locality. Robert H. Burgess, then exhibits curator of The Mariners Museum and well-acclaimed Chesapeake Bay historian, owns a nameboard from the 46-year-old craft.

Many local residents would enjoy a cruise on the James River today—if they could get it. It is sad that the way of life typified by the *Pocahontas* is so irrevocably past.

CHAPTER 2

(1894)

U.S. Gunboat *Nashville,*
the Ship that Fired the First Shot

The Newport News Shipbuilding and Dry Dock Company's initial venture in shipbuilding produced the tug, *Dorothy,* cited in the previous chapter. This 90-foot iron craft was completed and delivered on April 30, 1891, being followed by a tug of similar dimensions, the *El Toro,* less than a month later. Then came along a quartet of 7,360-ton cargo steamers for the Morgan Line in which yard founder Huntington had an interest. They were named *El Sud, El Norte, El Rio* and *El Cid* and were delivered between July, 1892, and August, 1893.

Collis Huntington realized, however, that although ship repair work was booming, the permanent success of his shipyard depended on obtaining new government construction work and, to this end, he requested President C.B. Orcutt to make every attempt to secure naval contracts as soon as possible. The Navy's Great White Fleet was then coming into being and the shipyard's first chance to bid in this area was for construction of the battleship, *Iowa,* and the armored cruiser, *Brooklyn.* Bids were opened December 15, 1892, but Cramps Shipyard of Philadelphia, a veteran and experienced concern, had underbid Newport News and, accordingly, got the jobs.

Orcutt was determined that this should not happen again. When the opportunity came to bid on three gunboats for the Navy the following year, he was ready and Newport News submitted the lowest bid. Contract for the *Nashville,* Newport News Hull No. 7, the first of the three craft, was awarded January 22, 1894. Hull Nos. 8 and 9—the *Wilmington* and *Helena*—followed a week later.

As the first of what has subsequently been a long line of U.S. Navy supervisory people assigned to the yard, Constructor J.J. Woodward, U.S.N., arrived at Newport News at this time. One of his associates was Albert L. Hopkins. He became the shipyard's fourth president, only to lose his life a short time later in the sinking of the *Lusitania,* as related in Chapter 7.

The *Nashville* distinguished herself soon after commissioning by being the ship that fired the first shot of the Spanish-American War—Teddy Roosevelt's "Splendid Little War" which looks something less than glorious in historical perspective. That wasn't the *Nashville's* fault, however. She had a long and useful dual career—from 1895 to 1918 as a gunboat; from 1918 to 1957, more prosaically, as a barge.

The following "cradle-to-grave" account appeared in the United States Naval Institute *Proceedings'* "A Page from the Old Navy" in the June, 1958, issue.

In June, 1957, I made a sentimental pilgrimage to Camden Mills, Virginia, to see what was left of an old, historic ship before the bite of the shipbreaker's torch reduced her to

11

scrap metal. Fast on the muddy bottom of the southern branch of the Elizabeth River lay
the worn-out hull while the tide rose and fell inside her rust-streaked hold. Her long sharp
bow and sweptback, tumblehome sides bore the disfiguring marks of her final employment afloat as *Richmond Cedar Works No. 4*, a cut-down barge for carrying logs. She was,
however, the once proud U.S. Gunboat, *Nashville*, the ship that fired the first shot of the
Spanish-American War. Her other claim to fame was as the product of the first government contract awarded to the young and struggling Newport News Shipbuilding and Dry
Dock Company.

Launching of the U.S. Navy gunboat *Nashville* at Newport News, October 19, 1895. The
Nashville was the first ship built at the Newport News Shipbuilding and Dry Dock
Company for the Navy. *Shipyard photograph, courtesy of Mrs. Phyllis Kyle Stephenson.*

The significance of the contract to Newport News, signed on January 22, 1894, was of
greater consequence than might have then been imagined. For the little gunboat of only
1,371 tons displacement became the first of a long and illustrious line of naval vessels
built for Uncle Sam that is climaxed today by the *Forrestal* and *Ranger* and the atomic-
powered *Enterprise* now [1958] taking shape. The *Nashville's* 233-foot overall length was
not as great as the flight deck width of today's giant aircraft carriers.

The *Nashville's* keel was laid on August 9, 1894, and she was launched with much ceremony on October 19, 1895, being followed down the same shipways later in the day by the gunboat *Wilmington*, whose contract was signed only a week after the *Nashville's*.

The ship was characterized by two slim and extremely tall funnels and had the following dimensions as completed: 233'8" length overall, 220' length between perpendiculars, 38' beam, 25'1" depth, and 11' mean draft. She had two, quadruple expansion, reciprocating steam engines and developed 2,524 indicated horsepower on official trials. She had six Mosher boilers and bunker capacity for 363 tons of coal. Her armament consisted of eight 4-inch, 40-caliber, rapid-fire guns, and two each 6-, 3-, and 1-pounder, rapid fire guns. On her trials she logged 16.30 knots.

The *Nashville's* big moment came less than a year after her first commission. With war clouds fiercely gathering following the unprovoked destruction of the U.S. Battleship *Maine* in Havana Harbor, units of the Atlantic Fleet including the new gunboat were stationed at Key West, ready the moment that war was declared to establish a blockade of the Spanish West Indies. Finally, on the evening of April 21, 1898, the word came

The gunboat *Nashville* pursuing the Spanish freighter *Buena Ventura* at the outset of the Spanish-American War, April 22, 1898. *From a painting by Thomas C. Skinner, collection of The Mariners Museum.*

through to acting Rear Admiral W.T. Sampson, U.S.N., and the squadron prepared for departure early the next morning to blockade Cuba.

A sizable array of strength steamed out from Key West. It included the flagship, armored cruiser *New York*, battleships *Iowa* and *Indiana*, protected cruiser *Cincinnati*, small cruiser *Machias*, gunboats *Nashville*, *Newport*, and *Wilmington*, and torpedo boats *Foote*, *DuPont*, and *Porter*.

Early light revealed a merchant steamer flying Spanish colors and the *Nashville* steamed off to intercept. At 7:10 a.m. she went to general quarters and fired three shells across the Spanish steamer's bow. It would have been a pleasure to report that Commander Washburn Maynard's men of the *Nashville* fought an engagement of conspicuous gallantry, but it was a sadly one-sided affair. The Spanish steamer, ironically named *Buena Ventura*, hove to immediately and the *Nashville* sent an armed crew on board to escort her into Key West. Up to that point, the *Buena Ventura* had not even known that a war was on.

The first shot of the Spanish-American War was fired by the U.S.S. *Nashville* across the bow of the *Buena Ventura*. From a photograph, courtesy of *The Mariners Museum*.

For the remainder of the conflict, the *Nashville* rendered useful blockade duty off Cienfuegos and added another steamer and two sailing vessels to her list of captures. When the unpopular war was over, the *Nashville* went out to the Pacific and was there during the period of the Philippine Insurrection. For several stretches between 1903 and 1917 she was on active duty protecting American interests in the West Indies and Gulf of Mexico.

During World War I, the *Nashville* took up submarine patrol duty in the Mediterranean and later escort of convoy. She returned home from Gibraltar on July 15, 1918, and was decommissioned on October 29 of the same year, being sold out of the Navy three years later.

Recognizing the value of a staunch hull, the *Nashville* was acquired by the Richmond Cedar Works and was cut down to a barge for transporting logs from the shores of Albemarle Sound to the giant saws of the Richmond Cedar Works' mill in Norfolk County, now Chesapeake. In the process she lost her engines and all interior fittings. A wheelhouse with bargeman's quarters was set up on her fantail, and she was renamed

Log barge *Richmond Cedar Works No. 4,* formerly the U.S. gunboat *Nashville,* discharging logs at the sawmill of the Richmond Cedar Works at Camden Mills off the Intracoastal Waterway in Norfolk County, now Chesapeake, January 19, 1948.

Richmond Cedar Works No. 4, registered at 435 gross and 427 net tons. For thirty-odd years, the old gunboat served her owners well, if unspectacularly, riding along the calm waters of the Alligator River and Albemarle Sound at the end of a tow line, loaded with logs.

In 1954, the Richmond Cedar Works put her out to pasture, and in May, 1957, her remains were sold to Emmett Wiggins of Edenton, North Carolina, along with four or five other ancient hulls, most of them former iron steamers cut down to provide big open holds for carrying logs. In a shallow backwash of the river near Camden Mills and the busy Atlantic Intracoastal Waterway, this little ghost fleet is slowly dwindling away as its owner methodically proceeds to cut up the worn-out hulks into chunks of plate small enough to handle.

Top: Emmett Wiggins, right foreground, on the bow of the former gunboat *Nashville*. The ship was being scrapped in a backwash of the Southern Branch of the Elizabeth River at Camden Mills, Virginia, when this photograph was taken June 6, 1957. Bottom: Another view of the *Nashville* at Camden Mills. The deckhouse aft was added when the vessel was converted to carrying logs.

CHAPTER 3

(1895)

Newport News, the First Passenger Boat

Following the construction of the three gunboats cited in the previous chapter, the Newport News Shipyard provided machinery for a ferryboat and a passenger and cargo steamer, and then built a steam pilot boat and a tug, thus accounting for their Hull Nos. 10 through 13. Hull No. 14 was the shipyard's first passenger vessel—the Chesapeake Bay steamer *Newport News*, completed for the Norfolk and Washington Steamboat Company on June 15, 1895.

Apparently this vessel was the very first to carry the name Newport News, though several other craft came along between 1895 and 1947 when the magnificent heavy cruiser *Newport News* received her baptism in the James River. Other vessels honoring the city were listed in an account I prepared for the March 6, 1947, issue of the Newport News *Times-Herald* which was reprinted in the January-February, 1949, issue of *The Shipyard Bulletin*.

These ships included: (1) an 1899-built freight barge owned by the Old Dominion Line; (2) a Furness, Withy Company British-registered cargo steamer built in 1907; (3) the German steamship *Odenwald*, renamed U.S.S. *Newport News* when acquired by the U.S. Navy in 1917 as a World War I prize; (4) a side-wheel steam ferryboat, renamed *Newport News* when she came here in 1917 to serve as a Hampton Roads ferry; (5) the passenger and cargo liner, *City of Newport News*, of the Baltimore Mail Line, formerly the *Archer*, which inaugurated transatlantic service from Chesapeake Bay in 1931; and, (6) still another ferry renamed *Newport News* in 1943 when she was acquired by the Chesapeake Ferry Company. This diesel boat plied across Hampton Roads until abandonment of ferry service by the Virginia State Highway Department upon completion of the Hampton Roads Bridge-Tunnel in 1957.

The now venerable U.S. Cruiser, *Newport News*, certainly eclipsed all others of the name, having seen duty all over the world and chalked up outstanding records during the Vietnam War. Mrs. Homer L. Ferguson, wife of the shipyard president at that time, christened her March 6, 1947, on one of the proudest days in the city's history. Citizens had taken great pride in their namesake ship by contributing a beautiful silver service to her wardroom and by following her career with affectionate concern.

It is hoped that, when she is put out to pasture, she may be returned to the city of her berth to be enshrined as a "museum ship" similar to the battleship, *North Carolina*, at Wilmington. But even in the present day of rockets and missiles, the heavy cruiser's nine, eight-inch rifles would still pack an authoritative wallop, well worthy of retaining in the Navy, as was truly demonstrated off the coast of North Vietnam. It was announced early in February, 1974, however, that the Navy planned to decommission the 25-year-old ship during the fiscal year of 1975. Thus, the city has begun making overtures for her reception and ultimate display here.

The *Newport News* completed her final operational trip across the Atlantic arriving in Hampton Roads October 30, 1974. But plans that she be placed in her namesake city as a Bicentennial celebration attraction had to be held in abeyance, for the Navy apparently had no intention of declaring the vessel surplus and, until that does occur, the *Newport News* will remain a unit of the inactive fleet, subject to withdrawal and reactivation in the event of a national emergency.

The *"Grey Ghost"*—the last of America's heavy cruisers—was officially decommissioned Friday, June 27, 1975, in ceremonies held at the Navy's St.

U.S. heavy cruiser *Newport News* built by the Newport News Shipbuilding and Dry Dock Company and commissioned January 29, 1949. *U.S. Navy official photograph.*

Helena Annex in Portsmouth, Virginia, and she was turned over to Captain G.W. Walker, commanding officer of the Norfolk Naval Inactive Ships facility. At this writing, how long she will remain at St. Helena is anybody's guess. But one may be sure that Newport News will keep an eye on her, anyway.

The following narrative, however, is intended merely to cover the career of the early Bay steamboat, *Newport News.* Along with the story about the *Pocahontas,* this also originally appeared as one of the series discussing the steamboats of Hampton Roads of yesteryear and was published in the *Daily Press* of Sunday, September 6, 1959.

The first vessel of any consequence to carry the name Newport News was built in the "Gay Nineties" and, over the years, was well-known as a visitor to the local port. This steel, single-screw, 22-knot passenger steamer, the fourteenth product of the young local shipyard, was built for the Norfolk and Washington Steamboat Company for overnight service on Chesapeake Bay and the Potomac River.

Apparently the launching of the *Newport News* was an event of considerable moment, and the subject of great personal satisfaction to shipyard founder Collis P. Huntington, who believed that the new boat helped put Newport News on the map as a shipbuilding community. Records from the shipyard archives relate the event as follows:

The passenger steamer, *Newport News* (Hull No. 14) built for the Washington Line was launched on April 9, 1895, in the presence of several thousand people in holiday attire anxious to witness the bestowing of the name upon the city's namesake. A party of officials and invited guests of the owning company came from Washington on the

Launching of the Norfolk and Washington Steamboat *Newport News*, April 9, 1895. *Newport News Shipyard photograph, courtesy of The Mariners Museum.*

steamer, *Norfolk*, and was escorted to the Shipyard by local bands and militia. For this occasion [O happy day!] school children enjoyed a respite from classroom duties.

Miss Gertrude Woodbury, niece of Mr. Levi Woodbury, vice president of the owning company, becomingly christened the steamer at a few minutes before ten o'clock.

After the launching ceremonies a banquet was served on board the steamer, *Norfolk*, on the way to Norfolk. At this banquet Capt. John Callahan, general manager of the line, and under whose supervision the steamer was being built, paid high tribute to the shipbuilding company saying that the new steamer *Newport News* had no superior anywhere and expressing the hope that the company would meet with that success in the future to which their energy and skill entitled them.

As completed and turned over to her operators on June 15, the same year, the *Newport News* measured 1,535 gross tons and 1,043 net. The ship's dimensions were 274 feet in length, 46 feet in beam, and 14 feet deep. In appearance she was a typical, sparkling white Bay steamer with a gilded eagle mounted on the pilothouse poised for flight. Her bow, above the main deck, carried gold leaf decorations in spiral arabesque patterns. The steamboat's cabins were fitted out "in style" and she was a comfortable and useful vessel, although present dictates of good taste would probably condemn her as being overornate. But this was the late Victorian era and heavy carved work and plush fittings were in vogue, even though they constituted a considerable fire hazard. Indeed, a comparable vessel would be refused a Coast Guard certificate of seaworthiness today in short order.

For almost a quarter of a century, the *Newport News* regularly plied the overnight run between Norfolk, Old Point Comfort, Alexandria and Washington, alternating with her running mates, the *Norfolk* and *Washington*, and later, the new *Northland* and *Southland*. Being the extra boat on the line, the *Newport News* was frequently chartered for special excursions. In this capacity she often returned to her native city bringing parties down to attend local ship-launching ceremonies.

The steamer *Newport News* as completed by the Newport News Shipbuilding and Dry Dock Company, June 15, 1895. *Shipyard photograph, courtesy of The Mariners Museum.*

One of the gayest of these return visits occurred on the occasion of the launching of the Pacific Mail steamship, *Siberia*, on October 19, 1901. The *Siberia* was the sister ship of the *Korea*, which had received her baptism in the James River in the spring of the same year, and had been pronounced the largest ship ever launched on "this side of the ocean." The *Siberia*, "of the same huge dimensions," measured 572 feet in length, 63 feet in breadth, 40 feet in depth and displaced 18,600 tons.

Two railroad lines and the Norfolk and Washington Steamship Company teamed up to promote for some 500 West Virginians, a "Grand Seashore Excursion to the Magic City of the Atlantic Coast—Newport News." A night train left Cumberland at 11 p.m. to connect with the departure of the *Newport News* from Washington the next morning at 8 a.m., October 18. The boat took 12 hours to make the trip by daylight and laid over at Newport News until 10 a.m. on October 20, when she retraced her course back to Washington.

One of the attractions then offered passengers on the *Newport News* was the performance of a unique organization, the Mountain Beauty Band of Hendricks, West Virginia. This band was composed of eight sisters named Craven together with their instructor, Professor L.D. McCaulley. The *Daily Press* reported that when in Newport News they visited the shipyard in the morning for the launching, and spent the afternoon looking over the city. "The evening was spent in serenading," the report continued, "the Daily Press office coming in for its share of the music."

There is a great deal of talent in the band, but until about six weeks ago, not one of the young ladies had even taken a music lesson. They secured their instruments, however, sent for the professor, and have learned so rapidly that they now make a very creditable showing. The sisters dress [the account concluded] in a neat uniform of black cloth, tastefully trimmed with gold braid.

Steamboat *Newport News*, on fire and half-sunk at her Washington, D.C., pier, September 2, 1918. *Photograph courtesy of The Mariners Museum.*

Not all the *Newport News'* visits here were intended for pleasure. She came to the yard periodically for repairs and maintenance, and in March, 1910, she had to be dry-docked following a minor collision. More serious trouble developed later when she caught fire at her Washington pier on September 2, 1918. The fire started in a storage room and swept the wharf before being discovered. Since the *Newport News* was the reserve steamer, she was tied alongside with only a watchman on board. The fire destroyed the wharf and did $125,000 damage to the superstructure of the steamer. The watchman barely escaped and was rescued by a small boat on the outboard side.

Since the hull and engines of the *Newport News* were still structurally sound after the fire, her owners decided to rebuild. Accordingly, the steamer was towed to the Baltimore Dry Dock and Shipbuilding Company to have the work done, emerging the next year with a new name—the *Midland*. But unfortunately, the boat was now jinxed and fire destroyed her again on January 26, 1924. Her original owners had had enough. The remains were sold to Colonial Navigation of New York three months later.

These new owners kept the hull tied up at Alexandria for a number of years, but eventually decided that it was no longer worth fixing, so the boat ultimately passed into the hands of the Boston Iron Works for junking.

So was concluded the career of the first ship which carried proudly the name Newport News. The next time the name was used on a locally built vessel was when the magnificent U.S. Cruiser, *Newport News*, was christened on March 6, 1947. She was Hull No. 456—simple arithmetic discloses that the yard had the experience of building some 442 vessels since Hull No. 14 gracefully slid into the James on April 9, 1895.

CHAPTER 4

(1898)

Launching the Battleships
Kearsarge **and** *Kentucky*

When Newport News was laid out, an extensive tract of land between 25th and 29th Streets, lying between West Avenue and the river bluff, was set aside as a park. Soon after, the new Warwick Hotel, which opened at 24th Street and West Avenue on April 11, 1883, built as an annex, a bowling alley and casino at the southwest corner overlooking the James River. The Warwick Casino was the social center of the town and, long after it had come down in the World War I era, the undeveloped park was called—and still is by veteran Newport Newsans—the Casino Grounds.

In the years that followed, city development grabbed up more and more of the land until, when plans were being made for the statewide Jamestown 350th Anniversary, what was left was converted to a formal riverside garden area, two blocks long and about one hundred yards deep. A central bricked plaza is now embellished by a heroic size bronze statue of city founder Collis P. Huntington, designed and presented to the city by his most artistic daughter-in-law, the late Anna Hyatt Huntington (1876-1973). This is flanked on the downstream side by a large, outdoor mural painting housed in a weatherproof frame depicting the Confederacy's great naval victory of March 8, 1862, when the famous C.S. ironclad *Virginia*, the former U.S. steam frigate *Merimack*, rammed and sank the big wooden sloop of war, *Cumberland*, on the day before she engaged in her famous duel with the U.S.S. *Monitor*.

Soon after this painting was installed, the Newport News Historical Committee also commissioned artist Sidney King to create a matching portrait of still another great day for Virginians. This was when, on the same morning, the Newport News Shipyard launched the two great battleships, *Kearsarge* and *Kentucky*, described in the ensuing story. This appeared both in the *New Dominion* of June 26, 1966, and later in the August, 1967, issue of the U.S. Naval Institute *Proceedings*. Both painting and statue of Huntington were unveiled October 22, 1966.

Over the years, the city of Newport News has witnessed many stirring events within her borders. Never eclipsed, however, was that proud, crisp morning of Thursday, March 24, 1898—for the city, for the 12-year-old Newport News Shipbuilding and Dry Dock Company, and for its founder Collis P. Huntington—when the twin battleships, *Kearsarge* and *Kentucky*, slid down their launching ways into the James River.

These 11,500-ton, steel, "seagoing coastline battleships"—two of the nation's most powerful—had been authorized by Congress on March 2, 1895,

23

Top: Poised on their launching ways are the twin battleships *Kearsarge*, foreground, the first to be launched, and the *Kentucky*, March 24, 1898. *Newport News Shipyard photograph, courtesy of The Mariners Museum.* Bottom: The battleship *Kearsarge* enters the waters of the James River, March 24, 1898, while the *Kentucky* waits her turn. *From a painting by F. Cresson Shell in The Mariners Museum.*

three years earlier. They were designed "to carry the heaviest armor and most powerful ordnance."

Heeding shipyard founder Huntington's instructions to build "good ships," the yard secured the important contract only after careful bidding. Keels for the battlewagons, the yard's first capital ships, were laid on June 30, 1896. Only two weeks before the keel laying, the mushroomed community had separated from Warwick County, and on June 16 had been officially incorporated as a city by the Virginia General Assembly. The launching of the battleships two years later was indeed Newport News' coming of age.

As completed, the *Kearsarge* (BB-5) and *Kentucky* (BB-6) measured 375 feet, 4 inches in length, 72 feet, 2-inch beam, 34 feet, 5 inches deep, and were capable of steaming at 16 knots. They were respectively the shipyard's Hull Nos. 18 and 19. To show how far we have come since then, today's destroyers are not only longer, but go more than twice as fast. Three similar battleships in line could be placed on the present nuclear-powered aircraft carrier *Enterprise's* flight deck.

On February 15, 1898, the famous and memorable U.S. battleship, *Maine*, was mysteriously destroyed by an explosion in Havana harbor and relations between the United States and Spain were strained to the breaking point of a declaration of war on April 25.

Meanwhile, the launching of Newport News' twin battleships on March 24 occurred during a surge of patriotism embracing the entire nation, and vast carnival throngs, estimated at more than 20,000 persons, converged on the city to witness the unusual spectacle, taxing existing accommodations to the utmost. The Chesapeake and Ohio Railway ran several excursion trains in from the west, and chartered Chesapeake Bay steamers brought shiploads down from Baltimore and Washington. While crowds thronged the shipyard piers, river bluffs, and other points of vantage, personnel of the U.S. Navy had grandstand seats for the event from the cruiser, *Brooklyn*, and monitor, *Puritan*, at anchor off the yard.

The *Puritan*, incidentally, had been the first ship docked when the yard's Dry Dock No. 1 was officially opened nine years previously.

The *Kearsarge* was the first of the battleships to hit the water, christened by Mrs. Herbert Winslow, wife of Lieutenant Commander Winslow, U.S.N., and daughter-in-law of Admiral John A. Winslow. The latter Winslow commanded the famous U.S. sloop of war, *Kearsarge*, in her memorable Civil War duel with the C.S.S. *Alabama* off Cherbourg, France. The new *Kearsarge* had the traditional bottle of champagne smashed across her ram bow.

She was followed into the James by the *Kentucky*, whose sponsor was 19-year-old Christine Bradley, personable daughter of state governor William O. Bradley. Miss Bradley, attended by a full concourse of Kentucky colonels, was an ardent member of the Women's Christian Temperance Union. In deference to this lady's views on the subject of alcoholic beverages, the *Kentucky* was officially christened by breaking across her bows a cut glass decanter containing, as the press reported, pure water taken from the spring "at which Abraham Lincoln used to kneel to slake his thirst."

But the authorities had not reckoned with the spirit, resourcefulness and dedication of visiting members of the bourbon state, who considered the spring water "deal" both bad luck to the ship and an affront to all patriotic

Top: New York newspaper drawing showing the battleships *Kearsarge* and *Kentucky* ready to be launched at Newport News and, inset, the unofficial christening of the *Kentucky* with bourbon in addition to the "pure spring water" selected by the ship's sponsor, a member of the W.C.T.U. The inset in the upper drawing is enlarged below, to show the fusillade of small whisky bottles being hurled against the *Kentucky's* sides by eager "Kentucky colonels." *Courtesy of The Mariners Museum.*

Kentuckians. As their namesake vessel started down the launching ways, they cut loose with a veritable fusillade of small bottles labeled "Old Pepper Whisky" which they smashed against her armored sides. And so the mighty *Kentucky* entered the river dripping with bourbon. Not all the bottles broke, however. Two, recovered as souvenirs and still intact, are possessions of The Mariners Museum.

The magnitude of all these events did not go unrecorded. An eight-page "Special Launching Edition" of the Newport News *Daily Press* gave full coverage of the battleships, the Navy, the shipyard, Collis P. Huntington, the port, the railway and the city itself. Fully illustrated by woodcuts, much had

A photograph of the battleship *Kentucky* as completed in 1900, taken on a wash day, and one of the small bottles—labeled Old Pepper Whisky—which was used in the unofficial launching ceremony, but did not break. *Photograph taken by The Mariners Museum.*

to be written in advance; therefore no reference occurred of the *Kentucky's* unscheduled baptism, although mention was made of the fact that "no sparkling froth trickled down the cold steel prow." (This omission was rectified in the next edition, however.) Citing the successful double launching as "the crowning achievement of the Newport News Shipbuilding and Dry Dock Company," the *Daily Press* further editorialized that "few persons who

Top: A spirited view of the battleship *Kearsarge* under way at full speed. *From a pastel drawing by M.D. Dennis in the collection of The Mariners Museum.* Bottom: *U.S. Crane Ship No. 1,* formerly the battleship *Kearsarge* under way, May 14, 1944. The old battleship was rebuilt for a floating crane in 1920 and was on duty until 1955. *Official U.S. Navy photograph.*

saw these twin terrors of the deep as they glided from the ways have the faintest conception of the vast amount of thought, skill and labor required to place a large vessel in position to be launched."

Having handed out bouquets to all concerned, the newspaper reserved one for itself. "The *Daily Press* is a fixture among the institutions which are the pride of Newport News and it will continue to advance in popularity and influence as the city progresses along the path of commercial and industrial greatness," it prophesied with unabashed pride.

The soon-concluded Spanish-American War was fought and won some time before the first two Newport News battleships were completed. Commissioned respectively on February 2 and May 15, 1900, the twin craft joined the Atlantic Fleet and served their nation equally well in peace and war. They were included in Teddy Roosevelt's "Great White Fleet" of 16 battleships which made the triumphant round-the-world cruise from 1907 to

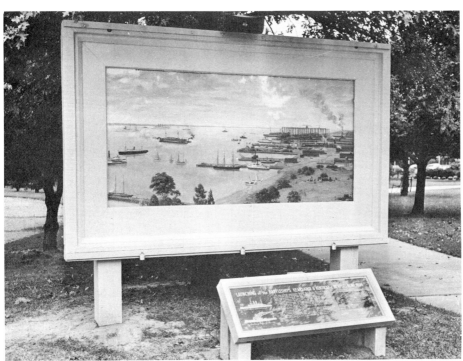

Outdoor mural painting by Sidney E. King in Christopher Newport Park depicts the launching March 24, 1898 of the twin battleships *Kearsarge* and *Kentucky*. The *Kentucky*, right, is shown entering the water. The *Kearsarge*, left, has already been taken in hand by shipyard tugs. The painting is a project of the Newport News Historical Committee.

1909. They subsequently gave valuable service to the Allied cause in World War I.

During the naval recession after the war, however, the *Kentucky* was stricken from the roster and scrapped in 1923. The *Kearsarge* lasted longer—more than 30 years in fact! At the Philadelphia Navy Yard, beginning in August, 1920, she was widened some 20 feet and her sturdy hull was converted to a self-propelled platform for a floating crane. With a lifting capacity of 250 tons, she was on duty until 1955 as U.S. *Crane Ship No. 1*. Seldom have the integrity and durability of a Newport News-built ship been so tellingly demonstrated as by the old *Kearsarge*.

Events of this memorable launching day in the history of Newport News have been recaptured in an outdoor mural painting by Sidney E. King of Caroline County, who is a specialist in this type of artistic historical reconstruction. King's works may be seen in many places on the Peninsula, notably at Jamestown Island and Yorktown where he was commissioned by the National Park Service to portray colonial day scenes and activities.

The shipyard view is installed in a heavy, weatherproof frame with special thick Plexiglas to screen out harmful ultraviolet rays. It is situated opposite King's painting in Christopher Newport Park of the Confederate ironclad ram *Virginia* (previously the U.S.S. *Merrimack*) at the moment of her greatest glory. On March 8, 1862, the day before her epic encounter with the U.S.S. *Monitor*, she dispatched with ease the two powerful Union ships of war, *Cumberland* and *Congress*, off Newport News.

Viewers of the *Merrimack* painting merely have to glance out over the river to see downstream the exact place where the memorable ramming of the *Cumberland* occurred. Similarly, viewers of the *Kearsarge-Kentucky* painting may look upriver to see the present shipyard in contrast to the 1898 panorama.

For the outdoor mural of the battleships, artist Sidney King has chosen the moment when the *Kentucky* had already started down the launching ways and was receiving her baptism in bourbon. The *Kearsarge*, already successfully launched at 10 a.m., has been taken in hand by the steam tugs, *Helen* and *Luckenback*, that will bring her to a south side outfitting pier.

In the distance lie the monitor, *Puritan*, and the cruiser, *Brooklyn*, while a variety of local and visiting craft line the shipyard piers and adjacent waters. Included in the roster of local craft is the James River steamboat, *Pocahontas*, and the Norfolk and Washington Steamboat Company's trim white steamer, *Newport News*.

Centered between the two paintings is the work of talented sculptress, Anna Hyatt Huntington. The full-size bronze statue of Collis Potter Huntington (1821-1900), founder of the modern city of Newport News, looks out over the James River and his twin empires, the C&O Railway and the shipyard.

Many changes have occurred along the Peninsula waterfront during the intervening years following that memorable launching day. Ships of both war and peace produced by the Newport News Shipbuilding and Dry Dock Company have grown in size, splendor and technical perfection. Yet here, captured on a spirited canvas, was the true beginning. It is a stirring record of a heritage in which today's local citizens may well take pride.

CHAPTER 5

(1908)

Steamboat Days on the Pagan River —
at Length a Steamer Named *Smithfield*

Steamers provided the town of Smithfield, Isle of Wight County, with dependable service for many years. In 1908, the 1901-built boat, *Hampton*, was rebuilt and enlarged and given the name of *Smithfield*—thus pleasing residents of the future ham capital of the world, who presented the steamer's owners with a large silver loving cup.

The accompanying article, one of the first I contributed to the Daily Press, Incorporated, new Sunday supplement entitled the *New Dominion*,

Side-wheel steamboat, *Hampton*, built in 1901 and rebuilt, lengthened and renamed *Smithfield* in 1908. This painting by Antonio Jacobsen was made in 1907 and is presently owned by John I. Cofer III, of Richmond. It was photographed in 1959.

appeared in two parts—March 31 and April 7, 1963—and covers Smithfield's steamboating days from the first recorded visits in the early 19th century, to abandonment of boat service in the middle 1930s. This topic was well recorded in Smithfield native, Parke Rouse, Jr.'s, delightful evocation of the area in *Below the James Lies Dixie*, published by the Dietz Press in 1968.

Parke's recollections of the joys of boat travel, through the eyes of a youngster, originally appearing in *The Commonwealth* magazine and, reprinted here by the author's permission, provide the most interesting part of the resulting account. Equally pleasant is the four-part series by Segar Cofer Dashiell entitled, "Olde Smithfield," covering the steamboats. This began in the weekly *Smithfield Times* on October 9, 1974. Mrs. Dashiell contends, and few would gainsay her, that the steamboat era was Smithfield's "golden age."

It has been almost a dozen years since the Chesapeake and Ohio Railway Company's little white passenger steamer, *Virginia*, was ignominiously towed away to Baltimore on July 3, 1951, to be scrapped. Many Tidewater partisans, who used to set their clocks on her mellifluous whistle, knew her as "Smoky Joe." She was the last of a long line of jaunty passenger boats which had plied Hampton Roads waters, without interruption, since the early 18th Century inception of steam navigation. When she departed, a colorful era of transport, geared to a leisurely way of life, came to an end. Another generation will know them no more.

It is difficult to realize the bustle and gaiety that once greeted the many arrivals and departures of steamboats calling at Newport News' C&O Passenger Pier, and at City Pier "A" stretching out into the James River at the foot of 25th Street, where Horne Brothers' plant is now located. Here came the floating links that bound the bustling young metropolis with her tidewater neighbors—Hampton, Old Point Comfort and Norfolk to the east and south, Smithfield and Suffolk westward, and Scotland, Jamestown and James River landings all the way to Richmond to the north and west.

Of the many services the steamers provided, probably none were more needed or, when they terminated, were more sadly mourned, than the Smithfield boats flying the Old Dominion Line house flag. Following the Civil War, they provided this Isle of Wight town with its sole, dependable, daily link with the outside world. Railroad interests subsequently cast sheep's eyes on Smithfield's rich hams, peanuts and other crops and explored the feasibility of connecting Smithfield by rail, but residents opposed them because the Old Dominion steamers provided all that was needed to handle existing passengers and local freight. A railroad would be superfluous, they argued.

One looks back—almost to Robert Fulton's day—to find the earliest recorded mention of a steamer sailing to Smithfield. This is contained in an advertisement placed by the James River Steam Boat Company in the Norfolk *American Beacon* in June, 1819. It appeared at a time when sightseeing excursions by water were just beginning to gain popularity among the American people, heretofore confined to the short distance one could go over rutted country roads. This trip brought enthusiastic passengers from Norfolk to Smithfield and Suffolk for a fare of $2. The following year in August, Captain Life Holden advertised a "party of pleasure" in his steamboat, *Powhatan*, also from Norfolk to Smithfield. Two years later, he proposed regular summer service three times a week to Smithfield in the 80-ton steamer, *Albemarle*, "if she meet with encouragement." Apparently she did—for a time at least. One passenger enthusiastically reported that the *Albemarle* was "a fine boat of her class," and went on to say that he "was particularly pleased with the politeness and unremitting attention of the commander, Captain Holden."

Still other little wooden-hulled side-wheel steamers—no larger than present C&O tugs—visited Smithfield in this early period. One, a hundred-tonner called the *Hampton*, the first of several boats so named, maintained a biweekly service during the summers of 1822 and 1823. And a few years later one notes in the Norfolk newspaper advertisements the services of both the *Surprise* and the *Governor Walcott*. A trip on board the latter elicited from one passenger the enthusiastic report that "we had scarcely cleared the dock before we were sensible of the exhilarating influence of the fine currents of air which the rapid passage of the boat through the water produced." Incidentally, "rapid" here should convey speeds no greater than ten miles an hour.

Still other steamboat visitors to Smithfield included the Norfolk ferryboat, *Portsmouth*, which left her regular run to take a party to Smithfield on June 11, 1832, for the cornerstone laying of the Protestant Episcopal Church there.

One of the gayest and best documented excursions to Smithfield in these early times was the visit of the Portsmouth Light Infantry Greys, who commemorated the Yorktown Surrender by a military excursion held on October 23, 1833. According to an account by a participant, the volunteer battalion at 8 a.m.:

embarked on board the steamboat, *Hampton*, and under a salute from the Artillery, while gliding over the waters of our gentle Elizabeth [River], departed for Smithfield. On the passage, the polite attention of Capt. Samuel Seldon, an occasional discharge from our cannon, and sentiment and song gave a pleasurable foretaste to the enjoyment which afterwards we found in reserve for us at the end of the journey over the waters.

At 12 o'clock, Smithfield was in view. Its elevated situation above the stream which washed its shores, gives it an imposing aspect, which was at the moment rendered more beautiful and animated by the number of ladies who were promenading the lovely green, which carpets the banks and surrounding high land. The attention of the troops seemed for a while to be diverted from the restrictions of military discipline, to contemplate the rural scenery around them. But as our vessel approached the wharf they were formed in handsome style on the decks, and commenced a salute, which was answered gun for gun, from the shore. . . .

Once disembarked, the visitors received a hearty welcome and after the usual parades and other ceremonies, they were escorted "to a beautiful retreat, where under a canopy formed by the rich foliage of majestic oaks, they partook of a plenteous collation provided by the hospitality of the citizens. . . ." Then came the departure:

The line was formed again at 3 o'clock, the Cavalry dismounted on the right, and after a short tour through the streets, a salute of 13 rounds, and a "feu-de-joie," the column was formed and moved to the steamboat; taking their departure amid the reiterated cheering of those whose hospitality had made upon their hearts, too strong an impression ever to be erased.

As the boat glided majestically down the stream, their eyes continued to linger upon Smithfield, while a hearty huzza could be heard from her shores, or the form of beauty be seen upon her green-clad hills.

The following year Smithfield residents greeted the arrival of still another new steamer. This was Captain Samuel Seldon's Norfolk-built, 194-ton *Old Dominion*, which up to that time was the most pretentious vessel ever to navigate the twisting bends of the narrow Pagan River leading up to Smithfield's busy town dock. But spasmodic sailings, mostly through the summer season, apparently were all that were needed for the little town in that leisurely antebellum period.

With the advent of the Civil War, however, the pace quickened. Federal forces controlled the lower James River following the capture of Norfolk

Top: The ill-fated steamboat *Isle of Wight*, built in 1893 and destroyed by fire at her wharf in Smithfield August 31, 1895, with a full cargo of peanuts on board. *Photograph courtesy of The Mariners Museum.* Bottom: A photograph of the 1896-built steamboat *Hampton Roads* shown at the Newport News Shipyard, October 31, 1901. *Photograph by E.P. Griffith, courtesy of The Mariners Museum.*

and the self-destruction of the famous Confederate ironclad, *Merrimack*, and Smithfield surrendered to superior Yankee strength in May of 1862. Matters then remained outwardly quiet in the vicinity with most of the former residents evacuated, but on February 1, 1864, the little steamer, *Smith Briggs*, then doubling as a Union gunboat, brought 150 troops to Smithfield to quell an alleged uprising. The *Smith Briggs* was subsequently beset by Confederate guerrillas who put some effective shots through the boat's boiler when she was tied to the Smithfield wharf, reembarking her Federal troops after an indecisive engagement. This permitted her to drift across the river where she stuck fast in the mud and subsequently caught fire and blew up.

Gradually things returned to a semblance of normalcy following the Civil War. Residents came back to take up their threads of life once more and agriculture and commerce began a slow, but sure, recovery. In February, 1867, the long-lived Old Dominion Steamship Company was formed and a line of seagoing side-wheel steamers was established to link Norfolk with New York. Soon feeder lines plying local waters came under the Old Dominion house flag and so it was that Smithfield received its first regular steamboat service with the arrival of the 1874-built steamer, *Hampton*, commanded by Captain George Schermerhorn. She plied four times a week on a daylight round trip run from Norfolk to Smithfield, Hampton and Old Point Comfort.

Before the *Hampton*, freight had been moved by a schooner named *The Three Sisters*, owned by P.D. Gwaltney, Sr., father of the packing house founder, and Captain O.G. Delk. Captain Delk soon joined the Old Dominion Line and became one of the most beloved of all the shipmasters to ply the James and Pagan Rivers, particularly since he was a Smithfield native.

In 1884, ten years after the *Hampton* came out, Captain Schermerhorn was in command of the steamer, *Accomack*, in the same four-times-a-week service. Although he admitted that she did "a fine business," Samuel Ward Stanton, editor of *Marine News* magazine, referred to the *Accomack* as a "horrible example of steamboat architecture."

With the extension of the Chesapeake and Ohio Railway line to the lower peninsula in the early 1880s, and the blossoming of the sleepy fishing village into the present busy city at its terminus, the Old Dominion Line's Smithfield-Norfolk steamboats commenced making regular stops at Newport News as well as at Hampton, the Old Soldiers' Home (Kecoughtan) and Old Point Comfort.

The next Old Dominion boat expressly built for this service unfortunately had a short and disastrous career. This was the 158-foot side-wheeler, *Isle of Wight*, constructed in Brooklyn, N.Y., in 1893 and commanded by Captain Delk. Two years later, on August 31, 1895, with a full load of peanuts on board ready for shipment, the *Isle of Wight* caught fire and burned to the waterline. The hulk was subsequently raised and brought across to the Newport News Shipbuilding and Dry Dock Company for repairs.

The first screw vessel designed for Smithfield service was the steel-hulled, 150-foot long, 450-tonner, *Hampton Roads*. She was built for the Old Dominion Line by Harlan and Hollingsworth of Wilmington, Del., in 1896, the year that Newport News officially became an incorporated city and withdrew from the County of Warwick, of which it had been a part since the pioneer days of the Jamestown colony. The *Hampton Roads* had the distinc-

tion of surviving the longest of all the steamboats, contriving to run on the
river until about 1935 when her fires were drawn for good. She idled out the
last five years of her existence molding away at a wharf in Berkley. In the
fall of 1940 she was removed from her berth and broken up.

Pictures convey better than words the appearance of both the *Hampton
Roads* and her running mate, a new side-wheeler, *Hampton*, built in 1901 for
the Old Dominion Line at Elizabeth, N.J., by Lewis Nixon. This last named
boat was originally 181 feet, 7 inches long and was powered by a Fletcher
beam engine. In 1908 she was rebuilt and lengthened to 202 feet, at which
time she was reappraised at 725 tons. But what particularly endeared this
fine old vessel to Isle of Wight residents was the fact that upon her emer-
gence from the shipyard she was renamed the *Smithfield*. A large reception

The steamboat *Smithfield* (formerly the *Hampton*), taken September 1919. *From the
Robert T. Little photograph collection, The Mariners Museum.*

was waiting for her upon her first return to the town, whose name she now
proudly carried, and a handsome 12-inch silver loving cup was, as the engraved inscription upon it certified, "presented to Steamer *Smithfield* by the
Citizens of Smithfield, Va., Novr. 18th, 1909."

This decade, until the advent of World War I, was the golden age of
steamboating for Smithfield as well as the other Tidewater localities served
by the Old Dominion boats. The Line's advertisement, as carried in the *Daily
Press* of December 3, 1909, cited two steamers in service. The *Smithfield*,
having just arrived from Smithfield, left Newport News' Pier "A" daily,
except Sunday, at 9 a.m. bound for Norfolk, whence she returned that
afternoon, going on to Smithfield at 4:30 p.m., where she tied up overnight.

Meanwhile, the *Accomack* arrived at Newport News from Norfolk, also at 9 in the morning, en route to Smithfield. She came back to Newport News that afternoon headed for Norfolk and her layover there. W.H. Landon was Newport News' agent at Pier "A."

It could not be more appropriate here than to quote directly from the recollections of two reminiscent people who were former devoted patrons of the Smithfield line. Dorothy H. Robbins contributed a colorful chapter to a history of Smithfield, published as part of the town's bicentennial celebration of September 9-13, 1952, in which she observed in her title, "Smithfield Oldtimers Shed Nostalgic Tears Over Halcyon Days of the Romantic Steamboat." After describing the physical appearance of the steamers, "built along trim, graceful lines," she took her readers on board one at Smithfield early in the morning for the 30-mile trip to Norfolk. She wrote:

Once on board, the passenger found himself welcomed as an honored guest by Captain Delk, who was always nattily turned out in a navy blue uniform with the brass buttons of the steamship line and a jaunty cap with gold braid. The boat would barely get under way on the sparkling, white-capped waves before the tantalizing aroma of breakfast was tickling the noses of the hungry passengers, and they would soon be sitting down to crisply fried oysters or Ocean View spots, Smithfield ham and fluffy scrambled eggs, accompanied by piping hot biscuits and strong coffee. The boat in the meantime was advancing out into the river, and made its first stop at Battery Park, where the villagers would come down to the wharves to watch Negro deckhands unload the cargo. Here and there along the winding river could be seen beautiful gardens of some large Virginia estates running down to the water's edge.

Soon after the boat sailed out into the James, it passed the oyster beds and the passengers watched the colored fishermen tonging oysters from the river. The next stop was Newport News, and thence the boat visited the Soldiers' Home at Hampton, the Hampton Institute for Negroes, Old Point Comfort, Portsmouth and finally Norfolk. Lunch was not served on board, and the passengers left the boat promptly to do their shopping or visiting within the three hours remaining before the boat was to return to Smithfield. The boat left Norfolk on the return trip around the middle of the afternoon, and reached Smithfield in the early evening. Dinner was served on the boat as well as breakfast, and was one of the most pleasurable highlights of the trip.

Virginia historian, Parke Rouse, Jr., born in Smithfield and reared at Newport News, recalled vividly the delights of a boyhood trip across the James to Smithfield to visit grandma and the old family homestead. He stated in an article in the December, 1960, issue of *The Commonwealth* magazine:

The steamboat's homeward voyage in the afternoon was even more gala. Surrounded by bundles from Norfolk or Newport News stores, Smithfield matrons would gloat over their purchases in folding chairs on deck (or in the red-upholstered saloon, in cold weather), while husbands went below to settle up with the purser or drink a glass of iced tea. [Could it have been bourbon?]

The most excited passengers were the children. A trip on the *Hampton Roads* to see Grandmother was an adventure to anticipate all during the school year. After moving rapidly up the channel of the James, the boat would slow noticeably to enter the shallower water of the Pagan River. If the tide were low, the vessel would vibrate ominously as it passed over sandbars. With whistle blowing to warn fishermen and oystermen around the bend, the *Hampton Roads* would glide through the tortuous channel, banking so steeply as it turned sharp bends in the river that seats skidded across the deck and passengers almost fell into the marsh cattails. (Four young passengers from Newport News kept hoping the ship would turn over, just to see what would happen, but it never did.)

The arrival at Smithfield was the ultimate thrill. If you were young and the captain knew your daddy, he might lead you into the pilothouse to hang on the whistle rope and blow for the landing. This the captain accomplished simply by hoisting you up on the

Outdoor mural painting by Sidney E. King, depicting the Newport News waterfront about 1910 as seen from the old Hotel Warwick, installed at the Victory Arch Plaza, Memorial Day, 1969, by the Newport News Historical Committee. Smithfield steamers and others are shown.

whistle chain and letting you hang there for the desired duration. The necessary number of "Booooooops" accomplished, the young mariner would be detached and would rush from the pilothouse, shouting, "Mother! Daddy! I blowed the wissel!"

For such little kindnesses the captains—and especially Captain Delk, who was Smithfield's own—are remembered by patrons of the Old Dominion Line.

The steamboat's "Here-I-Come" blast at Red Point was the signal for Smithfielders of all ages and degrees to rise from their porches and saunter down Main or Church Streets to "see who's on the boat." For years before the automobile made sophisticates of all Americans over the age of 12, the landing was a week-day ritual in the lives of Smithfield's old and young. Townspeople on the dock would scan the deck for familiar faces. Those on board would look for those who had come to meet them. While the dock crew made hawsers secure and laid down the gangway, news was shouted between deck and dock and youngsters were held up for inspection by their kin.

For those like Parke Rouse, possessing a nostalgic yen for the "good old days," the rest of the story of steamboating to Smithfield is a sad one. Transportation services of all kinds found themselves in a thoroughly demoralized condition following operation by Uncle Sam's National Railroad Administration during World War I. The Old Dominion Line had fared

Antonio Jacobsen's 1907 painting of the steamboat *Hampton Roads*, presently owned by John I. Cofer III, of Richmond.

similarly to the railroads and other coastwise ship lines. But the announcement by Old Dominion president H.B. Walker appearing in the *Daily Press* on April 6, 1920, that his company was "practically suspended" and that "all steamers on river lines will cease to function after the trip today" came as a shocking surprise.

To Smithfield, with no railroad and no more than dirt country roads, it spelled catastrophe. The Old Dominion boats alone had brought the necessities to the town and taken its agricultural products to market—200 tons of cargo per trip fully loaded, the equivalent of seven or eight railroad cars of peanuts and meat.

While Newport News delegates and Norfolk businessmen, including shipyard president Homer L. Ferguson, Judge John B. Locke and John A. Shannahan, hastened to Washington to see what could be done to revive the Old Dominion Line, hurriedly convened mass meetings, designed to size up the "critical situation," were held in Smithfield. They quickly laid the ground-work for the formation of a Smithfield company to take over and operate the vital service. Capital of $200,000 was pledged by Smithfield and Isle of Wight farmers and producers, making it possible to purchase from the de-clining Old Dominion Steamship Company one of the two regular steamers, the *Hampton Roads*, for $90,000 and the Smithfield wharf for $25,000. A charter was secured from the State Corporation Commission and the *Daily Press* of April 18, 1920, proudly reported the creation of the Smithfield, Newport News and Norfolk Steamship Company. A directorate of 25 men was formed. B.P. Gay was named president, C.W. Warren, vice president, and John I. Cofer, Sr., secretary-treasurer.

The *Hampton Roads*, with Captain Albert Gard at the helm, made her first trip under this local ownership on April 22, 1920, leaving Newport News' Pier "A" at 2:30 p.m., with an imposing company of prominent citizens of the Peninsula and invited guests on board. A mass meeting was held at the Smithfield Town Hall upon the boat's arrival, and all present pledged continued support of the new line. By April 26, regular steamer service was back again after an interval of barely three weeks. The *Daily Press* the next day proudly reported the line off to "a good start" with heavy freight moving in both directions.

Meanwhile, the Old Dominion Steamship Company wound up its affairs, disposing of all eight of its other local river craft, including the James River night boats and the Eastern Shore and Mobjack Bay steamers. Mathews County interests took an option on the steamer, *Ocracoke*, but most of the boats were taken north to finish their years in New York and New Jersey waters. The *Smithfield* was acquired by the Keansburg Steamboat Company and, retaining her proud name, plied a New York commuter run until, on September 15, 1944, she was so badly mauled by a hurricane that she was towed away to a mud flat at Matawan, near Keyport, N.J., and abandoned.

The new Smithfield line maintained service faithfully with its steamer, *Hampton Roads*, despite such critical setbacks as the burning on August 17, 1921, of Smithfield's enormous, community-vital peanut plant located on the waterfront. Since peanuts had been Smithfield's chief business for 50 years, the loss of the plant seemed to spell disaster for the town. However, it was in the wake of this fire that Smithfield's present and highly prosperous product—Smithfield ham, for which it enjoys worldwide fame—became popular.

Automobiles, trucks and more improved highway systems inexorably ap-peared in increasing numbers in Isle of Wight and adjacent counties. When the James River Bridge was opened on November 17, 1928, it was no longer necessary for Newport News passengers, and freight for Smithfield, to travel by water. However, despite the new bridge competition, the Smithfield, Newport News and Norfolk Steamship Company managed to stay in business until about 1934.

By then, the writing on the wall was all too clear. But, John I. Cofer, Sr., the line's secretary-treasurer, was still not yet ready to quit. Accordingly, he bought the defunct company and proceeded to incorporate the Smithfield Boat Line in its place. The *Hampton Roads* was offered for charter while he continued to operate some small gasoline-powered freight boats on the James and Pagan Rivers for still another decade.

John I. Cofer, Jr., of Smithfield, holds the silver cup presented to the steamer *Smithfield* by the citizens of the town, November 18, 1909.

In addition to acquiring the *Hampton Roads*, Mr. Cofer obtained the handsome silver loving cup and two oil paintings expressly made for the Old Dominion Line by the noted marine artist, Antonio Jacobsen, of West Hoboken, N.J. These were formerly hung in the ship's main saloon and depicted the *Hampton Roads* under full steam, and the *Hampton*, prior to her conversion to the *Smithfield*. For some years the paintings were stored in the old Isle of Wight Courthouse, now restored. They are presently owned by John I. Cofer III.

Today the once-busy town wharf is virtually abandoned. Adjacent buildings with hogged-back roofs are in a sad state of repair. Rotting, broken-off piles, partially awash in the stream, provide a hazard to the occasional small tanker or handful of fishing or oystering boats that occasionally come in to moor. Smithfield, however, has not suffered from the change. Vast fleets of trailer trucks rumbling through its streets transport pigs to the busy packing houses and haul away the succulent hams and other

Decaying steamboat wharfs line the Pagan River at Smithfield as evidence of the former glory of the town's Steamboat Days, October 23, 1959.

food products ("everything but the squeak" is reclaimed) that have given the recently expanded town its enviable reputation.

The new Smithfield, nevertheless, has turned its back on the river that nurtured it, and the steamboats' paddle wheels are forever stilled. But, pleasant memories remain as most older area residents will readily attest.

CHAPTER 6

(1915)

World War I Came Early to Newport News

It is not generally appreciated that the first overt act of war at sea, perpetrated by Germany against the United States in World War I, was the sinking in January, 1915, of the American bark, *William P. Frye*, a splendid big sailing vessel. Disenchantment with the Kaiser had been mounting in the United States, but it was the destruction of the famous *Lusitania* three months later, with considerable loss of American lives, that aroused national resentment, although the actual declaration of war did not come until early in 1917.

Immediately upon the outbreak of war in Europe, Germany equipped and sent to sea a fleet of commerce raiders to prey on Allied shipping. Tidewater Virginia got a preview of this desperate conflict with the arrival in Hampton Roads of two of these vessels which, already battle-scarred, slipped in to escape from British cruisers pursuing them in the western Atlantic. One had sunk the *William P. Frye*.

The following account was written for a special World War I commemorative issue of the *New Dominion* published November 10, 1968. Material on "Dutch Village"—a project of the interned German crews of the raiders at the Portsmouth Navy Yard—was kindly supplied by Curator Marshall W. Butt of the Portsmouth Naval Shipyard Museum and author of *Portsmouth Under Four Flags*.

Although the United States did not go to war with Germany until the spring of 1917, war, in fact, had come to Newport News two years before. Early on the morning of March 10, 1915—not quite nine months after the assassination of Austrian Archduke Franz Ferdinand had plunged Europe into bitter conflict—a grim and battle-stained German commerce raider steamed into Hampton Roads and anchored off what was known as Newport News' Casino Grounds.

Those familiar with maritime affairs recognized her as the former North German Lloyd liner, *Prinz Eitel Friedrich*, built in 1904 for luxury transatlantic passenger service and named for Kaiser Wilhelm's second son. But those were not carefree passengers crowding her rails. On board were more than 300 prisoners of war—men, women and children—the passengers and crewmen who had been taken off unsuspecting Allied merchant vessels intercepted by the raider and sent to the bottom by gunfire.

The enormity of Europe's conflict was realized with the fact that on board this sleek "terror of the sea"—as a contemporary reporter termed the German cruiser—were 23 Americans, members of the ship's company of the American four-masted steel bark, *William P. Frye*, of Bath, Maine. This handsome square-rigger was sunk, with her 5,000-ton cargo of wheat aboard, in the South Atlantic on January 27, 1915, in what proved to be Germany's first of many overt acts of war against the American people. The *Lusitania* sinking came on May 7 the same year. All of this increasing harassment of neutral America led ultimately to our declaration of war on April 6, 1917.

But Newport News experienced it first.

John Spencer, writing a 40-year anniversary story in the *Virginian Pilot* of March 6, 1955, described vividly how the momentous news broke on the Virginia Peninsula:

The morning of Wednesday, March 10, 1915, was just another brisk and sunshiny March day.

The news staff of the Newport News *Times-Herald* was busy getting out the afternoon paper. No news of particular importance was breaking. It was true that there was a war going on in Europe as it had been off and on for a thousand or more years, only this time on a bigger scale. . . .

The telephone on the news desk rang. Unhurriedly, the news editor reached for the receiver with the indifference born of long experience. That telephone call, however, was to set off a chain reaction around the civilized world.

World War I German commerce raider *Prinz Eitel Friedrich*, formerly a crack Atlantic passenger liner, shown subsequent to her arrival, March 10, 1915, at the Newport News Shipyard. Inset depicts her commander, Max Thierichens. *From a photograph owned by Miss Jeanette W. Cooksey, courtesy of The Mariners Museum.*

That afternoon's *Times-Herald* confirmed the call with a page-one banner head which blared the story: "German Cruiser Steams Unexpectedly Into Port Here."

And, in one of the many subheads that were common newspaper makeup practice in those days, it said: "Like Phantom from the Deep, Vessel Appears in the Roads."

Local news stories were quickly composed to cover the *Prinz Eitel Friedrich* from every angle. It developed that the darkened raider, steaming in at full speed from the open sea, had arrived off Cape Henry late on Tuesday, March 9, and was brought into the quarantine station inside Old Point Comfort by Virginia Pilot Capt. A.B. Topping early the next morning.

Having been promptly cleared by the port physician, Dr. Hal W. McCafferty, the ship then proceeded to an anchorage off the Warwick Machine Company pier at the foot of 32nd Street, Newport News. The U.S. Coast Guard cutter, *Onondaga*, followed closely while thousands of local residents lined the shores to watch the belligerent vessel's approach.

The Times-Herald reported:

Marine circles were startled when the long, slick ship, easily distinguishable by the outlines of a North German Lloyd liner, steamed up the Bay and into Hampton Roads.

Scarred by the red rust and salt of her months at sea, the German auxiliary was painted white on one side and black on the other. It was reported she had been chased to the three-mile limit by a British cruiser, but as the German captain [Comdr. Max Thierichens] had sealed the lips of his officers, that was not confirmed.

Actually, the *Prinz Eitel* had eluded units of the Royal Navy out in force to intercept her. Apparently the unusual two-tone paint job was designed to further obscure the liner's identity as a man-of-war.

The paper then vividly reported that the *Prinz Eitel's* 300 prisoners— French, English, Russian, Portuguese, Turkish and American—"many of whom had not set foot on dry land for more than six months" were "gazing with wistful eyes on the shore" as the vessel came to anchor.

The story continued:

Most of the French prisoners were taken from the passenger liner, *Floride*, before she was sent to the bottom with shells from the six-inch guns of the Germans. . . . All the prisoners, with the exception of four who have refused to sign a certificate that they will not take up arms against Germany or her allies, will be allowed to leave the ship at Newport News.

The Chesapeake and Ohio piers at Newport News already held two vessels loyal to the Kaiser—the German *Arcadia*, with a cargo of toys on board, and the Austrian-Hungarian *Budapest*. These ships had voluntarily interned themselves in a neutral American port fearing certain capture by the British Navy on the high seas. They proudly dipped their flags as the two-stack *Prinz Eitel* steamed by. But the effect of the raider's arrival on some Allied ships, also in port and then loading cargo to take overseas, was somewhat different.

An amusing feature of the arrival here of the grim looking vessel of war occurred when the ship slowly rounded the outer edge of the coal piers of the Chesapeake and Ohio, and the German flag broke to the startled gaze of the crewmen of several British steamers moored to the piers loading horses and grain for France and England. The crew gasped in amazement, as they had no idea that a ship with a belligerent nation was within a thousand miles of Newport News. Some, it is said, became frightened and began a mad scramble for safety on the beach before they stopped to think that Newport News is a neutral port.

Upon arrival, Captain Thierichens sent a full report to the German ambassador in Washington, who was incidentally, as surprised as anyone to learn of the raider's arrival in the United States. Application was also made for drydocking at the Newport News Shipbuilding and Dry Dock Company, which immediately telegraphed Washington for instructions on how to proceed with the ship repairs.

Meanwhile, collector of customs, Norman R. Hamilton (subsequently publisher of the Portsmouth *Star)*, began putting pressure on the Germans, reminding them that as combatants their ship would be allowed to remain in port only 24 hours beyond taking on supplies and the completion of urgent repairs. Captain Thierichens quickly countered with the declaration that it would take at least six weeks to put the *Prinz Eitel* in seaworthy condition.

The sinking of the American ship added a serious complexion to the matter, however. For this was Germany's first deliberate attack on a neutral American vessel in World War I, and Washington was accurately described as being "profoundly stirred." The incident was further characterized with remarkable understatement as being an "unfriendly act."

Captain Thierichens played it cool and, for a full month, kept everyone guessing as to his intentions with the ship. Actually, her hard-driven service had made a major overhaul a complete necessity. Starting at the German Asiatic treaty port of Tsingtao on Kaichow Bay, China, on October 7, 1914, the 488-foot former passenger liner had been continuously used ever since. At Tsingtao she received her naval crew—13 officers and 356 men, and armament—two six-inch rifles, four four-inchers and four howitzers. Then she headed across the Pacific, rounded Cape Horn and entered the South Atlantic where juicy game was plentiful. En route, she put into port only once, at Valparaiso, getting supplies and coal for her voracious boilers from ships she encountered on the way, before dispatching them to "Davy Jones' Locker." Eleven ships were so sunk—five British, four French, one Russian and, the one which made her situation in a United States port a sticky diplomatic issue, the American bark, *William P. Frye.*

Before the Kaiser's U-boats changed the complexion of humane warfare, the war at sea conducted by German raiders was carried out in much the same manner as the procedure of Civil War Captain Raphael Semmes and his famous Confederate raider, *Alabama.* This was with punctilious courtesy and almost courtly gallantry. Sincere apologies were given to the masters and crews of the captured vessels for their inconvenience. It was explained that the exigencies of war regrettably required the sinking of their ships. But this was not mere verbosity on the part of the Germans, for not a single life was lost on the *Prinz Eitel's* cruise and this invariably involved potentially hazardous high seas transfers of personnel by small boat. But the increasing number of prisoners on board the raider, though well-treated and fed, posed a serious problem for the German commander.

Captain Herman H. Kiehne of the *William P. Frye,* and his wife and two young sons who were making the voyage from Seattle to Queenstown with him, became close friends of Captain Thierichens. They were very moved when the German skipper returned to them the flag of the American bark. Captain Kiehne had intended to leave the colors flying as the ship sank. At the last moment, before lighting the fuse which would send the bark to the bottom, a German sailor hauled down the flag to save as a memento. Ultimately, the American skipper, familiar with area waters, proved himself extremely useful piloting the *Prinz Eitel* into Chesapeake Bay.

Local readers were somewhat shocked to read on March 20 how the Germans had previously solved the prisoner problem. The paper reported that the Norwegian steamer, *Nordica,* had just arrived at Panama with 25 English and 18 French of the *Prinz Eitel's* earlier prisoners on board. These men, taken off two barks the raider sank in the South Pacific four months before, were marooned on lonely Easter Island. They considered themselves extremely lucky that a friendly ship happened to come close enough to the desert island for them to attract her attention.

Despite the newspaper's first mention that all the *Prinz Eitel's* other prisoners would be set ashore immediately, it was not until March 25—over two weeks after the raider's arrival at Newport News—that the last 66 persons were taken off and provided further transportation. Most of these people were extremely poor immigrants—undesirable aliens, the contemporary press dubbed them—from the French steamer, *Floride*, who were en route to South America when their ship was sunk.

Divested at last of his encumbrances, Captain Thierichens began the bluff that was to keep the port in an uproar and hold a powerful squadron of British cruisers idly standing by near the Virginia Capes, hoping to intercept the raider should she attempt to slip out to sea. Coal and stores were loaded on the *Prinz Eitel* under U.S. government supervision, thus disguising the German commander's actual intention of interning his already expended warship. It was rumored that the Germans were awaiting the arrival of the U.S. battleship, *Alabama*, to escort their ship to the three-mile limit to allow her a sporting chance to escape from the British. Excitement reached a fever pitch when on March 27, as the paper reported: "Hampton Roads took on a real war-like appearance last night when the entire garrison of Fort Monroe and Fort Wool were called to quarters. The men took their positions at the big guns at Monroe and searchlights shot their rays far out to sea."

On March 29, a special eight-car train arrived from Richmond with some 600 excursionists, expressly to see the German raider. The businesslike U.S.S. *Alabama* showed up off Old Point the next day on her mission to enforce neutrality.

Another week of tension passed and, finally, on April 8, the German commander announced the decision (which he had planned all along) to intern his ship for the duration of the war. He gave the flimsy excuse that German warships he had expected to rendezvous with in the Atlantic had failed to materialize. But a headline in the paper succinctly summed it up: "Thierichens Cost British Ships Big Sum." As long as the raider might elect to go to sea, other foreign vessels must stay in port. "Shipping Here Has Been at a Standstill," was the paper's summation.

On April 9, the now-tamed raider, again escorted by the U.S. Coast Guard, quietly departed for Portsmouth and internment at the navy yard. Before leaving, the skipper thanked the people of Newport News for their hospitality. So calmly ended part one of a two-part drama that kept the area disturbed for more than a month.

Part two followed shortly thereafter. Only four days after the *Prinz Eitel's* departure for Portsmouth, a *Times-Herald* headline of April 13 once more announced: "German Commerce Destroyer Safe at Newport News."

This time it was the German auxiliary cruiser, *Kronprinz Wilhelm*, which sought sanctuary in a neutral port. Suddenly appearing near Old Point in the midst of the U.S. fleet anchored there, she had barely eluded the British cruiser, *Suffolk*, on blockade duty near the Virginia Capes.

The record of the *Kronprinz Wilhelm* as a commerce raider surpassed even the amazing performance of the *Prinz Eitel Friedrich*. During some 255 days at sea, she dispatched 14 enemy vessels and one neutral Norwegian, alleged to be carrying contraband. Still another ship, the *Chasehill*, captured in the South Atlantic on February 22, was freighted by the 294 prisoners which the raider had accumulated in seven months' cruising. She was sent to Pernambuco. When the *Kronprinz* arrived at Newport News, she had only 61 prisoners on board.

Top: World War I German commerce raider *Kronprinz Wilhelm*, shown at anchor in Hampton Roads April 11, 1915, after her arrival from sea having eluded British cruisers waiting to catch her. *H.O. Brown photograph, courtesy of The Mariners Museum.* Bottom: Officers and crew of the German commerce raider *Kronprinz Wilhelm* taken on board the ship at Newport News, April 1915. *Photograph by Charles C. Epes, courtesy of The Mariners Museum.*

The *Kronprinz Wilhelm* was well-suited to her belligerent role. Built in 1901 for the North German Lloyd's crack Atlantic service and named for the Kaiser's eldest son, the four-stack coal-burning liner chalked up an Atlantic speed record for a passage from Cherbourg to Sandy Hook that averaged more than 23 knots. She was in New York harbor when the war broke out, and quietly slipped away from her Hoboken pier on August 3, 1914, taking with her the entire crew of more than 500 men, including a large steward's department.

Plans were to rendezvous with the German cruiser, *Karlsruhe*, off the coast of Cuba. Here, three days later, she received guns and ammunition as well as a new skipper, Lt. Comdr. Paul Thierfelder of the Imperial German Navy. The *Kronprinz* had just taken on board two 3.4-inch guns, 290 rounds of ammunition for them, and some machine guns when the ships were surprised by H.M.S. *Suffolk*. The "panic stations" then resulting may well be imagined. Crews scrambled back to their respective ships, lines were hastily slipped and the vessels separated. Naturally, the *Suffolk* went after the more formidable game, the *Karlsruhe* (which contrived to elude her), and the *Kronprinz Wilhelm* hastened at maximum turns in the opposite direction. But she was to regret that she never received from the cruiser the larger rifles intended for her use.

From that time on the *Kronprinz* lived off her enemies' supplies. Consuming 500 tons of coal a day, it was, of course, vitally necessary for her to capture as many Allied steamers as possible. Once brought to with a shot across their bows, they were quickly lashed alongside and the backbreaking and monotonous routine of transferring coal began. This the Germans were to know all too well ere the trip ended. Once they had taken off everything they wanted and all personnel were safely on board the raider, the *Kronprinz* either sank her quarry with gunfire, or rammed it amidships, cracking the hull open. In the process, the once immaculate queen of the Atlantic became a scarred, dirty and leaky scavenger of the seas.

She eluded numerous encounters with British warships attempting to track her down. At length, however, after sinking the wheat-loaded steamship, *Coleby*, on March 27, Captain Thierfelder decided to give up the struggle. The condition his vessel was in was admirably described by J.H. Isherwood in the British magazine *Sea Breezes* of January, 1957:

There were no more supply ships. His ship and his crew were in bad shape. The *Kronprinz Wilhelm's* hull was battered and dented with the endless banging alongside of her succession of colliers, while her bows were strained, bent and leaky from the ramming. The engines were in a poor state from lack of proper maintenance, the boilers from continuous steaming and no chance to clean. The crew were largely becoming sick men due to lack of fresh food, the constant mental strain and incessant labor. The captain decided on Newport News as the port to run to, although he knew that the coast and approaches were patrolled by British warships. . . .

On April 11, the *Kronprinz Wilhelm* made her final effort, worked up to every ounce of speed she had left and in pitch darkness at 5 a.m. in the morning eluded H.M.S. *Suffolk* and made the entrance to the port.

Apparently, this time there was no question of the raider being refitted and slipping off to sea again. She was drydocked by the Newport News Shipyard from April 19 to 22, and her bottom was cleaned, but new boiler tubes which were so necessary were unavailable locally. Since the greater part of the ship's damage was obviously war-incurred during her nine months' service as a raider, the United States refused by international law to

Top: So-called German Village, named by its creators "Eitel Wilhelm," was built at the Portsmouth Navy Yard in the summer of 1915 by the lonely interned crews of the commerce raiders, *Prinz Eitel Friedrich* (which is closest to the camera) and *Kronprinz Wilhelm. Photograph courtesy of Portsmouth Naval Shipyard Museum.* Bottom: Close view of some of the cottages of German Village at the Portsmouth Navy Yard, 1915, with the *Prinz Eitel Friedrich* in the background. *Photograph courtesy of Portsmouth Naval Shipyard Museum.*

perform anything beyond correcting superficial damage. Under these circumstances, to put to sea again would have been suicidal. And so the battered, former Atlantic queen was interned, joining the *Prinz Eitel Friedrich* alongside a lay-up pier at the Portsmouth Navy Yard.

Since no American ships or nationals had been involved in the *Kronprinz Wilhelm's* spectacular war career, there was little tension in this community. But considerable worry was conveyed by the fact that, when she arrived, there were more than a hundred cases of beri-beri among her crew. Local citizens were reassured by the U.S. Public Health Service that there was nothing to fear, as the noncontagious disease was caused by vitamin deficiency, due to the crew's monotonous diet lacking fresh fruit and vegetables.

Once moored harmlessly at Portsmouth, time passed endlessly for the homesick German crews. Scrounging odd pieces of lumber and other materials found around the yard, the sailors proceeded to build a miniature village of about 50 small German houses, planting gardens around them. The

A view of German Village at the Portsmouth Navy Yard as seen from the deck of the interned liner *Prinz Eitel Friedrich. Photograph courtesy of the Portsmouth Naval Shipyard Museum.*

village included a windmill, a little church, and a printing shop where they published their own newspaper. They named their city "Eitel Wilhelm," but to local residents it was known as "German Village." People traveled from afar to see it.

With America's entry into the war, the status of the 500 crewmen changed from loosely-guarded internees to regular prisoners of war. Presumably still yearning for return to the "Vaterland," they were taken to various P.O.W. camps throughout the country. Previously, some half dozen of the men had managed to obtain a small sailing yacht and put out to sea. They were never heard from again, thus, a hoped-for rendezvous with a German U-boat never materialized and their actual fate is unknown.

Since the land within the navy yard compound was urgently needed for other purposes, picturesque "German Village," with its neat houses and gardens was razed. Both of the former commerce raiders were immediately taken over by the U.S. Navy along with 85 other German vessels then interned in various American ports. Soon converted to troop transports, the *Kronprinz Wilhelm* became the U.S.S. *Von Steuben* and the *Prinz Eitel Friedrich*, the U.S.S. *DeKalb*. It was with fitting justice that the *Prinz Eitel*, the ship which had sunk the first American vessel in the war, should, as an American transport, have the honor to be included in the convoy carrying the initial wave of doughboys of the American Expeditionary Force to France. In addition to embarking the A.E.F. in 1918, at the war's end the *DeKalb* made eight voyages to Hampton Roads returning home more than 20,000 American troops. Both ex-raiders survived the war, but were subsequently scrapped—the hard-driven *Kronprinz* in 1923 and the *Prinz Eitel*, renamed the *Mount Clay*, in 1934.

Thus, on that distant spring morning in March, 1915, the impact of the "Great War" to make the world safe for democracy first came to the Peninsula and nation. But there still remained a long time before it would be "all over, over there." Actually, of course, it isn't over yet and may never be.

CHAPTER 7

(1915)

Shipyard President Hopkins
Goes Down with the *Lusitania*

The magnitude of the *Lusitania* catastrophe needs no embellishment for Newport News well remembers that Albert L. Hopkins, the young and promising president of the Newport News Shipbuilding and Dry Dock Company, was among the casualties. Over the years, vast amounts of literature have been produced about the torpedoing of the huge British liner—both at the time of that fateful day, and, more recently in two well-received volumes. The first, *The Lusitania*, by Colin Simpson, a London *Sunday Times* correspondent, came out in London in 1972, was given wide coverage in an excerpt in the October 13, 1972 issue of *Life* magazine, and was republished in full by Little, Brown and Company the following spring. Co-authors of the second book, *The Lusitania Disaster*, jointly published during the autumn of 1975 by Collier-Macmillan in London and The Free Press in New York, bring more impressive credentials. They are Professor Emeritus Thomas A. Bailey of Stamford and retired U.S. Navy Captain Paul B. Ryan.

Both books uncover the story of a monumental exercise in political cynicism, sweeping under the rug a record of expediency, self-assurance and arrogance that indicts many high-ranking officials in the governments of both Britain and the United States. Simpson, however, makes the claim that the *Lusitania* was a well armed auxiliary of the Royal Navy and ready to do battle—a point severely denied by Messrs. Bailey and Ryan.

While preparing my review of the Simpson book for the *New Dominion* book section, it seemed reasonable, in the light of the English author's revelations to attempt a sort of footnote to his book from the aspect of those in Newport News, who anxiously awaited reports of President Hopkins' fate.

Researching this project in the shipyard archives, under the direction of librarian, Carl Cannon, I was delighted to discover a contemporary and possibly never-before-published account, written by Mr. Hopkins' companion, Fred J. Gauntlett, another shipyard official, who survived the fatal voyage. Mr. Gauntlett's story, incorporated in my Sunday, May 6, 1973, *Daily Press* account, imparts an immediacy to the tragedy that could scarcely be duplicated by any secondary reconstruction. The *Daily Press* article enjoyed wide readership, due to state-wide distribution by the Associated Press.

Three score years ago, a tremendous ocean liner sank near the southern coast of Ireland and 1,198 lives were lost. Though few today recall the

"Lusitania Passing Old Head of Kinsale" in time of peace. She was torpedoed by a German submarine May 7, 1915 within sight of the lighthouse, left. *From a print in the collection of The Mariners Museum.*

Last known photograph of the Cunard liner *Lusitania* standing down New York Harbor at the commencement of her ill-fated voyage of May 1915. *Courtesy of the Daily Press, Inc.*

ancient name of Portugal which the ship was christened, the name of the steamship—the *Lusitania*—will never be forgotten.

England and Germany were deeply embroiled in World War I, when on the afternoon of May 7, 1915, a carefully directed torpedo, fired by *U-20*, smashed into the starboard side of the unsuspecting liner, triggering a second explosion, claimed to have been caused either by another torpedo, ammunition the ship might have been carrying, or, more likely, ruptured boilers. This blew out the bottom, sinking the great four-stack liner in less than 20 minutes. It was one of the most fateful of all sea disasters, ranking with the *Titanic* as a monument to man's over-confidence and complacency.

As Britain fervently hoped, the United States, previously uncommitted, now started down the road which would eventuate in our declaring war against Germany on the side of the allies. It was almost as though the

Left: Newport News Shipyard president Albert L. Hopkins lost his life when the *Lusitania* went down. *Photograph courtesy of Newport News Shipbuilding.* Right: Shipyard official Fred J. Gauntlett was President Hopkins' companion on the ill-fated voyage. He survived. *Photograph courtesy of The Mariners Museum.*

Lusitania was specially dispatched for this purpose. The disaster had particular significance to Tidewater Virginia, for one of the 128 Americans, who lost their lives that infamous May afternoon, was Albert Lloyd Hopkins, president of the Newport News Shipbuilding and Dry Dock Company.

An account follows of the disaster from the local viewpoint, plus a "statement" by Hopkins' companion on that ill-fated voyage. Fred W. Gauntlett, Washington representative of the shipyard, survived the harrowing experience. His account is a gripping one, printed here in its entirety through the courtesy of Carl Cannon, librarian of Newport News Shipbuilding, who exhumed it from ancient company correspondence files. Similarly, John L.

Lochhead, librarian of The Mariners Museum, provided invaluable information.

Albert L. Hopkins, 44, recently appointed principal officer of the shipyard, was thought to face a brilliant shipbuilding career. Born at Glens Falls, New York, September 7, 1871, Hopkins graduated with honors from Rensselaer Polytechnic Institute in 1888, and first came to Newport News as a government naval constructor in 1894. In 1898 he joined the company as personal assistant to general superintendent, Walter F. Post. Hopkins progressively rose through the ranks, achieving the presidency in March, 1914. Approximately a year later he gave his life in a disaster, which was both unnecessary and preventable.

Hopkins' and Gauntlett's departure from the United States was apparently routine, but upon discovering that Hopkins was not among the survivors, his reasons for sailing were questioned. Expectedly, the shipyard's New York office acted coy. A New York *Herald* reporter wrote that "on inquiry at the office of the shipbuilding company, No. 233 Broadway, no one would discuss the details of Mr. Hopkins' business aboard." James Plummer, the shipyard's New York representative, did state, however, that although "it is true Mr. Hopkins left to attend to some business affairs for the company, it was not to be solely a business trip." And he continued that Hopkins hoped "to treat himself to a vacation while attending to his business affairs in Europe."

These findings did not preclude speculation and it was suggested that undoubtedly shipbuilding contracts were involved, and that possibly Hopkins' trip had something to do with a desire of the Newport News Shipbuilding and Dry Dock Company "to furnish the warring nations with armor plate."

Another reason emerged—Hopkins was to confer with representatives of the German government concerning the status of the two recently interned German liners, which had sought sanctuary in Hampton Roads. Both ships had been converted to successful commerce raiders and British cruisers had made every effort to capture them (Chapter 6).

First the *Prinz Eitel Friedrich* and then the *Kronprinz Wilhelm* came to Newport News on March 10 and April 11, 1915, respectively, and were berthed at the shipyard before being laid-up at the Portsmouth Navy Yard. After America's entry into the war two years later, they were promptly seized by the U.S. Navy and converted to transports for the A.E.F.

Actually, Mr. Hopkins' mission must have been a delicate matter, since outwardly a pose of neutrality was necessary, even though pro-allied sentiment prevailed in America. It is known, though, that Hopkins was also to visit officials of Hay Bylandtlaan at The Hague, Holland, in connection with two types of submarine designs on which the shipyard was expected to bid. The shipyard advised Mr. Marley F. Hay of Hopkins' death, and shortly thereafter he visited America to present his condolences personally to the yard, and to continue discussions.

The *Lusitania*, with Hopkins and Gauntlett on board, sailed from New York as scheduled on the morning of May 1. Some passengers, leery of a small advertisement placed by the Germany Embassy, cancelled their trips. The ad stated without mincing words "that a state of war exists between Germany and her allies and Great Britain and her allies" and travellers should know that "vessels flying the flag of Great Britain . . . are liable to destruction" and that they journey "at their own risk."

Since it was believed the *Lusitania* was an innocent merchant ship plying her accustomed waters, most passengers failed to heed the Kaiser's saber-rattling. They were not aware that by using the dodge of filing a late cargo manifest, it was possible to get by with loading small arms, ammunition and other forbidden cargo. By international law, then, Germany might be considered justified in sinking the ship without warning, which she did.

Once on board, the Newport News Shipyard men joined forces with Samuel M. Knox, president of the New York Shipbuilding Company, Camden, New Jersey, who was undoubtedly embarked on a similar mission in his company's behalf. The voyage was pleasant and uneventful until the fatal

NOTICE!

TRAVELLERS intending to embark on the Atlantic voyage are reminded that a state of war exists between Germany and her allies and Great Britain and her allies; that the zone of war includes the waters adjacent to the British Isles; that, in accordance with formal notice given by the Imperial German Government, vessels flying the flag of Great Britain, or of any of her allies, are liable to destruction in those waters and that travellers sailing in the war zone on ships of Great Britain or her allies do so at their own risk.

IMPERIAL GERMAN EMBASSY
WASHINGTON. D. C., APRIL 22. 1915.

Notice placed in New York newspapers, May 1, 1915, by the Imperial German Embassy warning prospective Atlantic travelers of the dangers attendant to a state of war between Germany and England. *Courtesy of The Mariners Museum.*

afternoon of May 7. Then, in rapid succession came the two explosions, first as the *U-20's* torpedo struck, and second (though another torpedo was credited) as the ship's boilers blew up.

Shortly after his safe arrival with other survivors in Queenstown, Ireland, Mr. Gauntlett prepared a "statement" for the American Consul, Wesley Frost, for transmittal to the United States State Department. Forwarding a copy to James Plummer on May 14, Gauntlett advised that it "is about as complete as I can make it and it gives about all of the knowledge I have on the subject." He asked Plummer to distribute additional copies to friends and shipyard executives.

His letter further stated:

Neither Knox nor myself were able to find Hopkins after he parted from us in the dining saloon, but this is not much to be wondered at when you consider that there were 2,000 people crowded on the boat deck, and some of them had gotten away when I arrived on deck, and of course the time was very limited.

I have offered a reward for the recovery of his body, but am afraid the chances are very poor. So far, less than 200 bodies have been recovered out of about 1,200.

The authorities were very slow in sending out boats to search for bodies, and I found it necessary to raise a good deal of fuss before I could get things started, but after that they took hold and have done fairly well.

Another American and myself took automobiles and covered between us 60 miles of the coast to the west . . . but so far the wind has been driving everything off the beach and to the Westward.

I have not cabled you very often during the past few days as there has been nothing to cable.

I have examined carefully every body so far brought in, given the necessary description to the proper authorities, and covered every point possible, and am satisfied I shall get advices at once if anything turns up.

I shall, of course, remain here until I am forced to give up all hope, but am hoping against hope that he [Hopkins] may have been picked up by some vessel going to a distant port and that we may still have good news.

I have had a number of letters from people in England making inquiries and expressing sympathy with Mrs. Hopkins, etc. As for my own feelings, it is needless for me to say how I feel, and my heartfelt sympathies go out to Mrs. H. under these awful conditions.

We were talking of the possibilities of being torpedoed at the table a few minutes before it happened, and we all agreed that such a thing was impossible.

With best wishes to all.

Sincerely yours,

FRED J. GAUNTLETT

STATEMENT OF MR. FRED J. GAUNTLETT COVERING EXPERIENCES IN CONNECTION WITH THE SINKING OF THE *LUSITANIA*.

I was at lunch with Mr. A.L. Hopkins and Mr. S.M. Knox in the first class dining saloon, when were were startled by a very heavy explosion, occurring on the starboard side of the vessel. My two friends above-mentioned, immediately left the room, while I stayed behind, calling to the stewards to close the ports, which call I repeated several times, but without effect, as so far as I could see no porthole was closed. I then left the dining room and made my way to the boat, or "A" deck, and left the companionway on the port side, which was the high side of the vessel, she having taken a very heavy list to starboard by this time, and being down by the head.

One of the lifeboats was about full of people, mostly men, and two of the crew were about to lower away, and I watched the lifeboat going down, when the man handling the forward falls lost control and the boat was dropped into the water, a distance of about 50 feet, the forward end being so much lower than the after end that the people were thrown either out of the boat altogether or into a struggling heap at the low or forward end. The boat was smashed and everyone thrown into the water.

I then helped to line up and put into the next boat a group of women and children, and then becoming convinced that the vessel was doomed to sink, decided to take a look at things from the starboard side. The starboard side had been comparatively deserted, and I walked forward and saw that the bow was underwater, and the vessel's starboard side very near to the water, and decided it was time to get my life belt. I then went to my stateroom and found my belt on the lower berth, the other one having been taken. From this I concluded that Mr. Hopkins (who shared my room) had already been there and secured his belt. I had not seen him since he left the dining saloon, nor have I seen him yet.

I then went up to "A" deck again on the starboard side, and by this time "B" deck was underwater, and in a minute at most the boat deck, or "A" deck, was submerged in the final roll of the vessel. I slid down the deck and grabbed a boat davit to save myself from being thrown into the water, and climbing on the rail swung myself by the fall from the deck of the *Lusitania* into a boat that was empty of people, and which no one had attempted to lower away.

A woman and a man with a baby were thrown into the water, and these I pulled into the boat, but the boat davits immediately came over on the boat and carried it down with the *Lusitania,* leaving me in the sea. I turned around and saw one of the funnels apparently coming right down on top of me and swam at once as fast as possible out of the way of it.

I was then caught across the back by one of the antennae of the wireless, and turned over and grabbed the wire with my hands, pushing myself away from it. I then took hold of an air tank, probably from one of the lifeboats that had been smashed, and looked around to see if there was not some more secure wreckage to which I could hang on until relief reached me.

I saw one of the collapsible lifeboats, canvas cover still on, a short distance from me and swam to it. I was the first person to reach it but found it impossible to get on board.

A lurid German print after a drawing by Claus Bergen, 1915, depicts the deaththroes of the British liner *Lusitania. Collection of The Mariners Museum.*

A steward soon joined me, and he was also unable to climb aboard without assistance. I helped him up and then did the same thing for Mr. [Charles E.] Lauriat, a passenger from Boston, and they together helped several people to get up and then they came and helped me.

We then cut off the canvas cover and tried to rig up the sides of the boat, but the working parts were so stiff or rusted that we found it impossible to do this, and some of the parts were broken, which made it impossible to raise the sides and seats so that they would stay up. We then picked up wreckage and put under the seats to prevent them from collapsing, rigging out the oars, and rowed about picking up people until we numbered 32 in all. Mr. Knox, my friend before mentioned, was the last person but one we picked up.

We then rowed a short distance to a fishing vessel to which we transferred. She had already picked up two other boatloads, making about 100 in all, and afterwards took in two other boatloads there being no room for more people on board. We were later met by the steam tender, *Flying Fish,* which in turn took us off and brought us to Queenstown where we arrived about 9:30 p.m.

The torpedo struck the *Lusitania* about 2:15 p.m. and she sank in about 18 minutes, as near as I can determine. None of the air ports [port holes] were closed, to the best of my knowledge and belief, and I am strongly of the opinion that had they been closed the life of the ship would have been prolonged somewhat.

I also wish to call attention to the fact that the canvas sides of the collapsible boat were torn in places and had a number of small holes in others.

I was in the water about 15 minutes, noticed a slight suction, which was not strong enough to prevent me swimming against it. I did not receive any injury, not so much as a scratch, but have two or three very slight bruises on my left leg, probably received climbing aboard the collapsible boat.

£50 REWARD.

FOR THE RECOVERY OF THE BODY OF

ALBERT L. HOPKINS,

1st Class Passenger.

Age 42. height 5 feet, 10½ inches, Weight about 130 lbs, slight build, clean shaven, dark hair.

CLOTHES—well made, probably Rogers, Peet & Co. Tailors.   Money and Papers in pockets, gold crest ring on finger.

Persons finding body are requested to put in Casket and notify at once by wire

Mr. FROST, American Consul,
AND   QUEENSTOWN·

Fred J. GAUNTLETT, Queen's Hotel,
Queenstown.

Handbill distributed by Fred J. Gauntlett seeking the recovery of Albert L. Hopkins' body shortly after the torpedoing of the *Lusitania*, May 7, 1915. *Courtesy of Newport News Shipbuilding.*

Charles E. Lauriat, the Boston bookseller mentioned in Mr. Gauntlett's statement, subsequently wrote his own version of the catastrophe, *The Lusitania's Last Voyage*, published by Houghton Mifflin, Boston, Mass., 1915. The passage describing boarding the lifeboat closely parallels the shipyard official's account:

> I saw a short distance away a collapsible lifeboat floating right-side-up, swam to it and climbed aboard. A seaman quickly followed. I heard my name called and for the moment I didn't realize whether it was a call from Heaven or from Hell, but when I turned in the direction of the voice I found the man to be G--, one of the three men [Gauntlett, Hopkins and Knox] with whom I had played cards each evening. I pulled him up on the boat and we three got out our jackknives and went at a kind of can-opening operation, which was really the removing of the canvas cover of the boat. . . .

> This man G-- was another good one too; he deserved his name. By this time we must have had 15 people in our "NON-collapsible boat" (Let us thank God for the NON).

Gauntlett was annoyed at the nonchalance shown by the British in instituting a systematic search for survivors and bodies of the drowned. From the Queen's Hotel at Queenstown, he immediately posted a £50 reward for the recovery of Hopkins' body, describing his physical appearance and clothing —"probably Rogers, Peet & Co. Tailors" of New York City.

Gauntlett, along with representatives of millionaire Alfred Gwynne Vanderbilt, who also drowned, hastily chartered a tug to search the coastal waters. But not until May 14 was Hopkins' body recovered. It was among 28 victims brought in that night by a British torpedo boat and the tug, *Stormcock*.

A newspaper account stated that "undoubtedly the vigorous protest put up by Americans, among them F.J. Gauntlett of New York and Newport News, is responsible for the collection of the additional bodies."

Then came the sad task of shipping Mr. Hopkins' remains to the United States. His body was loaded on board the S.S. *Philadelphia* of the American Line for transmittal to Glens Falls, New York, where interment finally took place on June 5.

Messages of condolence over Hopkins' untimely death were legion. The shipyard had closed as a token of respect immediately after his fate became known. Mr. Henry Huntington, principal owner of the yard, summarized general emotions when he wrote "the company and all the employees share our sorrow and will mourn the loss of a splendid officer and a noble man."

Fred Gauntlett, who survived to relate sadly in person his recollections of the ship-sinking, continued in the company's service until he retired after a lengthy and honorable career on September 30, 1938. He died in Washington, August 9, 1951.

Some local residents well recall Gauntlett showing them his pocket knife, usually carried on the end of his watch chain. This was the knife with which he cut the canvas cover off the collapsible lifeboat of the *Lusitania*, thus saving his life.

Top: The so-called Shipyard Monument bearing the business philosophy of Shipyard founder Collis P. Huntington was unveiled New Years Day, 1917 in front of the yard's main office building by President Homer L. Ferguson and M.V.D. Doughty. *Shipyard photograph, courtesy of The Mariners Museum.* Bottom: A view of the Shipyard Monument as presently installed at The Mariners Museum after the transfer from the yard April 7, 1969.

CHAPTER 8

(1922)

"At a Loss if We Must . . ." — How the World's Largest Ship Saved Newport News

On September 4, 1968, amid rumors that the 80-year-old Newport News Shipbuilding and Dry Dock Company was suffering financial reverses from alleged mismanagement, the company's stockholders agreed to a merger with Tenneco, Incorporated. It then became, to use their term, a "component." The Houston-based conglomerate, thirteenth largest in the nation, was founded as an oil pipeline company in 1943, but quickly branched into a wide variety of other fields, now shipbuilding.

On January 1, 1969, the new shipyard organization was headed by various individuals from the Tenneco family, including personnel from the Walker Manufacturing Company of Racine, Wisconsin, builders of automobile parts. In reviewing urgent matters and revamping the yard's policy to be more profitable, one of the first items considered opprobrious by Tenneco's board chairman, was the half-century-old slogan inscribed on a bronze tablet mounted on a large block of granite set up near the southwest corner of the main office building. This stated:

> WE SHALL BUILD GOOD SHIPS HERE
> AT A PROFIT—IF WE CAN—
> AT A LOSS—IF WE MUST—
> BUT ALWAYS GOOD SHIPS.
> COLLIS POTTER HUNTINGTON

Apparently the "good ships" part was acceptable, but Tenneco would not endorse a philosophy that recognized the possibility of losing money under any circumstances. The new management demanded this be clearly defined.

The succinct, 22-word inscription for this so-called "Shipyard Monument" was composed 50 years earlier by President Homer L. Ferguson and yard attorney, Robert G. Bickford, (composer of the wording on the Newport News 1919 Victory Arch, erected to welcome returning World War I servicemen). It was unveiled on the yard side of the building by Mr. Ferguson and Mr. M.V.D. Doughty, a veteran employee whose service dated to the company's early days, while founder, Collis P. Huntington, was still alive. The date was January 1, 1917.

Although the text of the inscription was new, the sentiments of the words were derived from the often-stated policy of the yard founder in unequivocal terms. Superior workmanship in the new company was utmost in importance and, so well did he infuse that desire, that these intents transcended mere company policy and reflected a standard of perfection in all fields expected of the entire community. This definitely accounts for the name Newport News being symbolic of quality the world over.

As stated in previous chapters, the new company's first shipbuilding ventures in the 1890s included the construction of tugs and cargo ships, mainly for companies in which Huntington had an interest. But the founder soon realized that to progress, the shipyard must be involved in doing work for Uncle Sam. The first government bid placed by the yard came to naught with the work on the battleship, *Iowa*, and cruiser, *Brooklyn*, going to veteran Cramp's Shipyard in Philadelphia on December 15, 1892.

The following year the opportunity arose to bid on the construction of the three U.S. Navy gunboats, for which, this time, the Newport News yard was successful. Huntington wrote shipyard president C.B. Orcutt on October 18, 1893, as the bids were submitted:

> The price seems very low and more particularly so as you know my feeling is that every ship we build here should be first-class whether we make or lose on her. I think we have the best shipyard in the world. What I want to do is to have for it a reputation for building the best ships. So do not make any calculations for scrimping the works in any of their parts.

Again, on December 6, 1893, Huntington wrote to Orcutt in the same vein. The Newport News bids opened in October had been accepted, when he commented:

> I want you to turn out as good, or better ships of this class than have ever been built before for the Government. . . . I would rather lose money on a first-class ship than to make money on one that did not give satisfaction to the Government. The Yard is new, and what I want is to get a reputation for building first-class ships and then always build ships to sustain that reputation.

The Navy contracts executed in the latter part of January, 1894, eventuated in the U.S.S. *Nashville* (Chapter 2), the *Wilmington*, and the *Helena*. They fulfilled the founder's requests and served the nation long and well.

The aforementioned letters, plus others Collis P. Huntington wrote at various times to his people in Newport News, inspired President Ferguson, in the antebellum period of World War I, to compose 23 years later a slogan rallying the yard's workers to build "always good ships."

It seemed that with inexplicable myopia, the yard's new Tenneco management saw only in the patina-covered tablet the statement that ships might be built "at a loss if we must," a condonement of shoddy workmanship and license to perform profitless work. Newly arrived on the scene, they failed abysmally to comprehend the actual meaning of the yard's motto, dedication to quality work at all costs—even loss—that had long been the clarion call of Newport News workers.

Tenneco was in the saddle for only six months when the word percolated down from the top brass that the shipyard monument must go. "Get rid of it any way. Throw the damn thing in the James River," was how gossip reported the decision. In any event, a welcomed home for the monument was soon found in the collection of old guns and anchors at The Mariners Museum. The official lame-duck explanation, given by the Tenneco public relations people for the necessity of removing the boulder, was that they had to provide additional executive parking space near the building. Parenthetically, one may observe that all parking in the yard has since been abolished. Furthermore, they stated that the museum had long been pining to add the monument to its exhibit collection. Also transferred to the museum was a considerable quantity of cartons of paper matches with covers bearing the opprobrious inscription. Soon afterward, the new president came up with his own "Declaration of Status and Opportunity," which occupied a full page in the April, 1969, issue of the *Shipyard Bulletin.* Many concede this 397-word document—375 more than President Ferguson's inscription—conveyed far less.

Actual transfer of the granite block to the museum was made early Easter Monday morning, 1969, when the yard was closed for the long weekend. Cranes whisked up the 20-ton pedestal onto a flatbed truck and, a short time later, it was being shimmed onto its new base in front of The Mariners Museum.

Tenneco had not considered the results of this inept and unnecessary move, however, certainly a devastating one for a new organization hoping to begin in the community with an amicable relationship. To Newport News residents—and people around the world—the monument was sacred and to desecrate it was sinful. One amazed local lady, invoking holy writ, quoted Matthew 28:2—"And, behold, there was a great earthquake: for the angel of the Lord descended from heaven, and came and rolled back the stone. . . ."

In this climate of dismay, anger and disbelief that anyone would interfere with an unoffensive, time-honored talisman, I decided to recall for Newport News readers a classic story. Indeed, money could be, and was, lost honorably by the shipyard, with no connotation of incompetence or venality, but to save the entire city from disaster. Old-timers remember that in the spring of 1922, the yard purposely entered a below-cost bid to recondition the mighty steamship, *Leviathan*, to insure work for the almost-destitute community, suffering severely from post-war depression, compounded by cancelled naval contracts. President Ferguson, well recalling the inscription he installed only five years previously, when shipbuilding was profitable, entered a calculated low bid on an $8 million contract. He was awarded the job and considered a hero!

Recognizing that the Tenneco management would not appreciate a story timed with this implied criticism of their behavior toward older residents' sensibilities, and could consider it a slap in the face—which it was!—*Daily Press* editors, with something less than dedication to crusading journalism, refused the story as being too hot to handle. Alexander Pope once wrote, "Fools rush in where angels fear to tread."

Though this hurt has remained in the community, tempers simmered some before the factual story of the *Leviathan's* visit appeared in print in the December, 1969, issue of *The Commonwealth.* Backtracking on their previous decision, the *Daily Press New Dominion* of April 5, 1970, accepted it for reprinting.

With an authority standing in the wings, it was perhaps presumptuous to undertake relating matters involving the great *Leviathan*, even the brief part pertaining to the Newport News visit. A friend, marine author Frank O. Braynard, for many years has had a "passionate love affair" with the German liner, and was recording the full story of its remarkable career. The first of a projected five-volume history was published by the South Street Seaport Museum in New York on November 12, 1972, describing the ship's early years from 1913 to 1919. Volume II was printed two years later and covers the liner's Newport News visit as related here, and her subsequent re-entry into the transatlantic passenger service.

We wish Frank Braynard every success in this Herculean task and crave his forgiveness for appropriating this segment of his ship's story.

The transfer of the monument to the museum is now an acknowledged fact. No better appraisal of its significance could possibly be given—for all the shipyard to see—than that of former Virginia Governor Colgate W. Darden, a former company director. He wrote:

> The Monument does not belong to the past and should not become a museum piece. It is really a dedication to industrial greatness and should have a place in the active life of the community that over the years has contributed so much to the Yard.

But Admiral Hiram G. Rickover, U.S.N. (Ret.), father of atomic ship propulsion and present director of the naval reactors of the U.S. Atomic Energy Commission, expressed his sentiments more bluntly. Not one to mince words, testifying before a House Appropriations Subcommittee on July 23, 1974, on the subject of conglomerate ownership of the nation's major shipyards, the crusty, aged admiral was quoted:

> Shipyard managers no longer seem to display much interest or expertise in ship construction [and] they seem to view shipyard operations as strictly a financial game. The managers actually in charge of shipyards are not technical managers, but legal, financial and contract experts. . . . In general they are not interested in ships, they are interested solely in profits.

Matters have changed since the Huntington-Ferguson days!

Wholesale cancellation of shipbuilding contracts, in a town whose principal product is ships, could be catastrophic. Such was the case in Newport News in 1922, when the Newport News Shipbuilding and Dry Dock Company, already pinched by the expected shipbuilding recession after World War I, received a shattering body blow. It was a feeble reward for the persons who had prodigiously built that vital "bridge of ships" that helped win the war, and provided the allies' answer to Kaiser Wilhelm's unrestricted U-boat sinkings.

According to the terms of the post-war Washington Arms Limitation Conference, the victorious nations of Britain, France, Japan and the United States pledged themselves to abandon virtually all naval construction. Thus, some $70 million worth of shipyard work at Newport News was officially scratched by telegram on February 8, 1922.

The immediate effect on the Peninsula's economy is perhaps difficult to realize in this affluent age of industrial development and diversification. The shipyard payroll, upon which the community depended, declined from 14,000 to 2,200 wage earners and the citizens of Newport News were desperate for work.

What saved the day both for Newport News and the shipyard, was the contract to convert the steamship *Leviathan*—a former German liner-turned-troopship—into a luxury passenger vessel once more. It was cited the "biggest ship repair job in the history of shipbuilding." The *Leviathan* played a vital role during the war years, safely ferrying more than 100,000 American servicemen across the Atlantic. She was driven strenuously on more than a dozen round-trip voyages to help win the victory. The *"Old Levi,"* as she was affectionately termed, carried one-twelfth of all members of the American Expeditionary Force "Over There."

Decommissioned by the U.S. Navy after the war, the well-spent craft was idled for two years at Hoboken, New Jersey, while the United States Shipping Board decided her outcome. On April 10, 1922, as an angel of mercy, she came to save Newport News.

The ship, launched at Hamburg, Germany, by Blohm and Voss on April 3, 1913, as the *Vaterland*, was the world's largest when she entered transatlantic service as flagship of the Hamburg-Amerika Line in the spring of 1914—during the lull that preceded the "Great War." The *Vaterland* measured 950 feet long overall by 100 wide, and was rated at 54,282 gross tons. Her two lofty steel masts rose 210 feet from the waterline, and the tops of her three enormous funnels were 184 feet above the keel. Four turbine-driven bronze propellers, 16 feet in diameter, propelled her at the commendable speed of 24 knots. A coal-burner, it required over 1,000 tons of coal a day to fire 46 voracious boilers.

War clouds had begun to swirl over Europe when the *Vaterland* entered service on the North Atlantic. Rather than risk interception by British warships, the liner was voluntarily interned in New York Harbor in August, 1914, after completing only the first half of her second passenger voyage. Despite the sharp eyes of a neutrality patrol assigned to all interned ships of belligerent nations, early in 1917, when war between the United States and Germany seemed inevitable, the German skeleton crew aboard contrived to dismantle a considerable amount of vital machinery, undoubtably under secret orders of the Kaiser's embassy.

On April 6, 1917, the United States declared war against Germany. Our government seized the *Vaterland* and shortly afterwards began to convert her to a mammoth troop transport. She was renamed *Leviathan* after the sea's largest creature. As a liner, she accommodated 3,400 passengers; as a trooper she carried three to four times that number. Considerable work was done to ready her and rectify the damage due to sabotage. This included reblading all main propulsion turbines and installing eight six-inch rifles for defense.

The *Leviathan* was accepted by the U.S. Navy and commissioned in July, 1917, sailing her maiden voyage from New York to Liverpool in December with 10,000 passengers. Then used for regular Atlantic shuttle, she performed yeoman duty throughout the war, and returned the boys home after the armistice. Her last troop voyage terminated at New York on September 8, 1919, when General Pershing and his staff disembarked. Then the "Old Levi" was put to pasture.

The U.S. Shipping Board decided that the United States Merchant Marine would operate the *Leviathan* under the American flag, in competition with Britain's R.M.S. *Majestic*, also a giant German-built vessel acquired through war reparations. But, when the Shipping Board applied to Blohm and Voss for plans of the *Vaterland* to follow during reconversion, the German shipbuilders stated the price was $1,000,000. This exorbitant offer was rejected. Instead, America's leading naval architect, William Francis Gibbs—designer of the famous liner, *United States*, 30 years later—undertook an all-but-impossible task. He measured every inch of the ship and prepared blueprints from these measurements—a job made more difficult because the liner was afloat, and all underwater measurements were taken from inside the hull.

Plans and specifications finally completed, the Shipping Board made its proposals for the colossal job of reconditioning the ship, including conversion from coal-burning to oil-fired. All American shipyards were suffering from the devastating effects of the ironically-termed "naval holiday," but conditions at Newport News were beyond comprehension. Shipyard President Homer L. Ferguson—who, five years earlier, had condensed the business

Top: The 950-foot *Leviathan* moored to the Shipyard's outfitting pier, April 1922, while work went forward to reconvert her to a luxury transatlantic liner. *Shipyard photograph by E.P. Griffith, courtesy of The Mariners Museum.* Bottom: The steamship *Leviathan*, reconditioning complete, ready to leave the Newport News Shipbuilding and Dry Dock Company to enter transatlantic passenger service, May, 1923. *Photograph courtesy of The Mariners Museum.*

philosophy of founder, Collis P. Huntington, into an inscription engraved on the Huntington Monument: "We shall build good ships here; At a profit if we can; At a loss if we must; But always good ships." He was determined to obtain this badly-needed job for Newport News—"At a loss if we must." He succeeded.

Local shipyard estimators sharpened their pencils and figured. When the nine bids submitted to the U.S. Shipping Board were opened, Newport News' offer was $2,000,000 below its nearest competitor, and half the amount of some other bidders. The Newport News yard's proposal was $6,110,000, the majority of which covered reconditioning and conversion to oil-burning ($5,595,000), and repairs to machinery ($515,000). The remainder of the $8,200,000 was for work subcontracted. It covered redecorating passenger accommodations, and rehabilitating and revamping the galleys and stewards' departments throughout. Upon completion of the work at Newport News, seemingly as a political ploy, the *Leviathan* was to be dry docked at the Boston Navy Yard—one of few facilities in the United States able to accommodate the enormous vessel. It would have been less expensive to perform this work across Hampton Roads at nearby Portsmouth Navy Yard, also equipped and able to handle the task. It was an open secret that the Newport News tender had been intentionally submitted considerably below actual cost of doing the work.

Excitement reached a frenzy during the period between submitting the bids and announcement of the company that was awarded the job. On February 15, 1922, the *Daily Press* printed an extra with the banner headline:

Leviathan Contract Is Awarded to the Newport News Shipyard—
Shipping Board Awards Contract to Lowest Bidder.

The story concluded that President Ferguson had already been called to Washington to sign the long-hoped-for agreement.

Even more exuberance was reflected in stories that appeared in newspapers the following morning: "Local People Are Delighted . . . Between One and Two Thousand To Be Employed . . . Five Million Dollars for Labor Alone. . . ." The lead editorial by Colonel W.S. Copeland said, in part: "Paying tribute to Citizen Ferguson is like boosting Newport News. We can not resist the impulse to express the sense of gratitude of this people for the most recent service Mr. Ferguson has rendered in securing a contract from the U.S. Shipping Board for reconditioning the greatest passenger ship afloat. Mr. Ferguson is a shipbuilder of national repute and he is a real man as everybody knows, but he is also a good citizen. . . . Shipbuilding is the greatest expression of the mechanical arts. . . . Many of the best ships . . . now afloat were planned and constructed from keel to mast in the yard whose motto is 'We shall build good ships here—At a profit if we can—At a loss if we must—But always good ships.' "

Stating that the Newport News tender was intentionally lower than the estimated cost of executing the work, the editorial continued:

This was done for the Shipyard, to be sure, but it was done for Newport News also. It was done to give employment to men who had served the yard faithfully but who, through no fault of their own, had been laid off by the inexorable agreements of the Arms Conference. . . ." It was a noble thing to do. It was a work of the heart as well as of the brain and we make the record to be preserved in the public print as a testimonial to the friendly consideration of the officers of the Newport News Shipbuilding and Dry Dock Company. Newport News is deeply sensible of the service they have rendered.

It was a time-consuming task to assemble and train a crew, and to ready the *Leviathan* for a self-propelled trip such as the 24-hour run from New York to Hampton Roads. One wonders that the ship was not towed by a brace of powerful oceangoing tugs. In anticipation of the ship's arrival at Newport News, the shipyard dredged (at a cost of $57,000) the slip on the north side of Pier One, where the deep-draft liner would spend the ensuing 13 months. Finally the ship was ready and at 5 p.m., Sunday, April 9, mooring lines were cast off from her Hoboken pier and she headed south under command of Capt. W.J. Bernard, her war-time pilot. Early the next morning off Cape Henry she picked up Capt. James Peake of the Virginia Pilot Association and slowly threaded her way up the channel to Newport News.

"Thousands lined the shore to see her in," the paper reported of the crowds assembled at 8 a.m. at the Casino Grounds and other vantage points to view the world's largest ship. At one period in her war career, the *Leviathan* sported camouflage colors. The great, brooding vessel which loomed through the morning mists was a dull somber gray.

Questioning her size, one wit was quoted: "How big? About six million dollars big!" To another, a tugboat alongside "looked like a barnacle." It was an emotion-fraught moment. Some waved, some wept, others gratefully acknowledged that there came the bread for their mouths.

Reminiscing many years later, Newport News hotelman, F. Ray Mewborn, recalled the *Leviathan* as "the most beautiful sight coming down the river that morning. Newport News was in such bad shape," he continued. It was "a reconditioning job that kept Newport News alive."

The tugs nudged the *Leviathan* alongside the shipyard's south side outfitting pier, and work began with a full crew of boilermakers to start the mammoth coal-to-oil conversion. Progressively other shipyard tradesmen assumed their tasks until a maximum of 2,500 workers swarmed over the vessel. With employment provided this number of knowledgeable shipbuilders, the yard management was able to pursue the adoption of various other kinds of work to terminate the shipbuilding slump. Rebuilding railroad freight cars and locomotives was one sideline undertaken by the yard and, during the spring of 1922, it entered the field of hydraulic turbine design and manufacture. The first contract was with the Virginia Railway and Power Company on November 10, 1922, involving the building of a power station near Petersburg. This type of business developed rapidly and became a major adjunct to the shipyard's capabilities, and fame.

Gradually the *Leviathan's* gray hulk, which dominated the Newport News waterfront, emerged from its chrysalis as a sleek, black-hulled liner with gleaming white superstructure, crowned by three enormous red funnels topped in bands of blue and white. The following spring, Capt. Herbert Hartley and his key officers were on hand as the final stages of the reconditioning project neared completion.

A delegation of Tidewater shipping men traveled to Washington to persuade the U.S. Shipping Board to dry dock the *Leviathan* at the Norfolk Navy Yard in Portsmouth rather than sending her to south Boston upon consummation of the Newport News work. The Shipping Board had promised the job to Boston, and refused to be moved by the $100,000 saving which would have accrued by eliminating the ocean voyage and having the job done virtually next door.

Upon completion of the rejuvenation and assembly of the crew, the ship readied to sail. According to the statement of Admiral W.S. Benson, chairman of the Shipping Board, although the Newport News Shipyard lost $1,200,000 on the job, the reconditioning was praiseworthy. But Homer Ferguson directed the compliments where he felt they were due. He stated that his shipyard "never could have done the job it did on the *Leviathan* without the voluntary and hearty cooperation of the workmen. I doubt if there has ever been a job that so taxed our utmost resources, patience and skill."

Is it any wonder a 1923 magazine article on the *Leviathan* was entitled: "But Always Good Ships"?

If Ferguson were loyal to his employees, so were the shipyard owners loyal to him. Founder Huntington's nephew, Henry E. Huntington, and his wife were the principal company stockholders. Frank O. Braynard, in his biography of ship designer, William Francis Gibbs, relates that when Mr. Ferguson—armed with a letter of resignation in his pocket—reported the shipyard's loss to Henry Huntington, the latter reassured him by saying, "My wife owns most of the stock in the shipyard, and she has not been feeling too well recently, so maybe we should say no more about."

The following year, however, a grateful Henry Huntington bestowed upon the city of Newport News the waterfront land which is now encompassed by Huntington Park.

The *Leviathan* was scheduled to leave Newport News for Boston early on May 15, 1923. That morning, however, low-hanging fog banks did not disperse until the advantage of high tide was lost and, rather than risk grounding the ship, drawing 38 feet 6 inches, it was decided to postpone the departure. In consideration, the shipyard dispatched a boat near the shore and announced to the throngs lining the banks that the sailing was delayed. On May 16, however, with veteran Virginia Pilot Captain James Peake again at the conn, the ship cleared the harbor and slowly steamed away. Again, crowds on the shore both cheered and wept.

Reporting the events, *The Times-Herald* of May 16 also presented a six-stanza poem composed for the occasion by local resident Henry E. Baker. It began:

She sails today, the *Leviathan*
    The mistress of the deep.
Her flag floats high on the freshening breeze
She sets her prow toward the Seven Seas
    Where wild the billows leap.

The remainder of the *Leviathan's* story may be quickly told. She reached South Boston, May 18, and was immediately dry docked. After having her bottom cleaned and painted, she embarked on an extensive trial trip from Boston to southern waters, from June 19, to 23. During this voyage, the refurbished liner broke the world's record by averaging 27.48 knots during 25 consecutive hours steaming.

Following these successful trials, the *Leviathan* arrived at her new terminal, Pier 86, North River, New York, and was readied for transatlantic passenger service. Her first voyage began on July 4, 1923, and for many years thereafter the world's largest steamship (the British White Star Line claimed their *Majestic* was larger, however) proudly flew the American flag on the Atlantic sea lanes under the management of the United States Lines.

By the 1930s, the old *Leviathan* had been outclassed by modern, more economical liners, and spent lengthy periods laid up before finally being sold to foreign ship-breakers. Having only a skeleton crew embarked, the 25-year-old ship made her last Atlantic crossing to Scotland in 1938 and was then scrapped.

Newport News will not forget the *Leviathan*. She brought work and wages; she kept alive the community's shipbuilding know-how. Several relics of her rest in The Mariners Museum and many older homes on the Peninsula may still have pieces of ponderous Teutonic furniture taken off the ship during the 1922-1923 conversion. Until razed in 1969, an ornate mirror, removed from what was claimed to be the Kaiser's suite, hung in the Tidewater Hotel barbershop in downtown Newport News.

A final note of proof of the dedication to fine workmanship shown in the *Leviathan*, spelled out by the inscription on the Huntington Monument, was cited in practically every contemporary article about the "new" ship. An editorial in *The Times-Herald* published on May 16, 1923, the day the *Leviathan* left Newport News for good, commented that the "company gave the government a first-class job and pocketed its losses without murmur." It also stated that the day the *Leviathan* sailed, the *President Buchanan*, an ex-troopship later named the *Republic*, entered the yard for similar reconditioning. She provided a year's employment for 2,000 shipbuilders.

A former company director recently summarized this with crystal clarity when he stated that building good ships, "at a profit if we can—at a loss if we must" is not merely the once-revered philosophy of a successful company—it still is the spirit of a community whose particular ingredient is quality workmanship for which the profit motive is secondary. To compromise on principle is unthinkable.

For this may the great *Leviathan* be long-remembered!

CHAPTER 9

(1934)

Fire on the *Morro Castle*

The shipyard built 45 passenger vessels between the *Newport News* of 1895 (Chapter 3) and completion of the *Morro Castle* in 1930. Though some had hard luck and *La Grande Duchesse* (Hull No. 15), proved unacceptable to her prospective owners when she failed to perform satisfactorily on her trial trip, no other Newport News-built ship suffered a more inglorious end than the Ward liner, *Morro Castle.*

This highly-respected ship, returning to New York from a Havana cruise, burned near the New Jersey coast on the stormy morning of September 8, 1934, causing 134 deaths. Newport News officials were concerned whether the fire was caused by defects in the vessel, for which the builders were responsible, or in its operation, for which the owners and unions were accountable. Local pride was saved when it was conclusively proven that the *Morro Castle* was not to blame, but, as a result, the government now demanded fire-resistant materials in all new ship construction.

The *Morro Castle* disaster inspired the production of three full-length books. *Fire at Sea*, by Thomas Gallagher, published in 1959 by Rinehart and Company, New York, 25 years after the event, is the best. More recent appearances are: *Shipwreck: The Strange Fate of the* Morro Castle, by Gordon Thomas and Max Morgan Witts published by Stein and Day, New York, in 1972, and The *Morro Castle*, by Hal Burton published by Viking Press, New York, in 1973. Additional perspective gained by the latter books proved more conclusively the hypothesis advanced by Gallagher that the ship's destruction was the work of a pyromaniac, identified as George White Rogers, the strange and later-demonstrated psychopathic radio officer of the ship. Rogers died in prison in 1958, while serving a life sentence for murdering an elderly man and his daughter, who had befriended him.

None of Rogers' subsequent career had been revealed when retired United Fruit Company chief engineer, William McFee, wrote an article on the *Morro Castle* disaster. McFee did not then know that fires seemed to continually occur in Rogers' vicinity and an associate in the police department of Bayonne, New Jersey, where he eventually worked as a radio technician, was badly injured by a diabolical mini-bomb which Rogers had set. McFee's article formed a chapter in a book entitled, *The Aspirin Age: 1919-1941*, edited by Isabel Leighton and published by Simon and Schuster, New York, in 1949. In it, the acclaimed author considered loss of the ship an "appalling record of incompetence and horror" for those responsible for the ship's conduct, who showed "excessively dull judgment." He also attributed the conflagration to the ineptness of the ship's engineering force toward the condition of the fireroom burners. The stacks overheated, thus transferring the excessive heat to inflammable plywood partitions in the passenger spaces which, had that been the case, obviously should have been better protected in the original design.

The following story was a twentieth anniversary account written for *The Times-Herald* of September 8, 1954. The theory of engineer-author McFee that the trouble was in the fire room was quoted. However, the facts uncovered by Gallagher in 1959 seem to exonerate the *Morro Castle's* firemen, in view of the unsavory reputation of radioman Rogers and the distinct possibility that he started the fire with a bomb similar to one he tried on a police associate. Despite all manner of circumstantial evidence, these charges remain "not proven." Newport News shipbuilders were relieved that nothing was revealed in the *Morro Castle's* design to cast aspersions on their reputation for "good ships" from Newport News.

At the time of the disaster, my brother-in-law, Dr. Francis J. Braceland, widely-honored senior consultant at The Institute of Living in Hartford, was a young resident at the Pennsylvania Hospital for Mental and Nervous Diseases in Philadelphia. With a group of friends, he was returning from a week's vacation at Bermuda on the Furness liner, *Monarch of Bermuda*, before starting on a Rockefeller Fellowship he was awarded. I recently asked him for his personal recollections on the *Morro Castle*, for the *Monarch* was among the first ships to arrive on the scene and performed prodigies of rescue work, before returning to New York with numerous survivors. I wanted a psychiatrist's professional opinion of radioman Rogers as well.

Although Dr. Braceland wrote that the catastrophe was "something which I had blotted out of my mind completely and never wrote about," the acclaimed hero dug into his store of recollections and produced a thrilling eight-page narrative letter which presents a novel approach not covered to any extent by the authors aforementioned. He wrote:

The night we were coming home, September 8, 1934, I think we must have been near New York's quarantine anchorage, and the girls and a few of the men were going to stay up and see us pick up the pilot. But it was rainy and cold and the fog horn was blowing mournfully, so I went to bed. About 4 a.m. I was awakened by a steward, who said the captain sent him to tell me to stand by as we were after a ship that was afire. I went up on deck and waited with some officers till we came upon her. I thought it was a freighter and I was not distressed until we came upon the *Morro Castle* at about 5 a.m. As we got near I could hear the screams of the people trapped between decks and could see them. Also I could see some folks jumping into the water, and learned that she was a cruise ship out of Havana.

I think we were the first ship to come up to the scene, though I soon saw a Luckenbach freighter which stood off, and as we came up our crew tried to get some of the boats away. The vaunted English seamanship was not working. They had trouble with the captain's gig—couldn't get it down at all. They also had trouble lowering the lifeboats, and we were an unconscionably long time.

Meanwhile, the people were screaming for us to come over. Finally our boats got into the water and brought the first load back. I was afraid that they were going to dump them, when they did get back, for one davit held and the other didn't, and the crew and survivors hung suspended. I was afraid they would all fall out. I regret to tell you that the first load was made up of men from the *Morro Castle* crew; no officers, only crewmen—several dozen of them.

I knew that the ship's doctor of the *Monarch of Bermuda*, a man named Kennedy, was a bit alcoholic. I had seen him in the early evening. I came down and stood by him and I was afraid he was a little more under the weather than was good for us. At any rate, the boats started to bring people back and while there was some shouting, there was nobody directing where the survivors should be sent, or what to do about them. Most of them were half-dressed and soaking wet. I tried to chase one crewman down to the hospital, for it was cold, rainy, and raw and he had no clothes but a pair of ragged pants. He had dropped his change and was wanting to pick it up, and I tried to stop him until one man said, "Doc, that's all he has left in the world." That sobered me up a bit.

You must keep in mind the fact that I was only a year out of the Chief Residency at Jefferson Hospital—a center city hospital which handled all of the downtown emergencies in Philadelphia—dozens of firemen felled by gas, people slashed in little neighborhood fights, bullets in policemen and others, and I was used to emergencies people brought in in a hurry by ambulances and patrol wagons. I tell you that, because before long, Dr. Kennedy came to me several times and asked me what to do about a couple of people. I made up my mind a little later that if he asked me one more question he was going to be working for me. He then asked me to look at a woman on the second-class deck. It was obvious that she was dead. I told him either to take the hospital, and let me land the patients on the afterdeck, or for him to land them and distribute them, and put me in the hospital, which was rapidly filling at that time. He wanted no part of the hospital, so I took it.

A lot of women arrived in several boatloads, and everybody I saw was parched from the salt water. I couldn't think what to do. They needed a demulcent, but I didn't want to give them oil and thus increase their problems. Then, finally, a little girl in her early twenties came up to me, told me she was an operating room nurse from New York, and could she give those passengers some milk. I said, "Milk, bless you!" Of course, that was what they needed and plenty of it. She came and asked another question pretty soon and I said to her, "Look, you are the only person on this ship who is thinking, so stay by me."

By that time there were fractures and all sorts of problems. She would disappear for five or ten minutes, and come back and say there is a woman who came aboard with a child on her back; the child was not hers. They are on "B Deck," such-and-such a room. Would I look at them both? She would be gone again, and tell me there was a fracture on "A Deck," such-and-such a room, and the man is in pain, would I take a look? Whoever she was, I never even knew her name, she was an angel from heaven.

I put the other nurses that I knew from Bermuda to work and, in doing so, incurred the wrath of stewardesses whom I thought took care of the rooms, but they let me know that they were wonderful nurses. I watched for a while and saw they were of no help, so I depended on the RNs.

One situation, which was almost unbelievable, was that the few times I had a chance to look out to sea, there was a man hanging on a rope amidships on the *Morro Castle*, and he hung there for I don't know how long—it seemed like hours—and how he hung on I don't know. He wore only skivvies. The small boat coxswains were fearful of going in to rescue him, for it took them too close to the burning ship. Finally, there was some kid at the tiller of a gig from one of the other ships; a red-headed kid with his cap pushed on the back of his head, cigarette in his mouth. He was, devil may care, standing up with the tiller in his hand. He was dashing around picking up people and finally he went up and, by some incredible effort, he took that man off the rope, got him in the gig, and tried to land him on our ship. But they couldn't get him aboard. He cursed everybody around and got him into some other ship. A Ford oiler had come up and several other ships were coming on the scene.

All the while, the *Monarch's* passengers were slowly becoming aware of what was happening. Early on, I heard a woman say, "Our breakfast will be late today, there goes our steward." But they rapidly sobered and behaved very well indeed. By that time it was getting to be daylight, and several times they had to move the *Monarch* because of the flames—she might have caught on fire.

In the meantime, down below in the hospital I had all sorts of things happening. Four people became psychotic; some were screaming. As is usual, there were some passengers who wanted to help and some really did. One obnoxious girl was insistent and was getting in my way, so I put her in charge of the psychotic patients who were carrying on—she didn't last long on that job! Dr. Kennedy came down once or twice and at about 11:00 or 12:00 noon asked me whether we shouldn't splint the fractures. That was a good idea, but I said it all depended on how long we were going to be there and when we were going to go into New York. There were planes over us by that time; some people from the *Morro Castle* trapped and still alive were screaming for somebody to do something.

I lost all track of time. Hospital and room visits with my nurse friend took all thought of anything else away from me. I just know there was muted excitement and before long an officer told me we were going to move into harbor. It must have been near 1 p.m., for the tugs took us in at about 2 p.m. Now, mind you, this was all only eight miles off the Jersey coast and some men on our ship were wondering why they didn't beach the burning ship. She was really afire, have no doubt about that, but did not have much of a list. I noticed that some of the people who had jumped on the seaward side didn't seem to appear again, and I am sure some of them were lost. Some who jumped on our side, I think, were knocked out by improperly fastened life jackets.

A newspaper clipping I saved says we brought back 72 patients [Gallagher's book says 71], but I think we brought back 103 all told. We lost nobody after we got them aboard alive, but some required a lot of work and worry. There was an old doctor aboard who annoyed me at first. He was a pediatrician, but there was little for him to do. I gave him a bottle of liquor and told him to give everybody a drink who seemed to need it. That got him out of my hair. I don't mean to be nasty, but he told me he was not very capable in situations like the one we were in.

As we moved closer to shore, the launches came with the New York police—some great big handsome Irishmen with eagles on their shoulders. They had a few reporters with them, tugs were coming up in profusion, and my only worry now was off-loading these people. I had lost my shirt somehow, and when we did tie up I was busy cursing someone who was handling a fracture roughly.

At that time an elderly lady passenger on the *Monarch* tapped me on the shoulder and said, "Young man, how are you getting along with your planting?" Proof that the truth will out! A friend, Dr. Bond, had warned me upon going to the St. George's Hotel in Bermuda that there would be lots of school teachers on the porch, and warned me not to tell the ladies there that I was a psychiatrist. So I told them I was a landscape artist, for there was no landscape there. Bond used to say he was a golf professional. So you can see—the old lady caught me. So much for telling the truth!

At any rate, we off-loaded the ship in New York. There were dozens of ambulances, bushels of doctors and nurses, and cops and newspapermen. I made my way through a group of relatives and friends—something I never want to go through again. They were white-faced and weeping and hoping, looking for information. I had none to give them.

As soon as I could get me a shirt from my bags ashore, I started for the Pennsylvania Railroad and went home. My hospital, meanwhile, had heard about the fire, knew somehow that I was on it and when I answered the phone that satisfied them. The newspapers the next morning caught me up on details and I found out that Captain Banyan of the *Monarch* had cited me.

It was some time later, of course, that Dr. Braceland reviewed the exciting events in which he had taken part and speculated on the cause of the holocaust. His letter concludes:

Now about Radioman Rogers. I read that book, *Fire at Sea*, and I remember that the newspapers at the time tried to fasten the trouble on a man named George Alagna, the other radio operator, who had started a little ruckus before the ship sailed, originally in order to get better food. He was designated apparently by Captain Wilmott as a Commie. But the captain was getting his information from Rogers. Alagna, therefore, was on the poop list. You know that Wilmott died on board the night before under strange circumstances. The more one thinks about it, the more Rogers had something to do with that, too.

I firmly believe, although not convicted of it, that Rogers set the ship on fire. They found some sort of incendiary pen on him later and fires seemed to start wherever he was. You know, when he got on the police force, that he told somebody that he would be the lieutenant of that force, and, before long, a bomb blew the fingers off the then lieutenant.

You know, too, about his defrauding that fine old man and his daughter who had befriended him, and how they died, and that later he died in prison. His death occurred just as they were fastening the net about him. He was a criminal psychopath, have no doubt about that, and I used to use him as an example in my classes at Yale, to tell them of the death and destruction which follows in the wake of such guys.

I haven't consulted anything but my memory about this. So I don't know whether I have missed something or not. I tried to blot it out and, even though I have subsequently been through a great deal in the hospital, this was a much more tragic and wretched affair.

It was all so badly handled, and the fire spread so quickly and so thoroughly, that it must have been set in my mind. I assure you that, despite the newspapers, I was no hero.

I was on the scene when they needed a doctor, and I was a Doc, and I did what I had been taught to do. Captain Banyon was the man who reported it to the newspapers and I, for a while, was a great friend of the Furness Line. But they soon forgot it all, even as I forgot it.

Even now, I am convinced that Dr. Braceland does not relish a hero's role. Yet, he performed his job skillfully and saved many lives. Curiously, none of the *Morro Castle* books carry the effects of the disaster one step further to mention the exhaustive experiments undertaken by the Newport News Shipyard in fireproofing techniques. They secured an aged, laid-up steamer, the *Nantasket*, in the James River Reserve Fleet Anchorage and, on board her, ship construction materials were acid-tested for fire-resistant qualities. When, shortly afterwards, the shipyard launched the liner, *America*, pride of the U.S. Merchant Marine and, at 723 feet, largest ship then built in this country, the only wood aboard was in the grand piano and the butcher's chopping block!

And so, like the International Ice Patrol which came in the wake of the *Titanic* sinking in 1914, the *Morro Castle*, 20 years later, did not die in vain. The federal government immediately required new and rigid standards in ship construction. A grandfather clause was applied which removed all vessels with wooden cabins from United States registry. A perennial exception has been the Mississippi River steamboat, *Delta Queen*, which has had many close encounters with condemnation procedures, but managed to avoid it through waivers.

However, the lack of fireproofing has not deterred foreign operators from procuring our obsolete ships and operating them for the sole benefit of transporting American passengers. They do not seem to know, or care, that the "new" Panamanian- or Greek-registered craft they booked passage aboard is classed legally in this country as a firetrap. It is with grim interest to note that the venerable Philadelphia-built *Yarmouth Castle* (Chapter 21)—originally the Eastern Steamship Company's *Evangeline*, but then under Panamanian registry—served American tourists exclusively on the overnight Miami-to-Nassau run. She caught fire on the night of November 13, 1965, in a holocaust that was ironically similar to the *Morro Castle*. One might shudder!

No Newport News-built ship ever suffered a more ignominious fate than the *Morro Castle*.

In the long history of building good ships in Newport News, many have ended their careers due to stranding, collision, or enemy action and a few have succumbed simply to old age and fatigue. But in 1934, the *Morro Castle*, a virtually new passenger steamer, operated by the Ward Line, was gutted by a *preventable* fire almost within sight of her home port. A total of 134 persons lost their lives.

Why did it happen? Who was to blame?

In the wake of any major disaster, the American people demand a scapegoat. But like the preventable disaster of Pearl Harbor, seven years later, no single person was to blame, although many of the crew behaved reprehensibly, and apparently the captain lost his head. The *Morro Castle* was unquestionably the victim of cumulative circumstances best summarized as personnel failure resulting in panic. It was actually more than that. The

Morro Castle was the victim of the times. The disaster was not caused through any defect in the ship (as the shipyard was anxious to have known); nor, was it the work, as some said, of Communist incendiaries alleged to have planted a bomb on board when she left Havana three days earlier. And, it was heart failure, not foul play, that, ironically, caused the *Morro Castle's* venerable captain to die only a few hours before the ship turned into a raging inferno. In command was an inexperienced first mate, hopelessly confused by the sudden responsibilities thrust upon him.

So erratic were the first reports that filtered in, that even the stock photograph of the vessel (reproduced in the Newport News *Times-Herald* on Saturday afternoon, September 8, 1934, and now filed in the *Daily Press* morgue) still carries the improbable notation on the back. *"Morro Castle*—struck by lightning and burned with heavy loss of life."

The *Morro Castle* leaving Newport News to enter service, as delivered August 15, 1930.
Shipyard photograph, courtesy of the Daily Press Library.

When the Newport News Shipbuilding and Dry Dock Company delivered the twin-screw, oil-burning *Morro Castle* and her sister ship, the *Oriente*, to the Ward Line in the autumn of 1930, the operating company received a superior pair of intermediate-size liners, displacing 16,113 tons and measuring 508 feet long by 70 feet wide and 39 feet deep. Though conceived in the carefree days before the "Great Depression," when American ship lines thrived in transporting affluent Americans to tropical islands where the scourge of prohibition was unknown, business was difficult in 1934 and apparently corners had to be cut to reduce operating costs.

There was a tremendous turnover in the crews on each voyage, and inexperienced men were the majority on board. Lifeboat drills, thorough inspections by the Steamboat Inspection Service, and other desirable and legal requirements were glossed over or, by-passed entirely. The United States

Merchant Marine was at a decidedly-low ebb and lacking in morale and responsibility. The profits from smuggling narcotics were sufficient to induce unscrupulous men to pay for the privilege of signing on as stewards and crewmen of West Indies cruise ships. One person responsible for hiring them, the Ward Line's shipping master, a native of Greece, supposedly could neither read nor write English.

Bow aerial view of the *Morro Castle* at anchor, September 8, 1934 following the disastrous fire that claimed 134 lives. *Acme photograph, courtesy of the Daily Press Library.*

Still another factor contributed to the horror of that early morning disaster. The traditional captain's dinner on Friday night, the eve of arrival, had numerous inebriated passengers and crew, contributing to the disorder and terror of the general alarm that woke still-befogged people to discover the vessel aflame. In the confusion, ship's officers lost contact with each

The *Morro Castle* shown completely burned out on the beach at Asbury Park, New Jersey. *Photograph courtesy of The Mariners Museum.*

Morro Castle survivors landing on the beach at Spring Lake, New Jersey, September 8, 1934. *Photograph from Eldridge Collection, The Mariners Museum.*

other; the novice captain gave contradictory orders; and, although the weather was stormy, the ship continued at full speed into a 20-knot breeze, thus fanning the flames furiously. Many of the lifeboats were burned as they lay in their chocks. One that was launched, though rated at a capacity of 70 people, contained only 16—all crewmen. The fine tradition of American supremacy and service afloat were not strengthened by the fact that the chief engineer skipped off earlier in Lifeboat No. 1, along with three passengers and 29 crew. The resultant inquest uncovered other unsavory details. The captain and his radio officer were not on speaking terms and there was a criminal delay in transmitting messages for assistance, despite the fact that passing ships could see the *Morro Castle* speeding by, shrouded in flames.

Between 2:55 (when the acting second mate noticed smoke billowing from the stokehole fiddley and pulled the fire alarm) and 3:30 a.m., the fire had gained in momentum, and the entire superstructure of the ship from the forward funnel to the mizzen mast was a furnace. Many people jumped, rather than being engulfed in flame, and many perished before they were located and rescued in the turbulent water.

Eventually the frantic dash that fanned the flames ended, and all power having failed, the *Morro Castle* was anchored near Sea Girt, New Jersey. It would have been more suitable, if she were allowed to drift broadside to the wind, for, at anchor, she lay head-on, the wind continuing to sweep the ship from stem to stern. Meanwhile neighboring vessels performed rescue work with their lifeboats and crews. The *Morro Castle's* captain and 14 loyal crewmen were the last to abandon the ship.

Later, the United States Coast Guard cutter, *Tampa*, took the burning hulk in tow, bound for New York. But, heavy seas parted the lines, and the smoldering charnel house drifted broadside onto the beach at Asbury Park, New Jersey, where she stuck fast during the afternoon.

As if the tragedy were not sufficiently horrible, the city manager of Asbury Park visualized, in the smoldering wreck, a gold-mine tourist attraction. The beach area was immediately fenced off and, as thousands of inquisitive citizens thronged to the Jersey resort to view the ship and watch the bodies drift ashore, they were assessed 25 cents per person for the privilege. So enthusiastically did the Asbury Park official pursue his monetary quest, that he attempted to assume control of the ship, claiming "riparian rights." He hindered considerably the work of the government officials, arriving at Asbury Park to attend the vessel.

The *Morro Castle* tragedy appeared on the front page of *The Times-Herald*, Saturday, April 8, and, since public concern over the inquest was so keen, the disaster appeared in print for two weeks—replaced by Bruno Hauptmann in the Lindbergh kidnap case on September 21. Reams of testimony were produced at the inquest, but the actual source or beginning of the fire was not then proven conclusively.

William McFee, one of America's renowned nautical authors, and a former Merchant Marine chief engineer, voiced the considered opinion that the cause was overheating of the funnel base, through neglect or incompetence of the fireroom watch, who failed to maintain the burners in the furnaces. Since the red-hot uptake passed behind a cupboard in the little-used writing room, it was possible the ship caught fire there, due to the abnormal heat. Thus, the fire got a good start before bursting into a full-grown monster bent on destruction.

Matters that would have lessened the tragedy were ignored. Elijah Baker, III, estimator at the shipyard, mentioned at a recent panel discussion on safety at sea, that, the ship was divided into fire zones by fire screen doors. But subsequent investigation showed that several were sliding-type and tended to be noisy when the ship rolled. To prevent disturbing the passengers, Baker reported some of the doors were wedged open. In any event, when the fire occurred the doors did not close, and, fanned by the continued progress of the ship through the water, plus a stiff head-on breeze, flames spread with amazing rapidity, gutting her virtually from stem to stern.

Though 134 perished, it was not futile, for new safeguards for passengers resulted from the disaster. Extensive experiments were conducted by the shipyard on the old S.S. *Nantasket*, thus abolishing the use of burnable material in cabins and public spaces on shipboard. When the *America* emerged in 1940, the recommendations of a committee, formed by Congress to discover preventive measures, were thoroughly complied with.

But, as previously noted, more than a seaworthy, fireproof ship is needed. With the renaissance of the United States Merchant Marine upon the establishment of the Maritime Commission preceding World War II, efficiency and morale returned.

But, as McFee summarizes with telling perception, "the lesson of the *Morro Castle* is so simple that it may quite possibly be misunderstood. It is that the price of a merchant marine, like the price of liberty, is eternal vigilance."

CHAPTER 10

(1941)

The Liberty Ship *Zebulon B. Vance* — from Cradle to Grave

On several visits to the James River Reserve Fleet Anchorage, I checked on the slow and inevitable decline of an old liberty ship moored there named the *Zebulon B. Vance*. In March, 1970, at a luncheon meeting of shipping people at the James River Country Club, fleet superintendent John Negrotto, replied when I asked him how the *Vance* was faring, that tugs were presently towing the aged ship to Hampton Roads. There she would be turned over to a Polish deep-sea tug which would tow her across the Atlantic to an Italian scrap yard. Before the lunch was finished, the little cavalcade was in view, and we watched as it slowly passed the windows.

This weary vessel was the first ship built by the long-defunct North Carolina Shipbuilding Company, the World War II emergency subsidiary yard established for the U.S. Maritime Commission at Wilmington, North Carolina, by the Newport News Shipbuilding and Dry Dock Company. Now, virtually forgotten, are both the first ship and the establishment that built it. But, as the rust-streaked hulk slowly disappeared around Newport News Point en route oblivion, I resolved that its story deserved recognition.

These efforts materialized in the October 1, 1970, issue of *The State*, a quasi-official North Carolina magazine published at Raleigh, and also in the Newport News *New Dominion* of October 11. Several nostalgic liberty ship buffs wrote to the editor of *The State* to point out additional items of information. Emma Jo Davis, historian and curator of the U.S. Army Transportation Museum at Fort Eustis, Virginia, supplied photographs of the *Vance*, as she appeared as the hospital ship, *John J. Meaney*. The photographs were taken by Captain Horace Brown, who had the distinction of being Marion Davies' husband, thus affording the ship additional momentary fame.

Though old soldiers "may never die, but simply fade away," certainly old shipbuilders die slightly whenever one of the vessels, to which they loaned head, heart and hand to create, sails over the horizon for the last time. So it was, then, for a few old hands along the local waterfront, the departure of the steamer, *Zebulon B. Vance*, brought nostalgic pangs.

What—and who, for that matter—was Zebulon B. Vance?

Obviously this old and rust-streaked liberty ship, which on March 30, 1970, left Hampton Roads ignominiously trailing at the end of a tow line, bore no specific distinction beyond seeming well-deserving of her fate as scrap material. She was a sister ship to at least 2,580 other identical vessels, all hurriedly completed during World War II and most of them

83

Liberty ship *Zebulon B. Vance* on the launching ways of the North Carolina Shipbuilding Company, Wilmington, prior to launch December 6, 1941, as seen from the air. A big crowd gathered to witness the first North Carolina ship enter the Cape Fear River. *North Carolina Shipyard photograph, courtesy of The Mariners Museum.*

Officials and guests on the launching stand just prior to launching the *Zebulon B. Vance*, December 6, 1941, included, left to right: unidentified couple; Mrs. J. Melville Broughton; Captain Roger Williams, N.C. Shipbuilding Company president, standing behind the champagne bottle used to christen the ship; unidentified; Governor J. Melville Broughton; Homer L. Ferguson; Mrs. Homer L. Ferguson and Mrs. Roger Williams. A few hours later bombs rained down on Pearl Harbor. *North Carolina Shipyard photograph, courtesy of The Mariners Museum.*

already beyond recall. But, this particular ship carried to her end the name of one of North Carolina's most respected native sons. She was the first vessel built for a vital "Bridge of Ships" ultimately measuring, bow to stern, 21 miles in length, all of which were launched at Wilmington, North Carolina. These craft contributed a considerable part toward the allied victory in World War II.

As war clouds gathered over Europe, and Great Britain's desperate need for ships to maintain transoceanic lifelines increased, the United States recognized the acute necessity of building up its own merchant fleet to help her, lest the seemingly inevitable conflict should embroil this nation as well. Existing American shipyards—including the Newport News Shipbuilding and Dry Dock Company—were already taxed to capacity in constructing high-priority naval vessels. The United States Maritime Commission looked elsewhere for its merchant ships and so it was, that the government sponsored a series of new shipbuilding establishments devoted entirely to emergency cargo vessel construction.

These plants were set up and managed by existing shipyards and one of the most important was the North Carolina Shipbuilding Company at Wilmington, spawned and nurtured by the Newport News Shipyard. In the early 1940s 400 key personnel were loaned or transferred to the banks of the Cape Fear River to head a labor force comprising thousands of North Carolinians. The Newport News visitors spent the entire five-year war period in Wilmington before returning home. It was some of these men, who watched sadly as their first creation sailed away to oblivion.

The North Carolina yard was headed by president, Captain Roger Williams, executive vice president of the Newport News Shipyard. A 60-acre tract on the east bank of the Cape Fear River, below Wilmington, was selected and acquired by the government. The first local personnel packed and headed south in the autumn of 1940. Ground-breaking for the plant occurred on February 3, 1941, and the riverside woodland and tidal flats soon appeared as an enormous, bustling industrial establishment.

On March 18, 1941, the U.S. Maritime Commission formally announced that the first shipbuilding contract was awarded to the North Carolina shipyard for the construction of 25 liberty ships. This was the popular name for a modified design of a 2,500-horsepower, triple expansion, steam reciprocating engine-driven, 10,000-deadweight-ton cargo vessel, 441 feet long, 58 feet wide and draft of 27 feet. These ships lent themselves to mass production, but unfortunately were capable of steaming only ten knots. Each vessel was staffed by a crew of 40 officers and men, exclusive of a naval armed guard to handle the ship's defensive weapons. Initially, these consisted of a 3-inch 50 caliber antiaircraft gun on the forecastle head, and a 4-inch 50 caliber rifle on the fantail, both set in gun tubs. Twenty-millimeter machine guns were placed around the bridge structure, which was protected against small-arms fire by steel plates, backed by armor made of crushed stone and asphalt.

The formal designator of the liberty ship was EC2-S-C1 and, nearly 3,000 of them were built, before increased shipbuilding capabilities made it possible to convert to a sophisticated design producing more efficient turbine-driven vessels. But the slow, plodding liberties, with their antiquated "up-and-down" engines were the work horses of World War II.

Zebulon B. Vance (1830-1894), governor of North Carolina. *Photograph courtesy of the State Department of Archives and History, Raleigh, North Carolina.*

The first two liberty keels, laid at Wilmington on May 22, 1941, were designated *Zebulon B. Vance* and *Nathanael Greene*. Meanwhile, the company was awarded a contract to build several more liberties and was asked to expand its plant to provide increased facilities. Eight ships were laid down and construction on them was pushed by the time that the yard was ready to launch its first vessel, December 6, 1941. This occurred on a beautiful, sunny Saturday morning. Only hours away was the unexpected attack on Pearl Harbor, which plunged the nation into all-out war.

Sponsor of the *Zebulon B. Vance*, on that unseasonably warm and pleasant day, was Mrs. J. Melville Broughton of Raleigh, North Carolina, wife of the state governor. The ship's builders were gratified at the launching of their first ship in record time—only ten months after the ground for the shipyard had been a salt marsh.

The ship's eponym, Zebulon Baird Vance (1830-1894), was a worthy choice. A native of Buncombe County, N.C., Zeb Vance studied law at the University of North Carolina and had a private practice, with service in Washington in the U.S. Congress from 1858 until the Civil War's outbreak in 1861. As a Confederate colonel he returned to lead his state's government until the war's end in 1865. Postwar government service took him back to Washington as a United States senator, and again to Raleigh as state governor. He played a vital part in his state's return to prosperity within the Union. It was eminently fitting, that the first ship of the Wilmington yard would honor Zeb Vance, one of the Tar Heel State's most illustrious "First Citizens."

With World War II now raging, work at the North Carolina Shipyard was intensified. The *Vance* was immediately towed to an outfitting pier and a new liberty ship keel was laid on her recently-vacated shipway. When the yard began concentrated efforts, a new keel emerged each week.

By mid-February, 1942, the *Vance* was all but completed and, with a full crew embarked, she steamed down the Cape Fear River for a full day's trial trip. Entering the Atlantic near Southport, she plied a triangular course to test full power runs, crash stops, windlass gear and other equipment. German submarines were operating with apparent impunity on this side of the Atlantic, and a bomb-laden U.S. Army Air Corps plane followed the ship on her trials. The trial course passed near the dreaded "Torpedo Junction"—the area off Cape Hatteras and the Carolina banks islands, where the Nazi U-boats' slaughter was at its peak. Fortunately, no harm came to any North Carolina vessels while making trial runs.

On February 17, 1942, the *Zebulon B. Vance* was delivered to Uncle Sam, and sailed immediately from Wilmington to Philadelphia, to load a military cargo for Russia. She was commanded by a native of Mathews County, Virginia, Captain Charles N. Hudgins, and had a merchant marine crew of 48, plus a U.S. Navy armed guard of ten men with an ensign in charge. One of this Navy contingent was Champ Seeley, a Denbigh, Virginia, resident who vividly recalls his experiences aboard. He was a seaman gunner and was in the Navy five months before assignment to the *Vance.*

The cargo the ship loaded at Philadelphia included tanks, ammunition and foodstuffs, all desperatedly needed by the Russians. Though the United States had the material, transporting it to Russia was extremely difficult, with Norway and all the Baltic German-occupied, and U-boat wolf packs ranging the Atlantic. At Churchill's insistence, the famous PQ convoys to North Russia were instituted (designated QP southbound on their return). These provided one of the most desperate expedients of the war.

After loading at Philadelphia, the *Vance* departed the Delaware on March 15, and was ordered to join Convoy PQ-12. The convoy was formed at Halifax, Nova Scotia, and consisted of 14 other cargo ships and a Royal Navy escort comprised of a cruiser and four corvettes. After a 15-day delay, the ships proceeded without incident to Reykjavik, Iceland, where they remained another 15 days. Then, the tedious part of the journey began. Though they were on constant U-boat alert, no submarine attacked. But, Seeley reported that the convoy was bombed by Norway-based low-flying Nazi planes, some of which penetrated the screen and sank three ships. A proud moment for Seeley was when his antiaircraft gun, the 3-inch 50-caliber weapon mounted on the forecastle head, splashed one of the enemy bombers.

Eventually, the slow-moving ships rounded North Cape, Norway, and headed for Murmansk, their planned destination, Archangel, then still being frozen in. Seeley recalls that the Russians were quite friendly to the Americans, and they enjoyed liberty in the Arctic Russian port, despite its few amenities and the fact that the place was under continuous harassment by the Luftwaffe.

The return voyage, the ships ballasted with sea water, began on May 21. Halifax-bound Convoy QP-12 consisted of 14 ships plus escorts. Homeward bound, they were initially protected by unpleasant weather causing low visibility. But, actually, the Nazis were more interested in loaded outbound ships, and devoted their major efforts to attacking the eastbound PQ convoys.

Liberty ship *Zebulon B. Vance*, loaded and ready to sail August 21, 1942. *U.S. Coast Guard photograph, courtesy of The Mariners Museum.*

After a few tense days' steaming, the *Vance* and another vessel were detached from the convoy and ordered by the commodore to proceed independently to St. John's, Newfoundland. They were only separated a day when one of their escorts overtook them, and they were shepherded back into the convoy again. Intelligence reports indicated that a wolf pack was lying in wait.

No untoward events marked the remainder of the trip across the North Atlantic. Safely arriving at Halifax, the *Vance* was sent to St. John's, where she loaded a cargo of zinc concentrate for Norfolk. Her voyage down the coast was uneventful, Seeley recalls, but when she arrived in Virginia at the end of July, 1942, he was detached to enter the naval hospital there for major surgery. This concluded his affiliation with the North Carolina Shipyard's already battle-tested first ship. The *Vance*, however, again loaded a military cargo for North Russia and soon sailed once more on the dreaded Murmansk run.

Meanwhile, the Wilmington yard continued to grind out its liberty ships and built 126 of them by August 27, 1943, when the yard retooled to handle superior C-2 type cargo steamers. These, AKA's (attack cargo ships), and other military types contributed to a total of 253 ships launched into the Cape Fear River during the North Carolina Shipbuilding Company's five-year existence. The last vessel, the S.S. *Santa Isabel,* built as a Grace Line passenger-cargo-freighter, was launched April 16, 1946, when the once-teeming yard was relegated to caretaker status, and the men who performed such prodigies of shipbuilding returned home. Simultaneously, a reserve fleet anchorage for idled liberty ships was being prepared in the Cape Fear River.

U.S. Army hospital ship *John J. Meany,* converted July 1944, from the Liberty ship cargo carrier *Zebulon B. Vance,* as photographed by Captain Horace Brown on a Mediterranean voyage of August 1944. *Photograph courtesy of Mrs. Emma Jo Davis, Fort Eustis Transportation Museum.*

Although 27 North Carolina-built liberties were sunk by enemy action, the *Vance* led a charmed life and performed yeoman duty throughout the war. She had been transferred to the War Department in November, 1943, and converted to a fully-equipped U.S. Army hospital ship by the Bethlehem Steel Company in Boston in July, 1944, with the new name, *John J. Meany.* Cargo holds became sick bays, operating theaters, and off limits quarters for nurses. The ship's somber, all-over gray was repainted dazzling white with huge red crosses on sides and smokestack.

A present Yorktown resident, Mrs. Ruth Clegg Hogg, well remembers this service. From March until October, 1945, she was on board on duty

as a first lieutenant, Army Nurse Corps, sailing out of Charleston, South
Carolina.

I recall so well the wonderful G.I. patients who came home aboard this ship, and
their excitement as they once again sighted the U.S. mainland at Charleston and New
York. I shall never forget the tears of happiness and anticipation on the cheeks of our
soldiers, many on crutches or with casts, as the tugs with Army bands escorted our
ship into port. [And she concludes on a happy personal note:] Last, but not least, I
met my husband aboard this ship.

After such mercy mission duty, the *Zebulon B. Vance* (then the *John J.
Meany*) became an Army transport and, at war's end, was engaged through
1947 and most of 1948 in returning British and other war brides to
America, under her original name. This concluded the *Vance's* active
career, for the slow-steaming liberties were in oversupply with postwar

With her original name returned, the *Zebulon B. Vance* is shown laid up and paint peeling
in the James River Reserve Fleet, November 3, 1968. She was rated a U.S. Army Transport when she joined the "Idle Fleet."

markets found only for a few of the freighters among Greek ship owners.
Throughout the United States the government's idle fleet anchorages
swelled in size. The now-decommissioned *Vance* joined the already-packed
James River Reserve Fleet off Mulberry Island on December 10, 1948, and
remained there until the end of her career two dozen years later. For a
time, the *Vance* was moored with vessels which would possibly be returned to active service, but eventually she was relegated amidst those
whose fate was to be broken up for scrap. The relentless "tooth of time"
gnawed into her rust-streaked sides, paint flaked, and ultimately the unwanted old ship seemed the epitome of decay and neglect, her custodians
merely keeping her afloat until a customer should materialize.

This occurred when an Italian firm purchased the *Vance*, along with three other obsolete ships, for the sum of $470,000. It was stipulated by the Maritime Commission that the sale be for scrapping only. In mid-March, 1970, the Polish deep-sea tug, *Jantar*, arrived in Hampton Roads to pick up the *Vance*, and one other vessel, to tow them across to Italy for the account of the Cantieri Navali of Genoa. The *Jantar* was a large, efficient diesel-powered vessel, 215 feet in length and displacing 1,226 tons. She was built in England in 1958 for the Polish Ship Salvage Company, a property of the Polish government.

Port regulations kept the *Jantar* in Hampton Roads while a pair of local tugs brought the *Vance* from the Mulberry Island anchorage. At 11 a.m. on March 27, also an unseasonably pleasant day, the aged liberty ship was unshackled from her James River moorings, and towed down the river and under the bridge by the tugs, *Sparrows Point* and *Delaware*. Watching the outdated vessel slowly descend the James for her rendezvous with oblivion, one's "mind's eye" recalls those stirring days that witnessed her birth and wartime duty.

The *Zebulon B. Vance* rounding Newport News Point March 27, 1970 under tow. The next day an oceangoing tug took the *Vance* and another Liberty ship hulk in hand, towing them across to Italy to be scrapped.

Three days later, March 30, 1970, prepared with her consort for the long transoceanic haul by the *Jantar*, the *Zebulon B. Vance* left Hampton Roads at 9 a.m., bound for the Mediterranean port of La Spezia. Virginia Pilot Captain Robert H. Dozier, Jr., navigated the massive tug to the Virginia Capes, where he returned her to her master. At first, the two liberty ships were fastened side-by-side, each on a short tow line. Polish deck-hands were stationed on board the hulks to handle the lines, and a local harbor tug traveled along to help keep the tow in line. But once the vessels reached Cape Henry—a six-hour voyage at dead slow speed—the towing hawsers were let out and the ships disconnected so that one fell in line behind the other. After the accompanying tug retrieved the crewmen and delivered them to the *Jantar*, and Captain Dozier was picked up by his pilot launch, the three-ship cavalcade, now stretching out in tandem over a quarter of a mile of ocean, headed eastward for the long, wearisome passage across the Atlantic.

So it was, without a soul on board, that the *Zebulon B. Vance* and her mate made final departure from their native land.

Norfolk and Washington Steamboat Company steamer *Southland*, built at Newport News in 1909, was the oldest of the "Honeymoon Fleet" convoy of September, 1942. *Photograph courtesy of The Mariners Museum.*

Running mate on the Potomac River service was the *Northland*, built in 1911. *Robert T. Little photograph collection, The Mariners Museum.*

CHAPTER 11

(1942)

Bay Steamers Fight the Wolf Packs

The following story, headlined "Former Favorite Bay Steamers Battled Nazi Wolf Pack in World War II," appeared on the September 25, 1960, feature page of the Sunday *Daily Press*. With only a few minor changes, it was incorporated in the text of Chapter XII, "The Impact of World War II," in my book, *Steam Packets on the Chesapeake*, published by Cornell Maritime Press, Inc., of Cambridge, Maryland, in 1961.

In June of 1962, I received, "out of the blue," a letter from a Dr. Ernst Schmidt of Reinbek, West Germany, stating that he had acquired a copy of my book from his Hamburg bookshop under the following unusual circumstances, more suitably related in his own words:

In the late afternoon of February 17th [1962]—just a few hours after the flood catastrophe—I happened to pass the road along the port by boat. Then I decided to look for some people as to how their places were affected. Well, that bookshop had six feet of water and all sorts of objects in unbelievable quantities were floating up and down.

Right at the entrance there was your book in its blue dust jacket with my bookseller shouting, "Just hold it, and dry it as soon as possible—it's just what you want." He was always very friendly, so with a few other people we helped him shovel out the worst of the fishy stuff swimming around.

This copy of your book—in perfect condition again—has given me many hours of very, very interesting reading. . . .

Dr. Schmidt explained that he was a fellow member of the Steamship Historical Society of America and had a particular interest in the famous "Honeymoon Fleet" convoy of September, 1942. Composed of eight American former bay and river steamers, they battled German submarines on their trip across to England. Dr. Schmidt supplied all sorts of interesting nuggets of information from the German point of view, including the following transcript, now translated from the official German Wehrmacht High Command report of September 28, 1942:

As reported by special message, German submarines in the North Atlantic have destroyed for the most part an American troop transport on its way to England. They came upon a fast convoy of only a few large passenger ships, which were heavily protected and were loaded with troops, munitions and war materials. In many days of hard battle and rear guard engagement, they sank a 19,000 gross registered ton, two-funnel steamship of the *Viceroy of India* type, which, after three torpedo hits, capsized; a 17,000 gross registered ton two-funnel steamship of the *Reina Del Pacifico* type; a 11,000 gross registered ton transport of the *Derbyshire* type; and a destroyer of the convoy escort. Two other transports were damaged by torpedo hits.

With these successes, our submarines have inflicted a heavy blow on the enemy. The enemy transport navy have lost three especially valuable ships of altogether 47,000 gross registered tons, as they seek to put into action especially important and urgently needed troop transports.

Top: Chesapeake Steamship Company steamer *Yorktown*, built at Newport News in 1928, as delivered by the shipyard. *Newport News Shipyard photograph.* Bottom: The *Yorktown*, acquired by the Old Bay Line in 1940, as taken over for war service September 8, 1942. *U.S. Coast Guard photograph.*

Dr. Schmidt also forwarded from the Nazi newspaper, *Volkischer Beo-bachter*, of September 29, 1942, names and pictures from German sources of the three large British liners which, according to the German authorities quoted above, were destroyed. Actually, the ships they sank were the former Long Island Sound 1924-built two-funnel steamers, *Boston* and *New York*, and the 1928 Chesapeake Liner, *Yorktown*, incidentally the last passenger steamboat ever built at Newport News. *Boston* and *New York* measured 4,989 tons each and the *Yorktown* was 1,547. Their total tonnage, 11,525, was certainly far short of the 47,000 tons claimed by the Nazis.

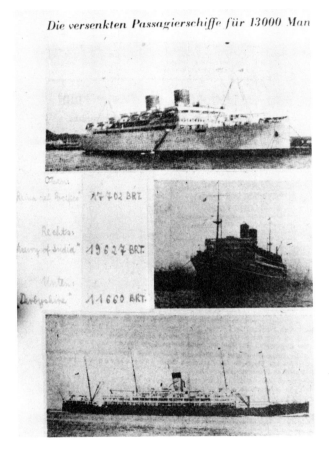

"The sunken passenger ships for 13,000 men." Nazi propaganda picture of the *Reina del Pacifico*, 17,702 gross registered tons; *Viceroy of India*, 19,627 g.r.t.; and *Derbyshire*, 11,660 g.r.t., which U-boats claimed to have sunk. From *Volkischer Boebachter*, September 29, 1942. *Courtesy of Dr. Ernest Schmidt.*

Later research performed in my behalf by Dr. Schmidt uncovered the information that German admiralty reports subsequently identified the casualties of the convoy—and this time the names were correct—designated RB 1 (River Boat). They were the *Boston*, sunk by *U-216* (Oberftleutnant K.O. Schultz); the *New York*, by *U-96* (Oberftleutnant Hellriegel); the *York-town*, by *U-619* (Oberftleutnant Makowski); and H.M.S. *Veteran*, one of their escorts, by *U-404* (Kapitanleutnant von Bulow).

None of these submarines survived the war, however. The *U-216* went down with no survivors on October 20, 1942, southwest of Ireland, victim of a British bombing raid. The *U-96* was sunk by bombing March 30, 1945, at her Wilhelmshaven base, with captain and crew escaping. H.M.S. *Viscount* sank *U-619* on October 15, 1942, southeast of Cape Farewell with no remaining survivors. And, *U-404* went down under American and British bombs on July 28, 1943, northwest of Cape Ortegal, also with no survivors.

Top: Eastern Steamship Company steamer *New York*, built in 1924 for New York to Boston service via the Cape Cod Canal. *William B. Taylor photograph, courtesy of The Mariners Museum.* Bottom: The sound steamer *New York*, convoy vice-commodore Captain C. Mayers, RN, in wartime dress, passing through the Cape Cod Canal en route to St. John's, Newfoundland, for departure in convoy RB-1, September 21, 1942. She was sunk by a German U-boat on September 26. *Rex R. Eldridge photograph, courtesy of The Mariners Museum.*

Dr. Schmidt sums up the story of the small convoy (eight steamboats and two destroyer escorts with an aggregate age of 155 years): "What bravery and courageous action of these steamers against 17 (seventeen) U-boats!!" There is certainly no argument there!

———————

Beyond the condemning and closing of the Old Point Comfort pier early in 1960 by the United States Army, there is still another extremely logical reason why the few remaining Chesapeake Bay steamers (none presently existing) no longer serve the Peninsula.

Top: Eastern Steamship Company steamer *Boston,* built in 1924 as a sister ship of the *New York,* June 30, 1935. *William B. Taylor photograph, courtesy of The Mariners Museum.* Bottom: The sound steamer *Boston,* convoy commodore Captain R.S. Young, RN, readied for war duty overseas, transiting the Cape Cod Canal in the summer of 1942. *Rex R. Eldridge photograph, courtesy of The Mariners Museum.*

Top: Baltimore Steam Packet Company steamer *President Warfield,* built at Wilmington, Delaware, in 1928, shown in 1939 at her pier in Norfolk. *Acme Photo Company print, courtesy of The Mariners Museum.* Bottom: The U.S.S. *President Warfield* returned to the Naval Operating Base, Norfolk, from overseas and was offered for sale by the U.S. Maritime Commission on September 19, 1945. *Official U.S. Navy photograph.*

Early in World War II the government requisitioned the majority of their fleets from all the bay carriers. Of seven regular Old Point visitors so pre-emptively taken, regrettably only one returned; one was sunk; one departed for Israel, two for China; and two remained in the Gulf of Mexico. One, the Pennsylvania Railroad Company's former Cape Charles steamer, *Virginia Lee*, returned later and was rebuilt as the diesel ferry, *Accomac*, for the Little Creek run. But, deplorably, the others were never replaced.

This account will attempt to cover the wartime history of commonplace vessels designed not for storm and shell, but merely to transport holiday-seekers and others on placid inland waters. Certainly battling Nazi wolf packs in mid-Atlantic was not a part of their original conception. Yet, they acquitted themselves bravely, adding an illustrious chapter to the record of American maritime enterprise.

In the early stages of World War II, with German U-boats raising havoc along the Atlantic sea lanes, the allies' need for virtually anything that would float was vital. Accordingly, early in 1942, the government, through the War Shipping Administration, having already seized oceangoing vessels from their owners, likewise attempted to requisition coastwise and sound-class steamers along the Atlantic seaboard. The major part of them were transferred to the British Ministry of War Transport for conveyance overseas where they could serve a variety of purposes such as training and barracks ships, hospital and command craft.

At this time the bay carriers, whose vessels made daily calls at Old Point, included the Norfolk and Washington Steamboat Company which had three vessels; the *Northland*, *Southland*, and *District of Columbia*. The Baltimore Steam Packet Company, recently merged with the Chesapeake Line, had six boats; the *State of Virginia*, *State of Maryland*, *President Warfield*, *Yorktown*, *City of Norfolk*, and the *City of Richmond*. The Pennsylvania Railroad operated two boats to Cape Charles, the *Virginia Lee* and the *Maryland*. A total of 11 boats regularly served the Peninsula.

When in fact the requisitioning was over, the Washington Line had one remaining vessel, the *District of Columbia*. The Old Bay Line (as the Baltimore Steam Packet Company is less formally known) possessed two, the *City of Norfolk* and the *City of Richmond*. The *Maryland* remained to do the best she could to handle the vastly mounting traffic over the Pennsylvania's Delmarva Division. The fleet was diminished to only four.

It seems somewhat extraordinary that those shoal-draft, inland water, essentially-pleasure boats were ever considered in the light of warships, and particularly so in the case of the Potomac River boats, both of which were more than 30 years old. When queried on the matter, the government issued an official euphemism that the *Northland* and *Southland* were required "for war purposes." Beyond that, no statement about them was released until the war's end.

The *State of Virginia* was the first of the local fleet to depart. She was requisitioned by the government in Baltimore on April 1, 1942, and was followed the next day by her sister ship, the *State of Maryland*. The *Maryland* was removed to the Newport News Shipyard and her passenger quarters and other appointments of peacetime employment were summarily ripped out, and she emerged several days later as a small cargo steamer. Similar treatment was accorded the *Virginia* in Baltimore. They were both then placed with the Army Transportation Service and served for the duration of the war as passenger and troop carriers in the Caribbean and South American waters.

On July 10, 1942, five more Chesapeake Bay boats were taken by the government—the *Southland* and *Northland*, cited previously, and the *President Warfield*, *Yorktown*, and *Virginia Lee*. These five, together with several Long Island Sound and other northern boats, were intended for use abroad.

To prepare them for transoceanic war duty, they, too, had considerable amounts of interior fittings and passenger accommodations removed. Foredecks were covered with turtleback sheathing, mooring chocks were plugged and open spaces boxed in with heavy planking. This effectively closed the areas between main and saloon decks aft, and between saloon and gallery decks forward. Armament was added and the boats were painted a somber gray from stems to sterns.

Though the need for the services of such a "dishpan fleet" across the Atlantic was increasing daily, remaining of course, was the slight matter of

New Bedford, Martha's Vineyard and Nantucket steamer *Naushon*, built in 1929 for the New England Steamship Company, July 6, 1940. *William B. Taylor photograph, courtesy of The Mariners Museum.*

transferring the boats there. And, many seasoned mariners doubted its completion, because the vessels were designed for navigating protected waters alone.

Captain R.T. Park, superintendent of Britain's Coast Lines, Ltd., of Liverpool, was of the opinion that the boats would prove dependable and sufficiently fast for the journey across, and that it would not be difficult to obtain volunteer crews to man them for the voyage, despite its obvious risks.

Accordingly, Captain Park was appointed a committee of one to implement the matter. Swiftly and effectively crews were collected in England, the masters and other officers coming from Coast Lines, Ltd.; ratings were drawn from the Liverpool shipping pool. A total of 550 Britishers were detailed to man the ships.

Meanwhile, the steamboats were hastily prepared in various East Coast American shipyards. Naturally there were heartbreaking disappointments. One steamer burned out at Philadelphia. The *Virginia Lee* developed structural problems, which could not be duly remedied for the fleet to be dispatched to Great Britain before the North Atlantic equinoctial season began, and decent weather passed. Accordingly, the *Virginia Lee* dropped out, and subsequently was repaired and sent south instead of north. Despite the compelling need for her in local waters, the government dispatched her to South America, and she operated throughout the war as an Amazon River passenger boat.

A fleet of some eight former steamboats, assembled at St. John's, Newfoundland, after proceeding up the East Coast independently, made ready to cross the submarine-infested North Atlantic in a convoy. Half of them were from the Chesapeake.

Eventually, all was ready and on September 21, 1942, in company with two British destroyer escorts, H.M.S. *Veteran* and *Vanoc*, the eight-ship

The Nantucket steamer *Naushon*, wearing her war paint, passing through the Cape Cod Canal bound for convoy rendezvous at St. John's, Newfoundland. *Photograph Rex R. Eldridge collection, courtesy of The Mariners Museum.*

convoy prepared for the grim business of war. It consisted of the *Boston*, *New York*, *Northland*, *Southland*, *President Warfield*, *Yorktown*, *Naushon* and *New Bedford*. A macabre humorist in the Admiralty assigned the code name, "Maniac," to the convoy, less colorfully designated RB-1. Apparently, security regulations were well-enforced in Newfoundland and no photographs seem available of what probably was the oddest appearing convoy that had ever collected to tackle the North Atlantic. But, residents of St. John's well recall the sailing of the courageous little fleet. It was a clear, crisp autumn day—a pleasant change on that usually fogbound coast—as the ships left fiord-like St. John's and assumed steaming positions outside the harbor. The course was set toward Iceland and the convoy commenced its perilous voyage at 15 knots.

Top: Nantucket Line steamboat *New Bedford*, July 6, 1940, built in 1928 for the New England Steamship Company. *William B. Taylor photograph, courtesy of The Mariners Museum.* Bottom: The *New Bedford*, readied for war, en route Down East via the Cape Cod Canal. *Photograph Rex R. Eldridge collection, courtesy of The Mariners Museum.*

The first two days were uneventful, but, on the third morning the disquieting news was received that a German surface raider was in the vicinity. Nothing materialized, but the following afternoon, in broad daylight without warning, two torpedoes slammed into the convoy commodore's ship, the *Boston*. She immediately heeled to starboard, but righted and started settling down on an even keel. Then, she slowly upended and slipped under, stern first. The former Washington boat, *Northland*, went to her assistance as the remainder of the convoy steamed ahead.

But this was merely a prelude to worsening conditions. The Nazi wolf packs had had their first taste of blood.

Then, it seemed that everything began to occur simultaneously. The steering gear of the *Northland* jammed in the excitement of taking evasive courses, after the *Boston* was torpedoed. Precisely at the time the *Northland* rectified the trouble, a surfaced submarine was sighted. Meanwhile, the other ex-Washington boat, the *Southland*, observed a periscope to starboard. So effective did her gunfire prove, that the U-boat was forced to submerge after 14 rapid rounds from a 12-pounder were hurled in its direction. Another periscope then appeared on the port hand, and once more the *Southland's* gunners went into action firing 18 rounds. When the skirmish ended, the Admiralty credited the *Southland* with a "probable kill"—not at all bad for a 1908-built riverboat, built at Newport News incidentally.

As this occurred, the Old Bay Liner *President Warfield* was being attacked and narrowly escaped, when a torpedo was sighted approaching abaft her port beam. Fast-moving helm action swung the steamer on a parallel course, and the lethal charge passed harmlessly by scarcely 30 feet away. Two minutes later, the *Warfield* sighted the outline of a submarine close on her port quarter and opened fire with her 12-pounder. The British escort ship *Veteran* joined the attack and the consensus was that still another submarine never made port.

All through the day, the desperate running battle continued, with a spirited defense being carried out by the now well-scattered fleet. But the Nazi U-boats were not entirely finished with the convoy, brazenly signaling the ships' positions to each other. The former Long Island Sound steamer, *New York*, was torpedoed at dusk on the fourth day and exploded in a sheet of flames. While searching for survivors, H.M.S. *Veteran* was struck and sunk with heavy loss of life, for she was carrying not only her own crew but also men rescued from other vessels.

The former Chesapeake Line steamer *Yorktown*, a 1928-product of the Newport News Shipyard, was the final casualty. On the evening of the sixth day, September 26, 1942, she was hit amidships on the port side; her superstructure collapsed and she went down in only three minutes. Survivors, including Captain W.P. Boylan, fortunately were discovered adrift on rafts the following day by a British patrol plane which dropped supplies to them. But the men remained on the rafts 46 hours in rough seas, and with a bitter wind, before a destroyer located and rescued them.

In the meantime, proceeding independently, the five surviving steamers reached various ports in the United Kingdom. Dr. Goebbels, Hitler's bombastic propaganda minister, was forced unwittingly to pay tribute to the spirited action of these little 300- and 400-foot vessels. He incidentally magnified them in his Radio Berlin broadcast, by claiming the sinking of "several ships of the *Queen Mary* class"—an accomplishment for the little Chesapeake Bay boats! Goebbels named as probabilities, the *Viceroy of India* and the *Reina Del Pacifico*, both massive, converted liners, neither of which was in the vicinity of Convoy RB-1 at the time. However, the German announcer observed that "the defense was so fierce that it could not be observed whether two or more of the transports hit, sank or not."

It was initially reported that the ships were deliberately dispatched as a decoy to lure enemy submarines from another more vital convoy carrying thousands of American troops to Britain. This was not the case, despite its frequent appearance in print.

Final tally showed three steamboats and one of their escorts were sunk, having 131 casualties. King George VI granted meritorious decorations and commendations to surviving officers and men of the fleet, and posthumous awards were presented for gallantry.

Thus, "Convoy Maniac" became one of the most shining episodes in the roster of courageous deeds of the British Merchant Service in World War II.

The U.S.S. *PC1233*, U.S.S. *Southland*, and U.S.S. *Leyden* (ex-*Northland*) moored side by side in the harbor of Cherbourg, France, August 11, 1944. *Official U.S. Navy photograph.*

Now, reasonably safe in English ports, the boats assumed their various and more prosaic military duties for the duration of the war.

The following months of the *President Warfield's* career were spent uneventfully at moorings near the English village of Instow on the Torridge River where, aground at ebb tide, she served as a combined operations training barracks ship for British commandoes and marines. The British subsequently decided this phase of operations was successfully concluded, so in July, 1943, she was gratefully returned to the United States Navy, along with the *Southland* and the *Northland*. The *Northland* was then renamed the U.S.S. *Leyden* (a U.S.S. *Northland* already appeared on the United States Naval roster). The *President Warfield* and the *Southland* retained their original names, however.

All three crossed to Normandy, following its successful invasion. At Omaha Beach, moored close to the artificial breakwater formed by sinking obsolete hulks and concrete block ships offshore, the former Old Bay Liner U.S.S. *President Warfield* became home for numerous U.S. Navy personnel. The men were attached to the port director unit, which operated the teeming beachhead and anchorage area. Some of her residents were well acquainted with her, from peacetime trips to Baltimore. One individual was assigned the identical cabin on board which he had occupied during his honeymoon. Appropriately, they nicknamed the *Warfield*, the U.S.S. *Statler*.

She later traveled the Seine transporting troops from Le Havre to Rouen. After the war ended, she returned across the Atlantic to the familiar waters of Hampton Roads. She arrived at the Norfolk Naval Operating Base on July 25, 1945, and was decommissioned and offered for sale by the Maritime Commission in September, 1945. After an inactive period in the James River Reserve Fleet she was quietly acquired by Haganah, the Jewish underground organization, and sailed back across the Atlantic. Renamed the *Exodus 1947*, she attempted to run immigrants to Palestine through the British blockade. This occurred prior to the establishment of the state of Israel.

The two Washington boats remained for a considerable time in Plymouth Harbor, England, and were ultimately acquired by Chinese interests. Their lengthy voyage was completed out to the Orient, via Suez, and the ships were renamed the *Hung Chong* and the *Hung Yung* upon arrival in 1947. They then disappeared behind the Bamboo Curtain and, though reputedly scrapped in 1955, their actual fates are unknown.

The *State of Maryland* and the *State of Virginia* found no purchaser after the war, and after a considerable period spent in idleness in the Mobile, Alabama, Reserve Fleet they, too, felt the bite of the shipwrecker's torch.

Thus, the careers of the former Chesapeake Bay steamers ended. Failing to return after the war was deplorable according to steamboat enthusiasts hereabouts. Meanwhile, transportation needs developed other channels. That still, cold night of December 30, 1959, when the *City of Richmond* docked for the last time at Old Point Comfort, marked the end of an era.

Mariner class dry cargo ship *Cracker State Mariner* at the Newport News Shipbuilding and Dry Dock Company south-side outfitting pier, May 24, 1954, as readied for her builder's trial trip.

CHAPTER 12

Trial Trip of the *Cracker State Mariner*

The following account of a trial trip of a Newport News-built ship was published in the Sunday feature section of the *Daily Press*, May 30, 1954, five days after it had taken place. This 17,500-ton, high-speed freighter was the last of five similar Mariner Class ships built at Newport News. The United States Maritime Administration produced the designs, for which Congress authorized $350,000,000, in the late summer of 1950. A total of 35 Mariners were constructed by various shipyards in the country between 1952 and 1954. Built as part of the Korean War effort, the average cost per ship was $8,441,332.

The Mariner ships were an immediate success. Eighteen remained in service as freighters, the U.S. Navy obtained three for fast cargo carriers and others were converted to passenger vessels for the Matson Line's Pacific service. The remaining vessels were held in reserve.

The *Cracker State Mariner* was acquired by the American President Lines from her initial Savannah operators and appeared as the *President Coolidge* in 1957, so perpetuating the name of a renowned Newport News-built passenger liner of the Dollar Line, built in 1931. Serving as a troop transport, the first *Coolidge* was blown up by a "friendly" mine on October 25, 1942, during World War II. Concerning the Mariner ship, the New York *Herald-Tribune* of February 1, 1959, is quoted: "The *President Coolidge* made cargo history by carrying an entire cement plant, including giant kiln sections weighing up to 92 tons."

The freighter remained in operation on the American President Lines' former 'round-the-world trade route until January, 1974, and shortly thereafter was chartered to the Military Sealift Command.

At periodic intervals, local shipyard workers set aside their plans and tools, go aboard ship and, temporarily become deep-sea sailors.

Shipyard mechanics, riggers, technical men and other vast numbers of crafts- and tradesmen required in shipbuilding, are transformed into mates and quartermasters, able-bodied seamen, engineers, firemen, oilers, wipers, cooks and stewards. Even a ship's surgeon and purser arrive on board at sailing time.

It is, of course, this group of highly-trained people that demonstrate its versatility by manning and operating the shipyard's vessels on their trial trips. This familiar procedure takes place prior to the completion and delivery of Newport News' legendary product—"good ships," preferably built at a profit.

Various sea trials of the yard's world famous vessels, such as the liner *United States*, attract widespread interest. In addition to the shipyard crew and other local key personnel, there are many invited guests, plus owners' representatives, government brass and other dignitaries. Through long-standing custom, it is invariably a stag party. Members of the press are invited, news conferences are held and messages are dispatched by ship-to-shore telephone to appear in papers and wire services across the nation. Carrier pigeons were once tried!

But the majority of trial trips attract little concern and are merely covered by brief press announcements of which ship sailed, who was in charge and other bare details for local consumption. The guests embarked on such routine vessels are limited to members of the trial board, the ship's principal officers who take charge on delivery, manufacturers' representatives and some shipyard officials and their friends, who enjoy an outing. Occasionally, a writer is aboard.

Such a trial trip was staged May 26, 1954, by the *Cracker State Mariner*—an excellent and useful (though hardly unique) high-speed, dry cargo steamer. As Hull No. 494, she was the last of five Mariner Class ships built at Newport News, from a total of 35 similar craft constructed in seven American shipyards. These vessels were allocated by the United States Maritime Administration in its 1951 program to bolster the quality of the nation's postwar merchant marine.

The *Cracker State* [Georgia] *Mariner* is a steel, single-screw steam turbine-driven vessel of 13,400 tons deadweight, launched by the Newport News yard on April 6, 1954. She is 528 feet long, 76 feet wide and 44 feet, six inches deep. Unloaded, she rides high on the water, drawing but 12 feet, four inches forward and 23 feet, three inches aft, carrying only fuel and water ballast.

Appropriately, the *Cracker State Mariner*'s home port, Savannah, is painted on her stern. Upon delivery she would be operated by the South Atlantic Steamship Line, Inc.

Although upon completion and readiness for sea trials, only minor adjustments remain to be made on a vessel, and all machinery and equipment have been individually tested alongside the outfitting pier, for the first time, the ship as a whole demonstrates her capabilities. A feeling of anxiety and anticipation prevails on the eve of any ship's sailing, even on commonplace voyages. But on the first trial trip there is a discernable tenseness as the crew quietly perform their varied duties preparing for departure.

The *Cracker State Mariner* was scheduled to leave the shipyard at 5 a.m., but we embarked the night before at 11 p.m. At the gangway we were greeted by Charles L. Soter, shipyard hull outfitting staff supervisor, who served as the ship's purser. We were presented a card listing our berth number, abandon-ship station and messing assignment. The majority of the ship's company was due to arrive the next morning prior to sailing time. Harold T. Bent, yard works manager in charge of the trials; Captain Elliott D. Edwards, veteran pilot of the Virginia Pilot Association and master for the *Cracker State Mariner*'s trip; George Abernathy, Ken Peebles, Tilly Smith, Red Baysden and several other yard officials and guests had previously boarded.

Before retiring we toured the ship from stem to stern and from flying bridge to shaft tunnel. The decks were brilliantly lit by clusters of lights attached to lofty flanking king posts, that support the intricate maze of booms and other cargo-handling gear suspended above the six cargo hatches, equipped with accordion-type steel hatch covers.

Below deck at midnight the firemen started lighting off boilers. Long-handled torches were thrust through holes in the ends, igniting the oil, and were then quickly withdrawn. Occasionally, a tongue of flame shot out into the fireroom before the peep-hole door could be closed. Steam pressure inched up the gauges as the effect was felt. At 2 a.m. the main engine was warmed up by running the turbines slowly, first ahead and then astern, while the ship strained at the lines securing her to the dock.

At progressive intervals throughout the night and early morning more people reported on board and assumed their various duties. An entry in the official bridge log read: "0415—all navigational equipment ready for sea."

Sunrise came at 4:45, the weather was pleasantly clear, with a moderate southwest breeze whipping up small whitecaps in the James River at the beginning of ebb tide. The shipyard tug *Huntington* was already alongside the ship and secured with heavy hawsers in readiness for undocking the steamer.

At precisely five o'clock, all card holders accounted for, a corrected passenger list was handed ashore, a crane whisked off the gangway, and the ship's siren emitted its deep-throated roar. The tugs tightened their lines and the *Cracker State Mariner*, gathering sternway, slipped back along the pier into the open river. The trial trip was underway.

Fifty-four minutes later, having carefully threaded her way through the maze of shipping anchored in Hampton Roads, the new freighter passed abeam of the lighthouse at Old Point Comfort and headed through Thimble Shoal Channel for Cape Henry and the open sea. The versatility of the shipyard afloat was now made apparent in still another manner. Breakfast produced the first of many demonstrations of this skill. J.W. Dickensen of the shipyard purchasing department, presently the chief steward heading a force of more than two dozen stewards, mess boys, cooks and pantrymen, provided the 250 people on board with a variety of excellent nutritious meals (fried chicken and Virginia ham for lunch; steak, tender and thick, for dinner). Including sandwiches, doughnuts and coffee continuously available on the ship, it was apparent that Dickensen's department was continuously diligent.

Cape Henry passed abaft the starboard beam at 6:45 a.m., and the *Cracker State Mariner* began to feel the slow and easy heave of the open sea. Meanwhile, speed was increased and the vessel skipped daintily along, leaving a wake of bubbling foam behind her. She took an easterly course towards the Chesapeake Lightship [since replaced by a light tower] anchored more or less permanently 15 miles off Cape Henry in the open Atlantic.

Arriving within half a mile of the lightship, preparations were made to calibrate the ship's radio direction finder by impulses broadcast from the lightship. Adjustment was made on the standard magnetic compass. In this age of mechanical marvels, specifically radar and gyrocompasses, the reliable magnetic compass is required, nevertheless. Automatic contrivances can suddenly fail, but once properly adjusted for deviation, the magnetic needle invariably points to the north magnetic pole.

Emil Smola, veteran compass adjuster and purveyor of nautical instruments in Newport News since 1917, a frequent passenger on trial ships from

Left: Virginia Pilot Association Captain Elliott D. ("Kid") Edwards, master of the *Cracker State Mariner* for her trial trip, May 26, 1954. *Shipyard photograph by B.J. Nixon.* Right: Veteran compass adjuster Emil Smola working on the standard magnetic compass of the Mariner freighter prior to the ship's high speed trial run. Mr. Smola came to Newport News prior to World War I on board the Hungarian freighter *Budapest* which was then interned here (*see page 45*). He elected to remain in America and became a U.S. citizen. *Shipyard photograph by B.J. Nixon.*

the ports of Hampton Roads commenced this job. The *Cracker State Mariner* slowly circled, flying the international code flags "J I" meaning "I am adjusting compass." While so "swinging ship," as the procedure is termed, Smola took rapid bearings of the sun and checked azimuth tables and portable chronometer as he noted the compass readings. Adjustments, first with the pencil-like magnets in the base of the binnacle, and then, the two soft iron balls (quadrantal spheres) on either side of it, gradually rectified the errors caused by induced magnetism in the ship.

In about three-quarters of an hour, adjustment of the compass completed, the freighter was readied for her initial machinery trials.

Checking the sounds of the main steam turbine rotor in the engine room of the *Cracker State Mariner* during a high speed run. *Shipyard photograph by B.J. Nixon.*

At this point it would be appropriate to go below deck with Charles F. Palen, shipyard superintendent of the machinery division and chief engineer for the trip, and others on the crowded starting platform before the instrument panel. With the engine room annunciator pointing full ahead, we watched various technicians moving about, adjusting various valves, noting a temperature reading, and occasionally listening intently with pointed steel rods, one end pressed on a turbine casing, the other tucked in an ear—similar to a doctor's examination with his stethoscope—as the power plant built up for the four-hour endurance run. This was commenced at 17,500 shaft horsepower, firing 14 to 15 nozzles on the boilers, and finally increased to 19,500 shaft horsepower, using 17 to 19 nozzles.

With revolutions per minute in the high-pressure turbine rotor now measuring in the thousands, and steam pressure in the main line from the boilers recorded in hundreds of pounds, the *Cracker State Mariner* was traveling more than 23 knots. This genuinely demonstrated evidence for her classification as a high-speed cargo carrier. Numerous luxury passenger vessels have to be content with considerably less. This speed was accomplished with virtually negligible commotion or vibration on the entire ship.

But, as the purpose of a trial trip is to demonstrate weaknesses as well as strength, it is rare that a trial trip is completed without malfunction. Though

View looking astern from the mainmast as the *Cracker State Mariner* makes a high speed turn to port during her builder's trials. *Shipyard photograph by B.J. Nixon.*

the end result was insignificant and in no way impaired the ship's quality and performance, the *Cracker State Mariner* suffered misfortune, considered by the shipyard to be more severe than average. Prior to completion of the first test run, the thrust bearing of the main high-pressure turbine burned out, necessitating postponement of further speed tests. Adjustments were made to blank off the high-pressure turbine and to introduce steam directly into the low pressure one. The task was time-consuming and meant that the original scheduled return home at 8 p.m. could not be met. Valuable experience was gained by the demonstrated ability of the craft to maintain approximately half of her designed speed on one turbine. The rate was now adjusted so that the *Cracker State Mariner* would re-schedule her arrival time for 6 a.m. the following morning. This enabled docking at a reasonable hour when tugs were available, thus obviating anchoring in the stream.

Returning to port during the night was one of the most memorable parts of the trial. In the stilled, darkened pilothouse, the officer on watch issued his muted commands to the quartermaster and, the lookouts progressively

Crewmen of the Newport News Shipyard catch a moment's rest in the evening as the *Cracker State Mariner* is returning from her trial trip. *Shipyard photograph by B.J. Nixon.*

reported the navigational lights burning satisfactorily. On the bridge wing, C.M. Rutter, Jr., superintendent shipyard hull outfitting division in charge on deck and "opposite number" to Charles Palen below, would be found talking to Captain Edwards. From this spot, with its canopy of brilliant stars above, we moved into the chart room, poured another cup of steaming black coffee, and pricked off courses and distances on the open chart. We peered into the miraculous eye of the radar and observed the sliver of light unerringly identify and locate the sundry ships in the vicinity. At midnight, the Chesapeake Lightship became a conspicuous "target" dead ahead. Within the 20-mile wand of light, the radar traced the configuration of the Chesapeake Bay entrance through the portals of Capes Henry and Charles.

Accordingly, through the night sailed the good Mariner ship with good men on watch, alow and aloft.

The sun was well above the horizon as we passed Old Point Comfort and stood down Hampton Roads for the Newport News channel. Two tugs, the yard tug *Huntington* and the Chesapeake and Ohio Railway tug, *R.J. Bowman*, came alongside as we approached the yard's south side outfitting pier. Without delay, the steamer's flanks were nudged into the dock, heaving lines were thrown to waiting hands, and slowly the hull moved in to "kiss" the camel fenders alongside. The *Cracker State Mariner's* initial ocean voyage was concluded. A useful life of service lay ahead. Immediately upon arrival, shore workers inspected the errant thrust bearing and on a second builder's trial held May 28, 1954, the ship passed all required tests with flying colors.

Back off the shipyard on May 27, 1954 after her trials, the Chesapeake and Ohio Railway Company's steam tug *R.J. Bowman* assists in docking the new steamship. *Shipyard photograph by B.J. Nixon.*

At supper the night before returning to the shipyard, I sat beside one of the veteran officers who was to assume control of the craft upon delivery. There's something about a Newport News-built ship, he said, that seafaring men can detect anywhere. And, those standards of reliability and honest workmanship are achieved in every product.

It is no wonder Newport News ships are highly esteemed on the sea lanes of the Seven Seas, and mariners consider themselves fortunate to sign aboard a vessel whose original voyage began in James River waters.

CHAPTER 13

La Belle France Came to Newport News

It would be futile even attempting to explain the mystic quality which made France's 1927-built, 33,000-ton liner, the *Ile de France*, one of the most appreciated ships in history. I believe that poet and critic John Malcolm Brinnin in his book, *The Sway of the Grand Saloon*, published by Delacorte Press, New York, 1971, has closely interpreted the Gallic *panache* of the beloved *Ile*—"huge, black-funneled and proud in the water."

He continued:

"No one would ever account for her matchless power to attract the talented and youthful, the stylish and the famous. No one could ever say why one ship, with appointments and dimensions neither better nor bigger than those of a dozen other ships, would win for herself devotion and affection that set her apart."

And he attributed it to the fact that she always seemed "at the center of things."

A local newspaper announcement that the fabulous *Ile* was sold to Japanese shipbreakers early in 1959, contributed to my decision to record in a Sunday *Daily Press* feature story of February 15, that year, my visit aboard the ship on the embarrassing occasion of her sole visit to Newport News two years previously. The *Ile* experienced a mishap while clearing the harbor of Fort-de-France, Martinique, on February 26, 1957, during a winter cruise to the West Indies. This was the basis for her unscheduled 1,600-mile trip to the shipyard in Newport News, under the escort of deep-sea tugs where she would be given emergency repairs. This was documented in the March-April, 1957, issue of the *Shipyard Bulletin*, as one of the yard's most extensive repair jobs.

But, even though ignominiously grounded in dry dock with passengers repatriated and boilers cold while replacement propellers were being shipped from France, this epitome of *La Belle France* continued to exert her undeniable spell as a "lady of quality," as I can unequivocally attest.

Maritime writer, George Horne of the *New York Times*, viewed in his article, "Fond Salute to a Great Lady," the approaching scrapping of the *Ile*, responsible for the French Line's slogan, "the longest gangplank in the world," as nothing short of "disquieting." But, as though converting the proud vessel into scrap metal was not sufficient anguish for her partisans around the world, she was to suffer even further ignominy. For, prior to being legitimately scrapped, she was to endure the ultimate depredation (Mr. Brinnin's words) of being "brutally wrecked, burned, exploded, vandalized and half sunk" in the interests of providing the vehicle for a "cinematic turkey" entitled *The Last Voyage*.

It seems that it was the lifelong yen of Hollywood producer, Andrew L. Stone, to use an actual vessel—not merely an ordinary one—to sink for moving picture realism. The *Ile de France* seemed the answer to his fervent prayer, and he immediately reached a settlement with the firm of Japanese shipbreakers for the opportunity to destroy the ship before they did. Despite French Line protests that the *Ile's* name should appear nowhere, under threat of banning MGM pictures entirely from French cinemas, the ship's identity was quite apparent and could not be disguised. This occurred much to the chagrin of her many aficionados who felt she was undeserving of such an ignoble fate.

In any event, in May of 1959, Producer Stone and his wife, Virginia, plus "Captain" George Sanders, Robert Stack, Dorothy Malone, Edmond O'Brien and other cast members "embarked" on the "S.S. *Claridon*"—adorned as a luxury liner "lamb" for the slaughter. At length, after a catastrophe "at sea," the old *Ile* was reduced to a "massive shambles" with holds and engine room flooded and, as the tour de force of drama, with one of the funnels exploded and toppled onto the deck. This appeared in a distant shot and a "doubting Thomas" friend of mine claims he could detect men pulling on the cables to haul it over.

"She went down in a blaze of Technicolor," exhaulted Producer Stone, claiming that his $4,000 per day rental of the ship was justified, and, actually his personnel had saved the wreckers considerable time and money by performing a lot of the work for them. Thus, the old *Ile de France* passed into history on the lamented "Last Voyage" that devastated her.

Some will claim that she was the North Atlantic's most gracious lady.

And, they say when the decision was made to dismantle the old vessel that members of her crew stood upon her deck and wept unashamed.

Only a small notice reached the Peninsula newspapers—*The Times-Herald* carried a 14-point headline and approximately 18 lines of type: "Paris, January 14, 1959—The *Ile de France* was sold today to a Japanese company for scrap iron," it began. But, a longer story remains in the hearts of countless devoted travelers who had enjoyed her floating hospitality for three decades—a lengthy life for a ship.

I will not readily forget my one visit to the *Ile de France* when she was undergoing repairs at the Newport News Shipyard in the spring of 1957. That was virtually an "Evening in Paris." One could scarcely come on board before sensing an indefinable aura, epitomizing the essence of *La Belle France*. Not only did one notice the splendid appointments of the ship, and the efficient bellboys running busy errands in their trim red coats—actually more a hunting pink—but the solicitous officers who were our hosts. Capitaine Lombard and Commissaire Duclos could be seen bending from the waist to kiss the hands of the lady visitors of the Peninsula, unaccustomed to continental courtliness.

"*Enchante, Madame*, and you, *Monsieur*. We are so happy to welcome you on board our *Ile de France*."

But it may be recalled that the 764-foot, 44,000-ton liner's visit here was not entirely for pleasure. In February, 1957, the *Ile de France* was cruising the Caribbean with more than 700 passengers embarked. Leaving Fort-de-France, Martinique, February 26, and backing to turn in the narrow harbor, she overshot the mark. Her graceful stern crashed into the breakwater, forcing her rudder and two of her four propellers against the rocks, twisting them into useless hunks of metal.

Many people refused at first to leave the ship, but it was all too obvious that the cruise was finished. Due to necessity, passengers and non-essential crew were repatriated and the liner, accompanied by tugs, began her long, slow 1,600-mile trek up to Newport News from the West Indies. Embarrassed, understandably, the French Line was skittish about divulging information concerning the incident, or allowing outsiders to observe for themselves. Few details were released to the papers and local reporters were persona non grata on board. Shipyard spokesmen remained silent, too. Yet,

Escorted by U.S.S. *DE 680*, the 44,000-ton French liner *Ile de France* passes Old Point Comfort March 18, 1957 en route to the Newport News Shipyard for emergency repairs to rudder and propellers. *Photograph courtesy of the Daily Press Library.*

when the *Ile* began her month-long stay in dry dock here, it was obvious that major repairs to her nether regions, involving a new rudder and two new propellers, were indicated.

Thus, with little to do, the ship's company settled back to enjoy its visit to Newport News, while the work continued with typical shipyard efficiency and dispatch. Preceding the liner's departure for New York to resume service, however, a soiree was held on board to repay local hospitality. A hundred invitees crossed the gangplank that evening and forthwith, miraculously found themselves in France. "The longest gangplank in the world" was how the French Line advertised its services in the carefree days of 1927 when the new liner, displaying the pinnacle of French artistic genius, entered service from the Penhoet Yard at Saint-Nazaire. "Step aboard in New York and you are already in Paris," became a slogan.

Never as rapid or flamboyant as many of her rivals to capture the cream of transatlantic travelers, nonetheless the *Ile de France* attracted more than her share of notables of both continents. Numerous passengers readjusted their travel schedules to enable them to take round-trip passage on her. They

Stern view in dry dock of the damaged rudder and propellers of the liner *Ile de France*, injured when she backed into the mole at Fort de France, Martinique. This photograph was taken March 21, 1957 prior to commencement of the repair work.
Shipyard photograph by B.J. Nixon.

wanted no other ship. For the most part her officers and crew came on board to live and, she became their permanent home. They were all but belligerently proud of her.

The war disrupted all that. The *Ile*, with all luxury fittings removed ashore for safekeeping, except the exquisite chapel built into the center of her hull, joined the ships of the Free World carrying countless allied troops abroad for duty in World War II. Then, once more in peacetime service, the elaborate fittings, paintings and pieces of sculpture were carefully reinstalled and she was again in the Atlantic parade.

During her later career she made a remarkable habit of helping ships in distress, thus earning a pleasant nickname—the Saint Bernard of the Atlantic. The *Ile's* most shining hour, of course, was when she triumphantly entered New York Harbor in July, 1956, bearing survivors of the ill-fated Italian liner, *Andrea Doria.*

The *Ile's* new schedule required leisurely transatlantic crossings in the summer, and winter cruises to the tropics. There was no attempt, nor could

As good as new again, the *Ile de France* turning in the James River as she leaves the shipyard to go up to New York to re-enter service, April 22, 1957. *Shipyard photograph by B.J. Nixon.*

there be, to compete with the swifter and newer liners such as America's Blue Ribbon winning record-breaker, the *United States.* Although not then recognized, undoubtedly the mishap at Martinique marked the beginning of the end. The *Ile* did not function long upon her return, after being out of service those few months. She was soon laid up by her owners as being too expensive to operate. Then, the final judgment was decreed.

But, let us return briefly to the ship's stay in Newport News.

On that warm evening in April, 1957, Peninsula guests were formally greeted by Le Commandant Lombard in the *Ile de France's* luxurious tourist class salon forward. The assemblage was then split into small groups to tour the ship. Our particular host was the chief engineer who had served aboard the liner since her return from war duty.

It was *très, très dommage;* he said that we should not see this beautiful ship as she would appear when actually in service. The promenade deck, for example, would seem like a fashionable boulevard in normal times, not deserted with lines of empty deck chairs. And, he apologized for the covers draped over most of the furniture.

But, he made us wait before going in the enormous first-class dining saloon, while he scampered ahead to turn on the lights, and so set the stage. We entered by way of an imposing staircase, undoubtedly the most elegant ever built in a ship, sweeping down to the center of a faultlessly furnished room. Imagine, he said, to the ladies of his party, that you are exquisitely gowned and coiffured, your escort in white tie and tails, of course, and you are about to make your *grand entrée.* The room is full and all eyes are turned to see you come. *Ah, magnifique,* he sighed and kissed his finger tips, blowing the kiss into the air with Gallic éclat.

And then, the food you would be served—dieting was prohibited on the *Ile Magnifique,* he said again, patting his midriff.

We passed from one elegant apartment to another, visited the kitchens and pantries, and sampled French pastries. We paused to glance into a first-class stateroom—this one recently occupied by the President of France. Descending more stairs to various apartments, we were escorted to the library, play room, reading room, theater, and then the so-very-French shops leading off the entrance foyer—Patou, Cartier, Coty—unfortunately all sealed by customs regulations.

In the foyer, mounted on either side of the chapel entrance, and encased in chaste silver frames were two medals, the well-merited awards given the ship—as though she were an actual living person—the *Croix de Guerre* for sterling service as a transport in World War II; the *Legion d'Honneur* for her role in the *Andrea Doria* catastrophe.

We were accompanied again to the elegant tourist lounge. Efficient waiters silently and swiftly circulated with trays of drinks and food—*canapés, glacés, bonbons, petit fours.* Our solicitous host commanded: *"Garçon, encore du vin pour Monsieur. Ah, c'est bon, n'est ce pas?"*

And then, at length the farewells. *"Voici un petit cadeau"*—a souvenir of your visit. *"Pour Madame"*—a tiny bottle of amber, a dram of *Ma Griffe, "Quel parfum délicat! Epatant!"* *"Et pour Monsieur"*—a medallion key ring, in bas-relief *La Belle France* surrounded by shields representing the dependencies of the *Ile de France,* the heart of the nation.

"Well, *au revoir."* "Yes, we will surely take the *Ile* when next we go abroad."

"Quel décor, quel service! Au revoir, merci, merci."

"Mais oui, très très formidable, ce jolie paquebot. Ile de France, I love you!"

Our "Evening in Paris" was over. It didn't seem quite right to be walking up to Washington Avenue by Newport News' far from elegant Colonial Hotel on the way back home.

CHAPTER 14

(1962)

The Fate of the Last of the Old Bay Liners

The following account of the last Chesapeake sailings of the dowager Old Bay Line steamboats, *City of Richmond* and *City of Norfolk*, was written on the evening that I had watched the *Norfolk* make her final departure for Baltimore, so concluding 122 years' service of the Baltimore Steam Packet Company. It appeared routinely as a *Daily Press* news story the next

The *City of Richmond* backing down to come alongside her Norfolk pier, April 10, 1962, during the last week of the Old Bay Line's operation.

morning, April 14, 1962, and was subsequently reprinted in the summer, 1962, issue (No. 82) of *Steamboat Bill*, the journal of the Steamship Historical Society of America.

Although my book, *Steam Packets on the Chesapeake*, covering the history of the Old Bay Line, had been published by Cornell Maritime Press Inc., in the autumn of 1961, only six months before, the book ended on a note of cautious optimism that it might be possible for the line to enjoy many more profitable years. I wrote:

A mirrored reflection of the *City of Richmond's* dining saloon viewed on her last visit to Norfolk flying the house flag of the Old Bay Line, April 10, 1962.

By and large, however, the grand old steamers have responded well to the loving care their owners have bestowed upon them over the years and night after night they continue to sail majestically up and down the Bay. One wishes that it might go on forever. Perhaps it will.

But this was not to be. The book had already chronicled that, by some zealous quirk of misplaced economy, the United States Army had elected to close the hexagonal-shaped, government-owned pier which projected into deep water at Old Point Comfort, effectively cutting off Peninsula shippers and travelers from their last direct contact with the line. The *City of Richmond* made the last northbound call at Old Point on the evening of December 30, 1959, and I was present to watch her sail, too.

With minor interruptions and the abandonment of weekend sailings, service continued entirely from the Norfolk-Portsmouth side of Hampton Roads. But labor problems were mounting, and the company was subjected to prolonged sessions with the National Labor Relations Board, and the boats made only spasmodic passenger trips through the winter of 1960-61. And, after September, 1961, they carried only freight.

However, both craft were spruced up to receive passengers in the spring of 1962, in expectation of a good summer with advance bookings and adequate freight business in store. Then, swiftly and decisively, the blow fell. A press announcement on April 3 reported that the company directors had decided that, rather than consume their remaining funds in crippling labor increases, it would be advantageous to quit immediately. Thus, there would still be sufficient assets to provide pensions for the line's hundred loyal employees whose jobs would be lost forever.

General Passenger Agent Raymond L. Jones explained to me that, by the U.S. Government's new wage and hour law, the crew members would be entitled to pay even when off duty and asleep. On this basis, a bellboy would be making from $17 to $18 per day and, to make matters worse, the men would not have been allowed to report on their own at 5:00 p.m. (to pick up tips) when the boats were opened to take on passengers—the time that the bellboys were most needed to help with luggage, and so forth. The steamers took 12 hours to make their runs, starting at 6:30 p.m. Purser's office department personnel were needed for at least a full hour before sailing time and, at the other end of the voyage the next morning, another hour to get the passengers off and to clean up. Charged as a 14-hour day with overtime, this made projected operating costs insupportable. Actually, the men were eager to continue working and the company could accept the new pay rate, but it did object to the clause requiring pay for off-duty personnel when they were occupying their bunks.

President Robert E. Dunn was naturally bitter. The Old Bay Line had never received operational subsidies from the United States Government, being entirely a domestic carrier. Yet, as a result of the enormous subsidies paid to American lines engaged in foreign services, "the wages of seamen and stevedores and, in fact, cost of ship construction and everything related to steamship service, went out of sight." This is how he explained the dilemma to maritime historian Robert H. Burgess in a letter dated July 27, 1959, quoted in Bob Burgess' and Graham Wood's, *Steamboats Out of Baltimore*, published by Tidewater Publishers, Cambridge, Md., 1968. And, Dunn concluded with the indictment: "The Unions, through increased and unreasonable costs, have the responsibility for destroying domestic shipping in this country."

Now, faced by the provisions of the new wage and hour law, it was just too much for the small company to handle. Thus, as a result of government and union harassment and apathy over its fate, a worthy American institution died. One can see no justice in it. President Dunn was to follow soon after. On June 2, 1963, he died at his home in Baltimore.

After the Old Bay Line failed, the company-owned ships, the 1911 *City of Norfolk* and the 1913 *City of Richmond*, together with the spare boat, the

Captain Patrick L. Parker of the steamer *City of Norfolk* prepares for the final run.

1925 *District of Columbia*, were offered for sale at Baltimore. They lasted only a few more years, however, before fires and shipwrecks claimed them.

Following quoting the news account relating to the final sailings of the boats from Norfolk, April 12 and 13, 1962, I will attempt to pick up the remaining threads of their story down to the bitter end.

It was, "All ashore that's going ashore" for the last time. At the Old Bay Line's pier in Norfolk, Friday night, April 13, 1962, the dowager steamboat, *City of Norfolk*, slipped her lines from the well-worn bollards and headed down the Elizabeth River towards Hampton Roads bound for Baltimore.

This was the final voyage of a ship flying the familiar house flag of the Baltimore Steam Packet Company which, for almost a century and a quarter,

City of Norfolk maneuvering in the Elizabeth River to come alongside her Norfolk pier prior to making her last run up the Chesapeake Bay to Baltimore.

had provided passenger and freight service on Chesapeake Bay. Despite strong attempts in various quarters to preserve the service, veterans of the line knew the end had come. With layoffs of ship and stevedore personnel and only a skeleton crew aboard, Captain Patrick L. Parker, the senior master of the Old Bay Line fleet, headed his vessel away from the dock for the last time.

An institution of 122 years' standing was so terminated. It was truly Friday the 13th for the few, but dedicated, steamboat line enthusiasts who came to see him off.

But, they too, were to be disappointed. The ship, scheduled to sail promptly at 6 p.m. as usual, was held to her dock by U.S. Coast Guard order until past the time that the waters of Hampton Roads were pronounced cleared to commercial traffic. This followed restrictions to navigation, imposed by the visit to the area of President John F. Kennedy, and his departure on an aircraft carrier.

It was dark when, later, off Thimble Shoals, the 51-year-old steam-powered *City of Norfolk* crossed the unseen track in the water just made by the nuclear-powered *Savannah*—the nation's first atomic-powered merchant ship—as she headed to her base at Yorktown following a demonstration cruise. So ended the old order as the new was ushered in.

The Old Bay Line's corporate existence began with the signing of a charter by the Maryland General Assembly in December, 1839. This authorized:

Notice of termination of employment posted on the Old Bay Line pier at Norfolk on Friday, April 13.

A corporate and body politic, by the name and title of the Baltimore Steam Packet Company . . . to do all such acts as shall be proper and necessary for the purpose of employing one or more steamboats . . . for the conveyance of passengers, towing of ships, vessels, rafts or arks, and the transportation of merchandise and other articles.

Even though no "arks" have been towed by Old Bay Liners within the memory of anyone presently living, the passenger and freight service was faithfully maintained—quietly, efficiently and safely—for a sufficient period for the line to acquire the affectionate designator "old." The first steamers were small wooden-hulled side-wheelers. They gradually gave way to "modern" steel-hulled propeller steamers, with the busy "up-and-down" reciprocating engines, whose rhythmical movements are appealing to steam-boat buffs.

The line suffered its first major mishap when, at the beginning of World War II, with a crying need for shipping of all kinds, the government requisitioned the foremost boats of the line. The company continued to operate two veterans, the *City of Norfolk* (1911) and *City of Richmond* (1913), which were scheduled to be scrapped. These two boats, plus the comparative youngster, *District of Columbia* (1925), acquired from the Norfolk & Washington Steamboat Company when it suspended in 1949, comprised the fleet when the line closed down April 13, 1962. Since it began in 1840, it has owned and operated more than 50 passenger and freight boats.

The Peninsula was effectively cut off from service by the line in 1959 when, having preemptively declared the Old Point Comfort wharf surplus, the U.S. Army decided to demolish it. Further reductions occurred in the

Early morning view, April 14, 1962, as the *City of Norfolk* approaches the Chesapeake Bay Bridge on her final run. *Hans Marx photograph.*

autumn of 1961, when the company elected to terminate passenger service—an economy measure during the winter. Passenger service was to be resumed again in the spring and the old boats were being spruced up to accommodate them. But, the official order came through that the Baltimore Steam Packet Company was going out of business. Cited were operational losses in both freight- and passenger-handling, despite available cargo and people who wished to travel by boat. The line had not been eligible for government subsidy of any sort since its short route was entirely in American waters.

The *City of Richmond*, under the command of veteran Captain Samuel Boyd Chapman, a native of Gloucester County, Virginia, completed her final run at Baltimore on Friday morning, April 13, having left Hampton Roads northbound for the last time on the night before. The *City of Norfolk* picked up the last freight at the Pinner's Point Terminal of the Southern Railway, Friday afternoon, before her final docking at the Bay Line's West

Captain Samuel Boyd Chapman, on the starboard docking bridge of the *City of Richmond*, gives the order to cast off the lines on the steamer's final departure from Norfolk to Baltimore, April 10, 1962.

Main Street wharf. Here she was delayed from her scheduled time of departure by the Coast Guard.

So passed into history, barely noticed by the space-conscious world of today, an institution—the American coastwise steamer—which helped mold the nation and will be mourned by many. The company could not have chosen a more suitable day—that Friday the 13th—to wind it up.

1962–1971
OLD BAY LINE EPILOGUE

Old Bay Line partisans were vocal in their distress concerning the closing of the 122-year-old service. Newspaper and magazine articles and editorials complained bitterly, and groups were immediately formed at both ends of the Bay to explore possibilities of restoring it. Many claimed that hidebound ownership of the line by the railroads had caused the trouble, others that automobiles and trucks were the principal culprits. And the roll-on/roll-off service of the former navy LST-converted bay freighters of the Baltimore, Norfolk and Carolina Line was also cited. Already quoted is Bay Line President Dunn's appraisal of the labor situation, and government apathy to the line's plight.

These groups explored every avenue available and had practically decided to abandon the two older boats, and concentrate on getting the newer *District of Columbia* back in service exclusively for summer passengers. When Washington industrialist, Benjamin J. Wills, owner of the Tolchester Lines, and a person of considerable experience in the steamboat excursion business, bought all three vessels in late May, 1962, for a reputed $185,000.

Wills stated that he would probably hold the two *Cities* for resale, but he planned to refurbish the *District of Columbia* immediately as an excursion vessel, and send her north to make the three-and-a-half-hour daylight run between Boston and Provincetown, Massachusetts, on the end of Cape Cod. After a quick trip to the Bethlehem Shipyard in Baltimore, the *District* emerged as the *Provincetown*, with 18 less state rooms, but with a corresponding increase in day parlors, a dance floor, and recreation area on the main deck, complete with bar and soda fountain.

Captain Patrick L. Parker, one of the many active members of the Save the Bay Line groups, was in command for the coastal trip to Massachusetts Bay and also initially for the ensuing Provincetown service. This began in mid-June and lasted all summer, with time out under charter to provide a grandstand ship for spectators at the America's Cup races off Newport, Rhode Island, in mid-September, when Australia's *Gretel* proved a worthy challenger to America's *Weatherly*.

The *Provincetown* then returned to lay-up status in Baltimore for the winter, but came back again for a second season of daylight runs to Cape Cod in the summer of 1963. But when she returned to Baltimore that fall, she was destined never again to run under her own power.

Meanwhile, the two *Cities* lay idle, gathering barnacles and rust alongside the Bay Line's Pier No. 3, Pratt Street. Although Wills announced that he was exploring the possibility of resuming bay sailings, and moved part of his personnel to the Old Bay Line's West Main Street pier at Norfolk in Septem-

The former Old Bay Liner *District of Columbia*, renamed *Provincetown* and used on Massachusetts Bay in the summers of 1962 and 1963, shown as a spectator craft at the America's Cup races off Newport, Rhode Island, September 15, 1962.

Journey's end for the Old Bay Line. The steamers *City of Norfolk* (left) and *City of Richmond* tied up at Pier No. 3, Pratt Street, Baltimore, to await their fates. *Eugene L. Diorio photograph.*

ber, 1962, nothing resulted. Two months later he stated once more that he planned to sell the boats.

The first actual move in that direction was in November, 1963, when the *City of Richmond* was sold to a pair of Washington restaurateurs, Herman and Daniel Price of the Occidental. They planned to refit the boat as a plush hotel-restaurant-night club and send her to Charlotte Amalie on St. Thomas, Virgin Islands. A vast quantity of equipment—700 tons—planned for her new role was gathered for installation upon arrival. All preparations completed, the Prices hoped to induce Captain Samuel Boyd Chapman, the *Richmond's* veteran master in Chesapeake Bay service, to take command for the trip to the Caribbean. He declined, which was just as well, however. Meanwhile, the refurbishing operation was under the direction of Carlos Queceda, the *maitre d'*

Former Old Bay liner *City of Richmond,* preparing for the long journey under tow to become a restaurant-hotel ship at St. Thomas, Virgin Islands, stops at Norfolk before leaving the Chesapeake. This August 1964 photograph is probably the last ever taken of the ship afloat. *Robert H. Burgess photograph.*

of the Occidental, who was to become the resident manager of the ship when renamed *Occidental,* and tied up for business at St. Thomas.

Baltimore steamboat enthusiast, John H. Shaum, Jr., hoped to ride the craft to her final destination, and he signed on to help load the boat on June 15. Ultimately he never made the trip, since delays increased the time and he had to resume his studies. However, he subsequently wrote a splendid life history of the steamer for *Steamboat Bill,* cited in the bibliography at the end of this section. He recalled feelingly the labors of himself and nine other young men hired to load aboard the 700 tons of cargo with 110° heat in the lower holds.

Shaum related that, to make her tow easier, the *City of Richmond's* propeller had been removed in Bethlehem Steel's dry dock and the rudder chocked amidships. After filling the lower hold to capacity, the watertight compartments were welded shut. They then proceeded to load more cargo, including hotel laundry equipment for the proposed establishment, together with three small trucks, on the main deck which was also sealed. Light cargo went into 20 cabins on the saloon deck, an anchor was rigged for lowering in an emergency, cables readied and the boat was set for her lengthy voyage under tow.

Originally scheduled to start the trip in June, the *City of Richmond*, towed by the *Lamberts Point*, finally left Baltimore on the first leg of her voyage to Norfolk on August 13, 1964, where she arrived the next day without mishap. But further delay came about due to bad weather prognostication in the wake of Hurricane Gladys. Several Peninsula steamboat enthusiasts took this opportunity to see the half-century-old craft before she left her native haunts forever. Bob Burgess' photograph reproduced in this edition might well be the last ever made of the ship afloat.

On September 23, with a new tug, the Florida-based *Sea Eagle* at the business end of the tow line, the old Bay steamer, now classified as a barge by the Coast Guard, slipped past Cape Henry for what was expected to be an eight- or ten-day open-ocean voyage to the islands. But this was not to be. While still off the coast of North Carolina, the *Sea Eagle* broke down and the Coast Guard cutter *Chilula* towed both vessels into Morehead City the following day. The trip was further delayed while a replacement tug was secured. At length, the 1,000-horsepower diesel tug, *Carville*, arrived on the scene and the *City of Richmond* set forth once more on October 3. It looked now as if everything were running smoothly. But two days later, the weather quickly deteriorated in the wake of Hurricane Hilda, and soon the aged vessel was in dire trouble.

Heavy, mounting seas pounded the laboring craft and she began at once to take on water in alarming quantities. Before long, it was obvious that she would have to be abandoned, although the tug was already heading for the nearest port. At 5:30 a.m., while still under tow, the derelict craft quickly rolled over and took her final plunge. The *Carville* successfully removed all seven of the thoroughly unnerved riding crew. The men reported that as she sank, trapped air blew out the entire starboard side.

The wreck's position was subsequently pinpointed at 33°, 2 minutes north latitude, by 78°, 55 minutes west longitude. It sank in 52 feet of water, about 18 miles southeast of the entrance to Georgetown Harbor, South Carolina, where the tug immediately headed with its castaway crew. Meanwhile, a Coast Guard cutter, the *Cape Morgan*, had sped to the scene and confirmed the heavy weather with seas of ten to 14 feet, and winds from the northwest up to 20 knots. Visibility was down to 300 yards due to rain squalls.

Personnel of both tug and steamer told their sad stories on arrival at Georgetown. It was, of course, obvious that the *City of Richmond* was a total loss. The only gainers were charter fishermen, who subsequently discovered the wreck, marked by a lighted buoy, was doing splendidly as an artificial fish reef. Amateur scuba divers, too, have had much enjoyment exploring the wreck and securing souvenirs. The late J. Sam Bellamy of nearby Pauleys Island, who made frequent visits to the wreck, claimed that in terms of fish population, the *City of Richmond* has proven fantastic as a fish lure.

This, perhaps, would have been the conclusion of the story, had not disgruntled owner Daniel Price elected in 1968 to bring the Allied Towing Company, owners of the *Carville*, into court. In a $575,000 damage suit, he charged them with liability in the loss of the steamer and cargo. The complaint was subsequently dismissed, there having been "no evidence sufficient to prove that the tug *Carville* was negligent in its navigation and handling of its tow."

Norfolk attorney, Hugh S. Meredith, who successfully defended Allied Towing, forwarded a copy of the U.S. District Judge John A. MacKenzie's fact-finding opinion dated January 10, 1969. These facts, regrettably, do not speak favorably for the loading of the ship or of her landlubber crew's seamanship.

It was aired in court that, although all six main deck cargo ports had presumably been secured, before midnight on October 4, in mounting seas, the lower half of the port side aft cargo door was caved in. Meanwhile, as the ship twisted and turned, items of the deck load began parting their lashings, and had carried away wedges securing wooden covers over the two freight elevator shafts leading to the lower hold, thus admitting a considerable quantity of water into the ship's bilges.

The following items from Judge MacKenzie's memorandum are quoted verbatim. This clearly showed how panic had gripped the unfortunate crew, under the leadership of riding master Olin Smokey Stover who "had never been to sea before except as a passenger," and whose testimony, alas, was "contradictory" and "confused." The judge's remarks stated:

The inexperience of the riding crew was a major factor in the catastrophe. The lack of experience of the crew is plainly shown in their conduct in the darkness in the hours just prior to the sinking of the vessel. For instance, [Carlos] Queceda (whose regular employment was as *maître d'* of the Occidental Restaurant in Washington), on the bridge of the *City of Richmond*, which was tossing about on the end of a 1,000-foot towline to the *Carville*, when unable to attract the attention of the *Carville* from the *City of Richmond* [previous communication between the vessels by walkie-talkie had been satisfactory], suggested that he get out his rifle and attempt to shoot out the running lights of the *Carville*. The impossibility of such a task and its absolute inappropriateness is illustrative of the conditions of panic existing aboard the *City of Richmond* in those early morning hours.

The inexperience of the crew is further illustrated by the fact that the master of the riding crew [Olin Smokey] Stover, about midnight on 4 October 1964, upon finding one of the trucks coming loose from its secured position on the cargo deck, chose to sit in the cab with his foot on the brake for ten minutes to keep the truck from moving, rather than seeing to its permanent securing and attending to the more pressing matter of the cargo port.

The boarding up and securing of the hull openings and the stowage of cargo were improperly directed and supervised by the United States Salvage Association. As an example of this, motor vehicles and equipment being transported were not properly fastened to the cargo deck and came loose on the very first day of heavy weather after leaving Morehead City. . . .

In summary, the Court finds that the *City of Richmond* was unseaworthy on at least four counts; namely, (a) the preparation for sea in the sealing of the elevator shafts was improperly planned, supervised and executed, (b) the cargo was improperly stowed and secured and the supervision of such stowage and securing was improper, (c) the provisions for pumping in the location of pumps and lack of installed suction pipes to the lower

Relics salvaged from the wreck of the former Old Bay Liner *City of Richmond* (sunk near Georgetown, S.C., October 5, 1964) by the late J. Sam Bellamy of Pauley's Island. This was equipment for the floating restaurant planned to be set up at St. Thomas. Bellamy retrieved the barnacle-encrusted objects during the summer of 1973. The cardinal bird was a table decoration.

Former Old Bay Liner *City of Norfolk* tied up at the Fieldsboro, New Jersey, scrap yard of the North American Salvage Company, May 30, 1966, as scrapping the old ship was about to begin. *Peter Gilchrist photograph, courtesy of Jack Shaum.*

holds was improper, and (d) with the ballasting and heavy cargo, the *City of Richmond* was overloaded from four to ten inches on a vessel of very limited freeboard. [Elsewhere cited as only three inches at the aft cargo ports.]

The crew was incompetent both in its failing to meet the requirements as to the number of rated AB Seamen aboard, and also in its failure to have been even cursorily instructed in the duties which would reasonably be expected to arise to a seaman as a matter of course. There were specifically no instructions to the men on board in how to use the pumps, or how or when to sound for water in the holds, and no instructions to inspect the interior of the ship and the stowed cargo for signs of shifting, nor any instructions in emergency procedures for damage control. The pumps themselves had never been tested on board the vessel. The weather encountered was not out of the ordinary for the area and the season of the year.

The *City of Richmond* existed no more and the Prices' dream for their plush resort was blown away in the spume-swept North Atlantic. But there was yet another element of tragedy in connection with the vessel. James S. Avery's weekly "Sea and Scene" articles appearing in the Newport News *Times-Herald* were a highly recommended feature of the newspaper and reconstructed the last voyage of the former Old Bay Liner in the issue of October 14, 1964, from dispatches from Georgetown. The final shock, he stated, was learning of the death at his home at Edgewater, Maryland—one week after the ship sank—of her former 70-year-old master, Captain Samuel Boyd Chapman. He had spent all, but the first 19 years, of his productive life afloat on Chesapeake Bay and was skipper of the *City of Richmond* from 1926 to 1962.

"Both man and boat had been around for something over half a century," Jim Avery observed, concluding, "perhaps it was time for each to depart within so short a span."

Lloyds' Weekly Casualty Report of October 13, 1964, noting the disaster, cited the loss of the *Occidental* (ex-*City of Richmond*). Writer Jack Shaum unashamedly confessed to a long-standing "love affair" with the old ship. "It is the *Occidental*, then, that lies at the bottom of the sea," he said. "The beloved *City of Richmond* sails on—in affectionate memory, in any event!"

As stated, the now ten-year-old wreck continues to provide magnificent grounds for South Carolina fishermen. The late Sam Bellamy, mentioned previously as a frequent underwater visitor, provided the following fish's-eye view of the *City of Richmond*. He wrote to me on February 14, 1974:

Her keel lies in about 52 feet of water in an east/west position—bow west—stern east. She sank and settled flat. Her present condition is nothing more than steel plating and decking on the hull section. All wooden parts have been eaten or eroded. I am not thoroughly familiar with what role she may have played in earlier years, but I can assure you she is definitely serving a useful purpose now, in making many fishermen and divers happy with the large catches of fish which swarm around her.

Bellamy sent along a couple of pieces of chinaware and a barnacle-encrusted cardinal bird decoration for the Occidental Restaurant that never came to fact. He retrieved these from the afterhold in the summer of 1973 as a memento of the venerable Old Bay Liner.

The remainder of the melancholy history of Old Bay Line ships may be more quickly related. Through the summer of 1964, the *City of Norfolk* and the *Provincetown* remained moored at Pratt Street, Baltimore. In November 1964, possibly inspired by the Price Brothers' plan to form a floating restaurant, Ben C. Dittenhofer, president of Nassau Marina, Inc., of Toms River, New Jersey, bought the *City of Norfolk* from Wills with the same purpose in mind. He planned to tow the boat to Philadelphia or New Jersey, or possibly keep her in Maryland, and to spend approximately $400,000 on her restoration as a first-class restaurant.

None of these dreams materialized and the following year it was reported that the *City of Norfolk* was re-sold to United States Bulk Carriers, Inc. This company had no plans for the actual use of the boat, other than to trade her in on an oceangoing ship under the Ships Exchange Act. Once that deal was consummated, Uncle Sam became sole owner of the steamboat under the U.S. Maritime Administration. Shortly afterwards, the Administration offered her for sale and there were several bidders, with the Lorain Construc-

The cathedral glass skylight of the *City of Norfolk* illuminating the main saloon looked like a Tiffany glass lampshade. A similar skylight was saved and is in The Mariners Museum today.

tion Company putting in the low bid of $5,100. J. Williams Sause, owner of this Baltimore firm, announced that he wanted the *City of Norfolk* to be part of a marina-motor inn complex he was planning for Kent Island, near the east end of the Chesapeake Bay Bridge.

However, the ship went to the North American Salvage Company of Fieldsboro, New Jersey, for scrapping. Their offer had been $6,883.

On May 24, 1966, the old ship left Baltimore under tow to the Delaware River scrapyard. Here, workers carefully removed both of the ship's handsome cathedral glass, dome-shaped skylights, illuminating the saloons fore and aft, and looking considerably like giant Tiffany-glass lamp shades. The smaller one has been installed in the ceiling of The Mariners Museum's Chesapeake Bay Room, along with one of the ship's name boards and her steam whistle. Visitors may be able to appreciate some of the grandeur that was commonplace on board the steamboats of yesteryear by these exhibits.

The shipbreakers had partially ripped away the *City of Norfolk's* wooden superstructure when, on August 17, 1966, she was struck by lightning during a severe thunderstorm, and caught fire. This consumed all the remaining woodwork and, after the hulk had cooled, the company completed their task of converting the once-proud steamboat to scrap.

The *District of Columbia (Provincetown)* survived slightly longer, but she, too, was destined to become a raging torch. Before that, however, steamboat enthusiasts were delighted to learn in January, 1965, that a Baltimore business group had acquired the steamer from Wills. Under the name Chesapeake Bay Line, Inc., they planned to refurbish the vessel for actual operation on the identical waters for which she was originally planned.

Plans to operate the *District of Columbia* as the "S.S. *Chesapeake*" during the summer of 1965 unfortunately came to naught. *From the advertising folder issued prior to the U.S. Coast Guard calling off the work, 1965, courtesy "Steamboat Bill."*

When the aged craft was renamed *Chesapeake*, Charles Hoffberger, spokesman for the group, announced that she would begin that summer to run twice-weekly, three-day cruises from Washington to Yorktown and Norfolk, with a daylight trip on the James River also. Forty thousand dollars was earmarked for the restoration. Leaflets were printed announcing the proposed service with outside cabins and all meals "for as little as $87.70." Historic sights of the lower Bay area, such as Williamsburg and Virginia Beach, would be served by charter buses included in the fare.

Jim Avery's January 4, 1965, article in *The Times-Herald* noted that Hoffberger's interest in reviving steamboat service was initiated by a reading of Bob Burgess' book of nautical lore, *This Was Chesapeake Bay*, published by Cornell Maritime Press in 1963. On the basis of the leaflet and word-of-mouth endorsement, the steamer was booked solid through May, June and July and included was a special charter by the Steamship Historical Society

Top: While being scrapped, the *City of Norfolk* was struck by lightning and set on fire August 17, 1966, which burned all her wooden upper works. Smoke and flame enveloped the ship. *Bill Hensley photograph, courtesy of The Mariners Museum.* Bottom: Firemen ineffectively battle the fire which swept the *City of Norfolk* at the Fieldsboro scrap yard. *Photograph courtesy of The Mariners Museum.*

of America. Meanwhile, the Old Bay Line's pier at the foot of Main Street, Norfolk, was razed the same summer, demanding the consideration of alternate terminal facilities.

Alas, alas! During the early renovation stages of the soon-to-become *Chesapeake*, the U.S. Coast Guard determined that more than $400,000 would be needed to meet their current seaworthiness regulations. This was more than the ship was worth, or the new company could pay, and on June 28, Hoffberger regretfully announced that he was abandoning his plans entirely and would sell the boat to the highest bidder. As with the other Old Bay Line craft, its use as a permanently moored floating restaurant-hotel was mentioned as a possibility.

As in the case of the *City of Norfolk*, the *District* became involved in another one of the Maritime Administration's ship-trade agreements, when the Waterman Line acquired the boat from Hoffberger, in exchange for a 1944-built freighter in the Reserve Fleet. Subsequently, the *District* was put up for bids by the Maritime Administration and was acquired in May, 1966, by George A. Mauro of Brielle, New Jersey, at a reputed $10,000.

Mauro's plans for the *District* included towing her to New Jersey, and up the Shark River to Brielle, and converting her to a restaurant-night club operation. Use of this location was squelched by the Central Railroad of New Jersey who, having had a bridge already put out of commission when a ferry owned by Mauro crashed into it, categorically refused to open their draw for the far larger *District*.

Mauro then searched for alternate locations and it was reported that as late as 1967 and 1968 he was still on the lookout. Early in 1969 a glimmer of hope appeared. Developers of Baltimore's inner harbor project announced the possibility that the *District* might be used as a restaurant and museum of the sea, in the home port she had never left since 1963.

But, on the hot and muggy summer afternoon of June 4, 1969, fire engines were summoned to Pier No. 3, Pratt Street to fight a raging fire that was believed to have been arson. Flames shot through the top of what was to have been named the Old Bay Line Inn, and soon the interior of the boat was completely gutted. Firemen on shore, and on the Baltimore fireboats, *P.W. Wilkinson* and *J. Harold Grady*, battled from 2:21 p.m. to 4:11 p.m., before the fire was declared extinguished. It was feared that the ship might capsize with the weight of water in her hull, therefore pumps were rigged to draw it out, as it was being sprayed in by the fire hoses.

Mr. Mauro gritted his teeth and bravely announced that he would restore the ship and proceed with his plans, regardless of circumstances. But with a great deal of her amidships interior burned out, it was obvious that much of the flavor and charm of the vessel was destroyed beyond repair, and restoration in modern style would be pointless. While this was being debated and Mauro was hedging on his future plans, the Baltimore harbormaster announced that the ship must be removed—she was not only an eyesore, but also a continuing fire hazard. She was then moved to Pier No. 6, only to suffer further abuse. In March, 1970, vandals—possibly the same trio of juveniles who had set her afire the year before—turned her adrift. Jack Shaum reported, the boat "spent a gay time meandering about the inner harbor before being returned to her pier by a tug."

The old *District of Columbia* was gutted by a six-alarm fire at her dock in Baltimore, June 5, 1969, dashing plans to convert the ship to a floating restaurant. *AP wirephoto, courtesy of the Daily Press Library.*

Abandoned and sunk, the once-proud *District of Columbia* rests on the mud in Curtis Bay near Baltimore. *March 10, 1973 photograph by Jack Shaum, Jr.*

Mauro was then ordered by the court to remove the boat from the harbor. But, before this ultimatum was heeded, vandals again set the pathetic old *District* on fire, thus burning out the stern section. By court order the hulk was then towed to the dead ship anchorage in Curtis Bay, outside Baltimore. Here she was anchored, and the "tooth of time" carried out its work. Six months later, on January 13, 1971, another leak developed and the once-proud *District of Columbia* quietly settled on the mud, leaving only her black funnel and part of her ravaged superstructure above the water. Each passing tide carries more of her away until, gradually she will be virtually unrecognizable.

And so, approximately 135 years after the original quartette of Old Bay Liners clipped the waves, making their accustomed rounds along Chesapeake Bay, the final members of a series of noble vessels have at length gone to rest. Their epilogue is now complete.

SIGNED ARTICLES WHICH HAVE APPEARED COVERING
THE DEMISE OF THE OLD BAY LINE
1961-1971

Blackford, Frank R., "Sailing the Chesapeake." *Virginian Pilot, Lighthouse,* Sunday, August 22, 1971.

Burgess, Robert H., "The *City of Norfolk* at Journey's End: Old Bay Line Steamboat was Baltimore's Last Maritime Link with Ocean Resort." Baltimore *Sunday Sun Magazine,* September 11, 1966.

———, "The Last of the Old Bay Line Steamers—End of an Era!" *Daily Press New Dominion Magazine,* September 11, 1966.

Cooper, David S., "Last Passenger Sailing of the *City of Richmond.*" *Steamboat Bill,* No. 119, Fall, 1971.

Hill, Don, "The End of the Old Bay Line." *The Commonwealth: Magazine of Virginia,* July, 1962.

———, "War, Storms, Time Ravage Bay Line Fleet." *Virginian Pilot, Lighthouse,* Sunday, November 22, 1964.

Lewis, Larry, "Steamboatin' Days on Chesapeake Bay Live on in the Memories of a New Steamship Society." *Maryland Living,* Sunday, February 23, 1969.

Rorer, Michael Arthur, "Vanishing Voices of Norfolk Harbor." *Virginia Cavalcade,* Vol. XI, No. 1, Summer, 1961.

Shaum, John H., Jr., "Steamer *City of Richmond.*" *Steamboat Bill,* No. 93. Spring, 1965.

———, "Restoring Lady of the Bay *(District of Columbia)* to Her Full Glory." Baltimore *News-American,* May 4, 1969.

———, "Steamer *District of Columbia.*" *Steamboat Bill,* No. 126. Summer, 1973.

Wing, William C., "The End of the Old Bay Line." New York *Herald-Tribune,* May 3, 1962.

U.S. tug crewman prepares to toss a heaving line up to the liner's fantail.

CHAPTER 15

Docking the Liner *United States* — a Tugman's View

Newport News' pride—indeed, once the pride of the whole nation—the sleek passenger liner *United States*, was more than ten years old when, being in New York, I was privileged to attend a routine docking maneuver of the boat upon her return from abroad. Even though transatlantic passengers were then increasingly taking to the skies, the ship was full, and few realized that in hardly more than a half a dozen years, the speediest and safest liner in the world would be permanently withdrawn from the sea.

Increasingly plagued by the irresponsible behavior of American seafaring labor unions, the *United States'* older, smaller running mate, the *America*, was taken from the run hardly more than a year after the following story of the routine docking of the *United States* was written. Following a period of inactivity of the *America*, in effect the United States Lines had said, "the hell with it!" and proceeded to sell the ship. Thus, the *America*, built at Newport News in 1940, became the *Australis* under the flag of Greece and with her majestic red-white-and-blue-topped funnels repainted entirely pale blue, the ship left Newport News on November 18, 1964, for the final time. Belatedly and ineffectively, she was picketed by some of the same unions that had contrived to drive her to a foreign flag.

The longshoremen again gave the *United States* a workover early in 1969, and she was sent to Newport News to wait out a period of costly negotiations, while she remained tied up, following annual overhaul by the shipyard. She resumed her services when agreements were reached, but returned to Newport News that fall and on November 15, 1969, her operators regretfully announced that she would now be laid up indefinitely. They had had it!

After occupying Pier No. 8 at the Newport News yard through the winter and spring of 1970, the ship was towed across Hampton Roads on June 19, by a battery of tugs and put in caretaker status at the Norfolk International Terminal. Here she is routinely observed by cruise passengers embarking on less glamorous, but more profitable, foreign liners as they gaily embark on West Indies cruises that the U.S. Merchant Marine apparently can not handle.

Curiously, in 1968, the carefully guarded secret details of the *United States'* incredible speed and power were suddenly, and inexplicably, revealed by the United States Navy. As custodian of the ship's national defense features, the Navy maintained security on matters pertaining to the ship's power and propulsion. Designer William Francis Gibbs, also a jealous guardian, had been dead a year when *New York Times* maritime writer, George Horne, cited in his column of August 16, 1968, that the Navy had rolled back its "brass curtain." They revealed that the *United States* pos-

sessed 240,000 shaft horsepower—over 100,000 more than any other liner—
and had steamed up to 41.75 knots (48 land miles an hour) during her
record-breaking maiden voyage of July 3 to 7, 1952, from Ambrose Light
Vessel to Bishop Rock near Cornwall, England. Also publicly stated for the
first time were details of the ship's four propellers, two four-bladed and two
five-bladed. Alas, they turn no more, except as statistics in current editions
of Guinness' *Book of World Records*, under the heading "Fastest Ships."

One item contributing to the *United States*' phenomenal speed was the
fact that she possessed two full sets of propellers. Each year, upon leaving
the Newport News Shipyard after annual overhaul, she was, in effect, using a
new set of props. Those installed on the boat when she arrived were
removed, and during the ensuing year were rebuilt and rebalanced. All pits

The *United States* returns to her birthplace for annual overhaul, December 21, 1957, as
tugs nudge her into dry dock at the Newport News Shipyard. *Shipyard photograph by
B.J. Nixon.*

and dents, caused by cavitation or striking underwater objects, were filled in
and reburnished to provide maximum efficiency.

Problematical is the future of the eminent and powerful liner. Abhorrent
to many, is the thought of merely kissing this talent good-bye to some
foreign shipowner, perhaps to have it utilized against us some time. But,
apparently other nations can operate passenger ships profitably, and the
United States cannot.

Meanwhile, the *United States* idles at her Norfolk pier, while rival pro-
moters disagree about such considerations as whether or not she should be
brought back to Newport News, or to the York River or Fort Monroe and

who would bear the expenses. Pressing arguments are advanced that the ship would be ideal as a floating showcase for exhibits from the 50 states, and would provide catering and hotel accommodations for hordes of visitors to the Bicentennial observances. As of this writing, the U.S. Maritime Administration, in whose custody she now reposes as a member of the James River Reserve Fleet, is about ready to give up. In 1973, the ship was turned over completely to the Administration which purchased her, hopefully for re-sale, at $12 million. Since then, "Marad" has had the ship available for sale on several occasions, but it did not receive any tenders that it considered responsible. (One man sent $1.00, despite the fact that it was stipulated minimum bids were to start at $12,100,000 and had to be accompanied by certified check in the amount of $150,000 as token of serious intent.)

Only recently the ship became involved in a flimflam operation. Early in June, 1975, a fly-by-night outfit calling itself W.W. Ventures, claimed it had fully acquired the vessel. They proceeded to place advertisements in prominent New York and Washington newspapers soliciting payments for a projected summer cruise at $500 per person. Marad had turned down W.W. Ventures in March when it attempted to buy the liner without putting up the required down payment. The mysterious Virginia organization stated that they planned to use the *United States* as a "floating condominium" for the extremely wealthy "to follow the sun" during the Bicentennial.

The organization's illusive promoter, William M. Wyant, claiming Howard Hughes' money backed him, could not be located for investigation of misrepresentation, mail fraud and false advertising, in what was obviously concocted as a swindle. The official Virginia state complaint against him listed his last-known address as the Baltimore County Jail at Towson, Maryland. Perhaps, he may be behind bars again when this account is published.

In any event, though Marad still hopes to find a responsible purchaser for the liner, it was stated that under no circumstances will W.W. Ventures be considered again as a potential buyer. And so, what to do with this apparent white elephant is still problematical. One earlier suggestion was to convert the ship to a floating retirement home for the aged. Another was for the State of Virginia to lease her at $1.00 per year from the federal government. Time alone will tell the outcome, but it is unlikely that those 240,000 "horses" imprisoned in her vitals will ever taste "oats" again.

It is interesting to note in the Secretary's Notes printed in the February, 1973, issue of the United States Naval Institute *Proceedings* that Paul Hall, president of the Seafarers International Union, was quoted as showing a slightly remorseful change of heart. While addressing the National Maritime Council in Seattle that year, he said in part:

> We recognize that in the labor movement that we haven't always done right by the American shipper. We understand it and we regret it, and we're trying to correct it. Where there have been tie-ups of American flag ships, cargoes have been tied up. We understand now as a result of the deterioration of this industry that . . . the labor movement has been wrong, that we have in many instances . . . acted irresponsibly. We understand this now and we are trying to correct it. . . .

Unfortunately, it is too late! If, perhaps, this attitude had prevailed as little as 20 years ago, the *America*, the *United States* and many other fine American ships might still be plying the world's sea lanes. But, it is finished now and the American flag passenger ship today is as dead as the dodo.

The following illustrated article appeared in the *New Dominion* on September 22, 1963, shortly after I had returned from New York, where I "helped" dock the liner.

For many, a New York visit is Broadway shows and nightclubs, exotic food, dazzling sights—the Statue of Liberty, the Empire State Building, the Metropolitan Opera, the Natural History Museum, the Yankee Stadium. New York, with its lofty spires and its teeming millions, can be varied things to numerous people. Not every visitor, then, realizes that New York is also one of the world's greatest harbors—home port to the world's distinguished ocean liners. These include, of course, the swift and sleek behemoth, the 990-foot *United States*, a supreme product of our Newport News shipbuilders' arts.

The liner *United States* steams up the Hudson River following her early morning arrival at New York after a routine transatlantic crossing, August 28, 1963. The padded snout of the tug *Alice M. Moran* is in the foreground.

As a guest of Moran Towing and Transportation Company's publicity director, Frank O. Braynard, a long-standing acquaintance, I was privileged recently to enjoy a somewhat unusual experience, not normally afforded the average tourist to Gotham. This comprised traveling aboard the steam tug, *Alice M. Moran*, granting me a tugman's view of the harbor. The *Alice*, along with her powerful diesel sisters, the *Moira Moran* and the *Julia C. Moran*, was delegated to assist in docking the *United States* at her home pier, No. 86, North River, on August 28, 1963, following a routine transatlantic crossing.

This was her 250th round trip since entering service with a record-breaking voyage in July of 1952. For the job, the three Moran tugs would assemble an aggregate of some 5,000 horsepower.

Our departure from Pier 1 at the Battery on the tip of Manhattan was early. Morning mists still lay close to the surface of the water, while horizontal fingers of sunlight probed through the labyrinth of skyscrapers selecting and bathing in a rosy glow, ships in the harbor and structures on the Jersey shore beyond.

Abruptly, the gigantic liner materialized from the haze down the bay, heading up the Hudson River, steaming on a mid-channel course. Patterns of light and shade played about her nearly 1,000-foot black hull, surmounted by its gleaming white superstructure, and crowned by the pair of lofty red, white and blue funnels.

The towers of Manhattan loom eerily in the morning mists as seen from the pilothouse of the tug *Alice M. Moran* with a steady hand at the wheel.

The 107-foot *Alice M. Moran* with veteran Norwegian-born waterman, Captain Johan E. Johansen at the helm, slipped her bow line from the well-worn bollard on the pier and gave chase up the river. Meanwhile, another tug bearing a white "M" emblazoned on her stack, and with docking pilot Captain Frederick W. Snyder on board, detached herself from the midtown Manhattan shore, and closed alongside the *United States'* starboard gangway port. The third Moran tug converged on the liner's port bow.

Approaching a point in the river nearly opposite the U.S. Lines' Pier 86, the ship's speed was reduced to a crawl as all three tugs took assigned positions alongside, nose in, to assist in turning the vessel at right angles.

A heaving line hangs from the starboard docking bridge aft as the *Alice M. Moran* closes under the liner's flank.

Dockmaster Snyder, on the liner's bridge, conversed with his brood by whistle signals and walkie-talkie, instructing them, with a ballet master's precision, just when to exert their pushing power against the ship and when to stop or shift position.

Initially, the *Alice M.* took station aft on the liner's starboard quarter. Once her padded nose was secured, the immense overhanging stern of the

The *Alice M. Moran* exerts full power to the *United States'* starboard quarter to pivot her around for a straight shot up into her slip.

United States practically covered the tug, snubbed in with her fender ready to shove the oversized girl's flank. Despite the earliness of the hour, quite a few of the *United States'* 1,758 passengers lined the rail, peering straight down on the tugboat company below. Whistles sounded and were answered,

The *Moira Moran* exerts a powerful shove to turn the *United States* as the liner's bow enters the slip at Pier No. 86, North River.

Captain Johansen gave his engine bells the full speed jingle, and a stream of water bubbled out behind the tug's fantail as her powerful 2,000 horsepower uniflow engine poured it on the screw. At first the *United States'* turning motion was hardly perceptible from the tug, but gradually the bearing changed and we could see that the ship was swinging farther and farther around.

Minutes later, the *Moira Moran*, our companion of the liner's starboard side, gave a final shove, then dropped back as the bow of the *United States* entered the dock. The 99-foot *Moira* raced around astern and assumed a new

A final shove from the *Alice M. Moran* positions the liner for docking as the shore crew hauls in the lines to secure her.

position to join the 107-foot *Julia C.* on the liner's port side amidships. Meanwhile, a kick ahead from the steamship's own screws sent her farther up into the slip.

Heaving lines rained down on the corner of the pier, were hauled ashore while hawsers followed. Then after a final toot, our *Alice* cast off, moments before she would have been caught and crushed between ship and shore. She, too, steamed around the liner's stern to stand by while the other two tugs contrived to straighten the ship's bearing parallel to the pier. There was no rubbing or squealing of steel grinding on wood as she swung around. The

Already looking somewhat delapidated, the liner *United States*, laid up at the Norfolk Marine Terminal, is viewed by members of the Steamship Historical Society from the bow of the tug *J. Speed Gray*, October 11, 1970.

A crewman on board the mini-cruise liner *New Shoreham*, bound for Florida waters via the Intracoastal Waterway, views the laid-up liner *United States* as the 125-foot diesel cruiser enters the Elizabeth River, November 5, 1972. At this time the *New Shoreham* was the largest passenger boat in service flying the American flag.

enormous craft came in and hardly kissed the floating camels which would hold her in position alongside the pier—a typical "ferryboat landing."

Chalk up a routine crossing for Captain Anderson of the *United States*, and a routine docking for Captain Johansen of the *Alice M. Moran*.

But a memorable experience it was for this correspondent.

A POSTSCRIPT ON THE DOCKING OF THE *UNITED STATES*
INCIDENTAL INTELLIGENCE—HARBORSIDE SEMANTICS DIVISION
(A note in *The American Neptune*, Vol. XXIV [April, 1964], p. 137)

As a guest of the Moran Transportation Company's steam tug *Alice M. Moran*, I had the privilege of observing at waterline level the docking of a large ocean liner. On August 28, 1963, we assisted in nudging the *United States* into her North River berth. In the process I noted a small sign painted in white on the black liner's port flank just above the waterline. The letters were outlined on the shell plates by a raised, welded bead so that when the ship was repainted, it would be no trouble to locate the letters and fill them in with white again. The sign read:

NO TUGS ABAFT
THIS LINE

Upon closer examination it could be observed that one word on the second line had not been painted in, although the outline beading still made it legible. The sign had originally appeared, albeit redundantly:

NO TUGS ABAFT
OF THIS LINE

The painter's correction, we are happy to note, is in accord with the dictum as set forth in Admiral Samuel E. Morison's "Notes on Writing Naval English," on the correct usage of the terms *abaft* and *astern*, appearing in *The American Neptune*, Vol. IX (January, 1949), p. 8. Towboat personnel in New York Harbor and Southampton thus receive their instructions good like an ocean liner should.

(Alas, the last time I had a chance to see the ship as laid up in Norfolk Harbor, the full lettering, including the redundant "of," was indicated.)

CHAPTER 16

(1963)

Final Curtain for the *President Warfield*

The bizarre, three-part career of the boat which began her life decorously plying the Chesapeake Bay as the *President Warfield*, flagship of the Old Bay Line, and ended as a burned-out hulk in the harbor of Haifa, Israel, has been frequently related. It was not until 1969, however, that the *President Warfield* was given the full-length, definitive treatment she deserved. David C. Holly did exactly this in his excellent book entitled—as was the ship at the end—*Exodus 1947*, published by Little, Brown & Co., Boston, Mass.

I covered virtually the entire career of the famous *Exodus* in *Steam Packets on the Chesapeake*, but approximately a year after the book was published, an Italian firm acquired salvage rights to the almost-entirely burned-out and sunken hulk and planned to raise it to reclaim its metal. This suggested retelling the story to include this final, but abortive episode. It appeared in the *New Dominion*, November 17, 1963, and, in slightly different form, in the Baltimore *Sunday Sun Magazine* of February 9, 1964.

This final event is briefly cited in Holly's book. Since my account was in print by that time, his dating the salvage attempt as of August 23, 1964, obviously made it a year's discrepancy. This is a small "nit to pick," in what is unquestionably an unequalled piece of nautical research and writing.

––––––––––

In the backwaters of an ancient seaport on the opposite side of the world, the final curtain rang on the extraordinary three-chapter career of a once-famous Chesapeake Bay steamer. On August 23, 1963, at the port of Haifa, Israel, the bow half of the former Old Bay Line flagship *President Warfield* sailed her last mile (actually only a few yards). Pumps kept her afloat long enough to nudge her closer to a breakwater in hopes that the ship wrecker's torches could reduce what remained of the burned-out hulk to scrap iron.

This was the proud steamer which, in 1928, started innocently on a utilitarian career designed to carry up and down Chesapeake Bay year-round passengers and freight overnight from Norfolk to Baltimore, with a Peninsula call at Old Point Comfort. Alas, no vestige of the service remains. First, the U.S. Army removed the wharf at Old Point, and then, in 1962, the 122-year-old line closed down for good.

None of this could have been envisaged when, on August 22, 1927, the Baltimore Steam Packet Company placed its order for a trim 320-foot, steel-hulled steamer at the shipbuilding yard of Pusey and Jones Corporation, Wilmington, Delaware. When completed, the ship carried the name of a late Old Bay Line president, S. Davies Warfield (not President Garfield as quick-witted newspaper re-write men invariably hastened to "correct" their copy to read). Incidentally, it was one of Mr. Warfield's nieces, Wallis, who gained international renown as the Duchess of Windsor.

On joining the Old Bay Line fleet in the summer of 1928, the *President Warfield* was manned by a master and crew of 69. She had 171 tastefully decorated state rooms trimmed in ivory and gold. She was licensed for a maximum capacity of 400 passengers, a figure which might be considered significant for comparative purposes in this story later on when, on her last spectacular voyage, she carried more than ten times that amount.

The *Warfield's* career on the Chesapeake could hardly be rated as wildly exciting. Although, prophetically it so happens, in view of her subsequent naval service, she received her baptism of fire during Prohibition Days when a U.S. Coast Guard cutter brought her to bay with a shot across the bow for suspected rum-running. This was a surprise to all concerned including the management, but principally to the owner of an automobile shipped as freight, which had 123 gallons of contraband gin in the rumble seat. This event was highly exceptional, however. For 14 years the *President Warfield*

First stage in the checkered career of the Old Bay Line flagship *President Warfield*. Shown alongside the steamboat wharf at Old Point Comfort, as viewed from the Hotel Chamberlin roof garden, June 23, 1939.

enjoyed routine smooth sailing on the Chesapeake. With the late Captain R.S. Foster, this writer took passage upon her on numerous occasions.

The advent of World War II in Europe changed the picture. As war approached, it was apparent that Britain would have desperate need of any type of craft obtainable. As a result, during the summer of 1942 the U.S. War Shipping Administration assumed control of the *President Warfield*, and other available American inland water steamers, for transfer to the British Ministry of War Transport. To make her a "warship," the *President Warfield* had cabins ripped out, open decks boxed in with heavy planking and a gun mounted on a platform aft. Gray paint replaced the traditional steamboat white.

On September 21, 1942, the *Warfield* and seven other former American sound- and river-type steamboats, not intended to ply the open ocean, departed from St. John's, Newfoundland, in a "skimming dish" convoy manned by British crews (Chapter 11). After four days of sailing and about 800 miles west of Ireland, Nazi submarine wolf packs shadowing the convoy, closed in for the kill. Three of the boats and their Royal Navy escort were sunk. But, the *Warfield* wriggled and turned, dodging torpedoes and firing her gun, and thus completed the voyage in comparative safety, whereupon she was moored in British coastal waters.

After using her for a Combined Operations training vessel for almost two years, the Royal Navy relinquished her to the United States Navy. She then officially became a unit of our fleet as the U.S.S. *President Warfield* (IX-169). Following the successful Normany landings, the *Warfield* crossed the channel to Omaha Beach in April of 1944. Here, affectionately nicknamed the U.S.S. *Statler*, she served as a station and accommodation ship for a U.S. Navy beach master's outfit. One of her most partisan residents, Naval Reserve junior lieutenant I.J. Matacia, occupied the same cabin he had used on his honeymoon a few years previously.

Back from war service in World War II, the former Old Bay liner was laid up in the James River Reserve Fleet, October 13, 1946. *Eugene Graves photograph, courtesy of The Mariners Museum.*

The war over, the *Warfield's* second trip on the Atlantic was less eventful. Returning home after a routine crossing, she arrived at the Norfolk Naval Operating Base on July 23, 1945. She was then decommissioned and offered for sale by the U.S. Maritime Commission later that year, concluding the second of her three incarnations.

The third chapter began shortly thereafter when, in November, 1946, the *President Warfield* was removed from her berth, gathering barnacles with the Idle Fleet in the James River, and was acquired by an innocent-seeming trading company. This organization actually served as "front" for Haganah, the Zionist underground movement that planned to use the former bay steamer as a blockade runner to Palestine. As a decoy, she was given the Honduran flag and an announced destination of Canton, China.

After many vicissitudes in getting off during which her true mission became known, the *President Warfield* steamed across the Atlantic for the third time and entered the Mediterranean. At the port of Cette on the French Riviera some 4,500 hopeful Jewish immigrants somehow wedged themselves on board and a pathetic odyssey of frustration began. Britain's unwelcome role in Palestine was to maintain the status quo during the United Nations' deliberations on the explosive Near East question. Representations were made to France to stop the sailing, but in the midst of them the dangerously overloaded steamer slipped out of port. Hardly had she left southern France headed eastward, when her new masters defiantly re-christened her *Exodus 1947*. Her front-page chronicled voyage, obviously impossible of success since she was from the first accompanied by powerful units of the Royal Navy, was intended essentially to focus world attention on the heart-rending

As the Jewish refugee ship *Exodus 1947*, the former Old Bay liner in her third career attempted to run the Palestine blockade with 4,500 illegal immigrants on board. She is shown entering Haifa Harbor, Israel, escorted by British warships, July 20, 1947. *British Admiralty photograph.*

plight of the Jews on this second great exodus. This occurred prior to the realization of the age-old dream of turning the Promised Land into the new Israeli nation.

Early on the eighth day after leaving Cette, Royal Navy destroyers closed not too gently on both sides of the crowded steamer as she was entering Palestinian territorial waters. There was a bitter, one-sided struggle before the ship, bearing a gaping wound on her port side, was taken and then conveyed submissively into Haifa. Here the "illegals" either went on to overcrowded detention camps at Cyprus, or were returned to their points of origin in Central Europe.

Time passed. At midnight, May 14, 1948, Israel became a new nation, at war with the surrounding Arab states. The rusting *Exodus*, moored to a breakwater across the harbor, took on a new and symbolic significance as a graphic representation of a nation's birth pangs. Fittingly, Leon Uris chose her as the title of his successful novel detailing these events. Israeli plans to use the boat as a museum to record the struggle, at first postponed owing to the more urgent and immediate preoccupation with defending her borders, were nullified when, on August 26, 1952, for reasons never discovered, the old steamer caught fire and burned to the waterline. When the flames subsided, the gutted hulk was towed away and abandoned at Shemen Beach. And there, virtually forgotten for another decade, she laid on the sandy bottom, her main deck awash with jagged pieces of steel protruding out of the water.

Early in 1963, salvage rights to the *Exodus* were acquired by an Italian firm. A salvage crew of 12, headed by Salvatore Perrotta of Savona, arrived

The *Exodus 1947* moored in Haifa Harbor shows the extent of the damage she sustained by the "nutcracker" movement of British destroyers intercepting her. *Photograph courtesy of Haifa Port Authority.*

at Haifa with their salvage vessel, *Giovanni Lertora*, and quietly began work on the abandoned hulk. One of their first tasks was to cut the hull completely in two. The ship had been badly strained where one of the destroyers rammed her on the port side. Time and decay had attacked this weakened area. It was felt that if an attempt were made to raise the corroded hulk in one piece, it would break across under stress.

And so, it was actually only half of the steamer which made that "last" voyage on August 23 and the stern section was planned to follow about two weeks later. With an appreciation for the historical proprieties, *Jerusalem Post* reporter Yaacov Friedler arranged for Itzak Aronowitz, the 22-year-old master of the *Exodus* on her incredible voyage 16 years earlier, to be on hand to see the old vessel "sail" again.

Two views of the *Exodus 1947* on fire in Haifa Harbor, August 26, 1952. She was reduced to a sunken hulk. *Photographs courtesy of Haifa Port Authority.*

"It brings back memories and touches the heart," the former skipper of the *Exodus* was quoted, as the forward half of the vessel gradually righted itself on an even keel and broke loose from the bottom while husky, bathing-trunk-clad salvage master Perrotta tended his pumps. But it was an anti-climax. The bow sank again without anything material having been accomplished.

The hulk of the *Exodus 1947* as it appeared early in 1963. *Photograph courtesy of Israel Ports Authority, Haifa Port Management.*

Italian salvage master Salvatore Perrotta attempting to refloat the hulk of the *Exodus 1947*. The "last voyage" occurred August 23, 1963 and the hulk sank again without anything being accomplished. *Photograph courtesy of Israel Ports Authority, Haifa Port Management.*

Perrotta reported that the ticklish salvage job on the much deteriorated *Exodus* had not been financially worthwhile. If enabled to complete the work, he planned to return to an attempt to raise an Italian submarine sunk in Haifa by shore batteries during World War II.

To all intents and purposes, the *Exodus* no longer exists, though pieces of her may subsequently turn up here and there as segments of bulkheads or seawalls while the balance is melted down for recasting as pig iron. Suffice to say, no ship has ever participated in more bizarre events, despite the long periods of inactivity that separated them. Thus, the little one-time passenger steamer, beloved here by countless Chesapeake travelers, became in turn a valiant warship serving the cause of peace, a desperate blockade runner dealing in human hopes, and finally, the symbol of the birth of a nation.

CHAPTER 17

(1965)

A Visit to the James River Ghost Fleet

Following the Armistice, the vast number of vessels, which had been rushed to completion in World War I to build a "Bridge of Ships" extending "Over There," suddenly became a fleet of white elephants. Though it was all over, and the world was presumably safe for democracy forever, the government wisely elected to maintain the vessels it had laboriously built in vast storage anchorages so that, if needed again, they could be made available with a minimum of reactivation work.

A distant view of the James River Reserve Fleet as seen from Mulberry Island. What appear to be individual ships are giant clusters of ten to twenty vessels moored side by side, bow to stern, stern to bow.

One of the largest of these reserve fleet anchorages was established immediately after the war on a wide bend of the James River, opposite Mulberry Island, west of the ship channel leading downstream to Newport News, a dozen miles away. It still remains, though the composition has changed many times. Two other surviving reserve fleets are at Beaumont, Texas, and Suisun Bay, San Francisco. Originally there were eight.

On many occasions I have cruised by what is popularly designated hereabouts as the "Idle Fleet"—a term which is anathema to its dedicated custodians, however. And I have never failed to be moved by the ghostly appearance of these neat rows upon rows of somber, seemingly-lifeless craft. But, though the uninformed might consider the area a graveyard, actually a tremendous amount of activity is continually going on. Maintenance work never stops and vessels are constantly being brought in or withdrawn for some purpose, and the numbers and composition of the fleet is a positive indicator of the maritime climate of the nation.

The present superintendent, Kenneth W. Fritsche, said that the fleet, at its greatest extent around 1948, contained 750 craft. This is now, early in 1975, down to around 150 odd vessels. The largest single classes were Liberty and Victory ship types of World War II, many of which were withdrawn for temporary reactivation, only to have the identical vessels find their ways back later.

In the autumn of 1965 I made my first actual visit aboard one of the ships, as a guest of Captain Raymond G. Brown. This is described in the ensuing account published in the *New Dominion* of November 28, that year. My old friend Jim Sampselle, then a marine surveyor, wished to have a close look at a moth-balled hospital ship, the *Blanche F. Sigman*, to explore the possibility of having her towed to South Korea for use again for that purpose, but this time to be permanently moored to the shore. The plan was never put into effect, however, and the former old Liberty ship has remained on in the fleet and was only recently sold to the Wender Company on speculation. As of the end of January, 1974, she was still at her accustomed moorings. But, that has changed and she has subsequently been taken away to be scrapped.

On the occasion of our initial visit, there was considerable activity going on at the fleet as Victory ships were being taken out to restore to duty for the Vietnam War sealift. I paid another visit to the James River Anchorage about six years later to watch some of these same three-war veterans—World War II, Korea and Vietnam—again return to pasture as described in Chapter 19. But of the earlier, less efficient Liberty ship types, now only a handful remains and, like the *Blanche*, they will soon disappear.

The ensuing article also mentions viewing the *Zebulon B. Vance*, which left to be scrapped in the spring of 1970, as related in Chapter 10.

Quite a few of the ships which comprise the U.S. Maritime Commission's 350-member James River Reserve Fleet recently ended their tranquil 20-year Rip Van Winkle sleep.

Although there is always something going on at the more than a mile-long anchorage in the curving James off Mulberry Island, the marked increase in military build-up at Vietnam has produced considerable additional activity. There is routine painting, maintenance and ship movements as replacements come in from other fleets, or vessels are shifted or temporarily withdrawn for one reason or another. From 1953 to 1964 they stored surplus grain in many of them, a total of some 165 being assigned for this purpose. Thus, ship tenders and maintenance men of Captain Raymond G. Brown's command are kept additionally busy as more vessels are pulled out to be put back into active service again.

Looking down a line of Reserve Fleet ships at anchor in the James River.

Though the Reserve Fleet is the proper name for the many gray craft of World War II vintage of which it is principally comprised, for most people who have observed the rows of motionless vessels strapped side-by-side at anchor, one generally hears the more popular name "Idle Fleet." But, those who work there fighting the inexorable "tooth of time" find it by no means idle. However, for the occasional visitor who is permitted aboard the lifeless craft, they seem more aptly to fit the gloomy designator, James River Ghost Fleet.

There is nothing more vibrantly alive than a ship in commission. But, stripped down and abandoned to be preserved in limbo against an uncertain

Heavy timber fenders are let down between the ships to keep them from rubbing together.

fate, nothing could be more abysmally lonely or creepy. First, there is the overwhelming silence on board that makes almost terrifying the occasional little sounds that do come through. Wavelets slapping alongside are magnified by the sounding box action of empty hulls to suggest rushing water, and a visitor briefly envisages himself trapped below in a sinking ship!

And, there is the sudden tortured squeal of raw steel rubbing raw steel, as the swell raised by a passing vessel already a mile down the channel, begins to make itself felt amongst the idle ships, and the metal gratings laid from

Marine surveyor Jim Sampselle crosses a grating between two laid-up ships after checking out the World War II Army hospital ship *Blanche F. Sigman.*

one deck to the next begin to work back and forth. Meanwhile, still other startling noises are emitted by the heavy timber grill-work fenders let down over the rails between the ships to separate them. These squeak and chatter as they rub their giant charges' flanks. Then, except for the sea gulls, all is quiet again and the solitude itself almost screams.

In 1965, this writer accompanied a good friend, Newport News marine surveyor, James V. Sampselle, of the U.S. Salvage Association, on a trip to

Outboard ships in each group are equipped with gangways so they may be readily boarded. A fleet tug is moored at the bottom.

the Ghost Fleet. Sampselle wished particularly to examine the condition of some World-War-II-built Liberty ships, originally freighters, but converted to floating hospitals during the later stages of the war.

We drove through Fort Eustis, down to the river shore where the Maritime Commission maintains busy office and maintenance facilities employing around 150 persons. Here administrative work for the fleet is carried out and the ship tender and workboat auxiliaries are moored. And here, before they

A pair of idle tankers of World War II vintage.

Three of a group of World War II Liberty ships. The one in the center is the *Zebulon B. Vance*, Hull No. 1 of the North Carolina Shipbuilding Company, as seen November 3, 1968.

embark on tug or tender to board the ships, visitors don coveralls and hard hats, and are provided with heavy leather belts onto which are clipped storage battery assemblies hooked up to provide current for powerful flash-lights. The cord is looped around the wearer's neck and the light stays on continuously until disassembled for recharging the batteries at day's end.

At least one outboard ship in each of the 17 clusters of craft, moored side-by-side, alternating bow to stern, to give maximum anchoring efficiency, has a gangway over the side. This gives access at main deck level to all vessels in that particular group, since the squealing gratings are laid across the spaces between the craft. High-voltage electric current is provided to certain clusters via submarine cable, not for power or illumination, but to actuate cathodic protection systems aimed to reduce corrosion of the hulls and discourage marine growth. Power for raising anchors or hauling cables when required

A pair of fleet tugs stand by at the headquarters dock on Mulberry Island.

must be brought in from outside. It is provided by one or the other of the two husky diesel tugs belonging to the facility. Depending upon what is required, one of the tugs is capable of providing electric power for laid-up ships having electric winches, the other compressed air for those equipped with steam windlasses.

Below, in the idle ships' machinery spaces, the engines and all auxiliary machinery have been converted to lumps of grease that gleamed in the errie half-light of our torches. Here, of course, in the still darkness, gloves and even hot coveralls are welcome.

Though the untrained eye may not detect it, in grouping the ships, those of the same type and age have generally been placed in a cluster—freighters, tankers, naval auxiliaries and so forth. Their conditions and availability range from those of high priority, maintained in a state of readiness (the ones which were to go to Vietnam), to those whose age and general debility is such that they are being retained afloat for scrapping purposes alone. Mention of one of the latter will evoke some nostalgic recollections in this community's shipbuilding fraternity. Looking very much the worse for wear was the former Army transport *Zebulon B. Vance*. This Liberty ship was Hull No. 1 of the North Carolina Shipbuilding Company, the World War II emergency shipyard established at Wilmington, N.C., for the U.S. Maritime Commission by the Newport News Shipbuilding and Dry Dock Company. The local yard supplied the key men and know-how for a sprawling plant, which quickly sprang up on the banks of the Cape Fear River and lasted for the duration of the war (Chapter 10).

Center vessel is the former Army hospital ship *Blanche F. Sigman*, a Liberty ship conversion. In her final duty the *Sigman* served as an Army transport for dependents and World War II brides coming to America, photographed February 24, 1971.

The good ship *Zebulon B. Vance*, named in honor of North Carolina's Reconstruction Period governor, was launched on Saturday, December 6, 1941, actually only a matter of hours before the Japanese planes zeroed in for their attack on Pearl Harbor. The *Vance* was delivered on February 17, 1942, and immediately transported vital war cargoes. After this extensive service as a freighter, she was converted to an Army hospital ship and renamed the *John J. Meany*. Later, after fulfilling her required missions of mercy, she was transferred to the U.S. Army Transportation Corps under her original name and, at the war's end, was happily engaged in bringing war brides back to the United States. She then joined the "Idle Fleet" and has remained there since.

Bypassing the *Vance* as not worth boarding, our first visit was to the S.S. *Blanche F. Sigman*, next to the last ship abreast in a cluster of vessels which might well be returning to active service if occasions warrant. Originally the Los Angeles-built Liberty ship *Stanford White*, but renamed for a heroic Army nurse killed in action at Anzio Beachhead, her namesake Lady Blanche, far from white, shows all too plainly her years of disuse and idle-

Patterns of mooring chains as viewed from the stern of the *Blanche F. Sigman*, 1965.

ness. To the untrained eye, she appeared a wreck, with decks buckled and paint flaking. Yet actually, she has been carefully preserved, and with an industrious shipyard work crew aboard, Surveyor Sampselle assured me she could be de-moth-balled and fully operational within a period of a fortnight or less.

Though all valuable furniture, equipment and stores had been taken ashore prior to the ship being laid up, she still gave vivid evidence of her former employment. It was surprising what odds and ends happened to be left on board when she was turned over to the Reserve Fleet custodians—such as a locker full of broken toilet seats. On the *Blanche*, corridor after corridor opened into hospital wards, with tiers of pipe-frame bunks with nearby pantries, washrooms, lockers and virtually miles of storage spaces and shelves.

As we climbed ladders and wandered along passageways, we discovered examination rooms, operating theaters, barber shop, commissaries, recreation rooms, mess halls, galleys, bake shops and vast iceboxes for frozen stores. Deep in the hold, there was one especially grim facility designed to transport cadavers under refrigeration in shallow stainless-steel trays. On upper decks were staterooms for officers, crew, and medical people. Quarters for nurses were still plainly marked "off limits except to assigned personnel." Below, we found a lock-up for prisoners, another, identified by flash-

Stern of a Liberty ship of the "Idle Fleet." Conspicuous "draft marks" are painted on the rudders and stems of all craft to show if they are in proper trim and have not taken on water.

light, contained cells, presumably for the insane. No skeletons of former inmates remained, but we were ready to jump and run if one came into view.

In short, here once was a fully-equipped facility designed to minister to the creature needs, well or ill, of a thousand people and to house a cargo of human emotion ranging from complete elation to abject despair. It was a moving experience to wander through such a ghost ship in the flickering light of torches.

What a story this ship could tell, or, for that matter, the bride-toting *Zebulon B. Vance* or any other of the 350 craft that then comprised the James River Ghost Fleet.

CHAPTER 18

(1968)

Farewell to the Queen; *Queen Elizabeth* (I)*
Leaves New York for the Last Time

One day in late September, 1967, a brief rendezvous took place in mid-Atlantic when Cunard's great *Queens, Mary* and *Elizabeth*, passed each other for the last time. Although venerable, the younger 82,997-ton *Queen Elizabeth* was westbound for New York on a routine service voyage. However, for the 81,237-ton *Queen Mary* it was her final trip back to England for, on October 31, that year, she would leave home waters for Long Beach, California, via the long way 'round Cape Horn. On arrival she was to become what has been described as a "floatel-museum." At that fleeting moment when the giant *Queens* met and parted in the North Atlantic, the most eminent passenger ships the world has known bade a tearful farewell.

Ever rivals in the field of promotion, Florida was miffed when California gained such a prize as the *Queen Mary*, for undoubtedly she would prove a bountiful tourist lure. Accordingly, when on January 31 the next year, Cunard announced that their second massive ship, the *Queen Elizabeth*, would be sold out of service (since her somewhat smaller but newer successor, the *Queen Elizabeth 2*, was ready to enter service) Fort Lauderdale made the successful bid to acquire her display liner, too. There were conditions to the sale which differed from the *Queen Mary*, however. Cunard retained part ownership and a share in any profits, in an arrangement highly-contested by Philadelphia interests as well, for the City of Brotherly Love had similar aspirations.

Alas for Florida. After they obtained her, the gigantic ship proved an embarrassment. She encountered further misadventures, which made many of her ardent partisans of transatlantic days wish that they had taken her out and sunk her in mid-ocean, instead.

The final departure from New York, of what undoubtedly would never be eclipsed as the world's most enormous passenger ship—though the new *France* would be considered a close contender—was certainly an event of moment. I was delighted, then, to accept the invitation of friend Frank O. Braynard, to ride one of the Moran Company tugs, slated to undock the vessel for the final time and escort her down New York harbor. This event also seemed worthy of taking my ten-year-old daughter, Johanna, from school to witness, on the assumption that she would derive a lesson in history far more meaningful than her current fifth grade assignment.

Accordingly, Johanna and I flew to New York from Newport News. We joined forces with another steamship buff, our friend Walter Lord, a person

*When the second liner to carry the name of England's Queen Elizabeth came out in 1968, she was officially designated *Queen Elizabeth 2*, popularly shortened to *QE2*. The first *Queen Elizabeth* (1940) naturally had no need for a numerical designator, but we have inserted the customary Roman numeral (I) in this account so the identities of the ships may not be confused. See also page 189.

of extraordinary talents, and author of the best seller, *A Night to Remember*, published by Henry Holt & Co., New York, 1955, covering the fatal voyage of the *Titanic*. As directed, we arrived for an early morning departure from Manhattan's Pier One on board the good tug *Doris Moran*.

My subsequent pictorial account of the *Queen Elizabeth's* departure was written upon my return to Newport News, and was printed in the *New Dominion* on December 1, 1968. Naturally, it was assumed that the old Cunarder's approaching career would more or less parallel that of her older sister *Mary* at Long Beach. But, the results were quite different. Returning to England after the routine voyage we witnessed the beginning, the *Queen Elizabeth* was readied for her next role as Florida's floating convention center and ship hotel. Recrossing the Atlantic via a more southerly route, the aged ship arrived and, though it was a tight squeeze, she was successfully moored in Fort Lauderdale's Port Everglades on December 8.

The vessel's career in Florida was short, unhappy, and too involved to relate here. Suffice to say, in September of 1970 she was sold for $3.2 million to a Chinese shipping magnate, C.Y. Tung. Her new owner planned to sail the liner around to the Pacific and spend an additional $4.5 million, to outfit her as a floating university and cruise ship, to be administered by Los Angeles' Chapman College. To this end, the *Queen Elizabeth* left Florida for Hong Kong, arriving off the China coast July 16, 1971, where her forthcoming conversion could be performed at far less expense than in the United States. Renamed *Seawise University*, shipowner Tung assigned her to his new-found Seawise Foundation.

Her debut as a floating college was planned for early March of 1972, but on January 9, just hours before the massive liner's planned departure from Hong Kong to Japan to go into the Orient's only sufficiently sizeable dry dock, fire suddenly erupted on board. Seemingly, it broke out on the entire ship at once. Approximately 2,000 workmen and visitors then on board miraculously escaped and only ten men were injured. But, all of Hong Kong's available firefighting craft could not contain the holocaust which burned out of control for 24 hours before, with tons of water pumped into her by fire fighters, the ship rolled over on her side and sank in 57 feet of water.

Airborne cameramen were out in force and the intense fury of the blaze, well depicted in a series of photographs, with a vivid accompanying account by Peter T. Eisele, appeared, among other places, in the summer, 1972 issue of *Steamboat Bill*, prestigious journal of the Steamship Historical Society of America.

Sabotage was immediately suspected, and so determined at the ensuing official inquiry, though reason and culprit may well remain a mystery forever. Hurriedly, ways of salvaging the enormous ship were proposed and discussed, but eventually abandoned. The *Queen Elizabeth* was simply too bulky. A dispatch from Hong Kong dated January 4, 1974, stated that, as of that date, workers had begun cutting up the rusting wreck, which arson had claimed two years previously. Thus, the death knell of the once-prideful liner was sounded. Because much of the ship would have to be cut up underwater, it was estimated that it would take at least three years to complete the job.

An interim report of June 8, 1975, relates that only a few hundred feet of charred steel is all that was visible above water. An enormous quantity of scrap steel has been reclaimed and sold throughout Asia. But, according to D.A. Sandison, the senior maritime officer whose department administers Hong Kong harbor, it will probably take three more years to remove the ship's mid-section from its casket of mud. Only then will the *Queen Elizabeth* be no more.

Two weeks ago, as this is being written [October 30, 1968], your correspondent made a sentimental pilgrimage to New York City to witness the abdication of a queen. The regal personage in question was Britain's 83,000-ton Royal Mail Steamship *Queen Elizabeth*. As widely reported, this, the world's largest merchant ship, was concluding almost three decades of service on the North Atlantic and is presently headed for a more questionable career in retired status as a floating hotel and convention center for Port Everglades, Florida. Ship lovers of the old school, however, were vocal in their suggestion that it might be far better for the grand old lady to be taken out into deep water and sent to the bottom!

Both the *Queen Elizabeth* and her slightly older sister ship *Queen Mary*—now already embarked on a similar retirement program at Long Beach, California—were conceived in the period prior to World War II when there was no transatlantic air service and those who chose to reach Europe as quickly as possible traveled by luxury liner. In this present air age, however, the enormous size and weight of the *Queens*, both over a thousand feet in length, became a liability. Those in a hurry to cross the "pond" would take a jet anyway and the *Queens* were not well-suited for alternate duty as leisurely tropical cruisers—witness the discomfort of those aboard the *Queen Mary* crossing the equator on her final voyage out to California.

The departure from Gotham of the last of the old *Queens*—even though the Cunard Line will soon have a new and smaller (58,000 tons) *Queen Elizabeth 2* in service—marked the end of an era. Thousands of New Yorkers recognized this and arrived in vast numbers to do her honor as she sailed away for the last time.

By invitation, we witnessed the great ship's departure from a grandstand seat—the deck of one of several Moran Towing and Transportation Company's tugboats, which assisted in undocking the liner and then accompanied her down the harbor to the salutes of virtually every vessel in port.

With other invited guests (including such well-known writers of the sea as Walter Lord of *A Night to Remember* fame; Leonard A. Stevens, author of a new book, *The Elizabeth: Passage of a Queen*, published by Alfred A. Knopf, New York, 1968, about the *Queen Elizabeth* herself; and our genial host Frank O. Braynard, Moran public relations chief, and author of *Lives of the Liners*, published by Cornell Maritime Press, Inc., 1947, and other books) we climbed on board the sturdy 4,290-horsepower diesel-powered tug *Doris Moran* at ten a.m. From Pier One at the tip of Manhattan Island, we steamed up the Hudson River to the Cunard Line's Pier 92, where the *Queen Elizabeth* was being readied for departure.

It was a glorious morning. The alchemy of brilliant sunlight and a crisp fresh cross wind converted the usually turgid harbor water to burnished silver. And occasional tiny rainbows darted through the *Doris Moran's* frothy bow waves and wake. Great masses of cumulous clouds were piled around

Johanna H. Brown awaits the arrival at Pier No. 1, the Battery, New York City, of the diesel tug *Doris Moran* which will assist in undocking the mighty liner *Queen Elizabeth* (I), making her final voyage back to England, October 30, 1968.

Pennants whipping in the breeze, the *Queen Elizabeth* is moments away from casting off her lines to start her voyage back to England.

A Moran towboat comes alongside the *Queen Elizabeth* to take off the docking pilot, as crewmen on the venerable liner break out the 280-foot Homeward Bound pennant from the mainmast truck, symbol of her final departure in transatlantic service.

the horizon, spreading changing patterns of light and shade across Manhattan's towers and the harbor at their feet.

The *Queen* was gaily dressed for the occasion. Strings of colorful international code flags whipping in the breeze, reached from liner's stem to foremast truck and from the base of the second of her two enormous black-topped red funnels to the mainmast. The ship looked beautiful poised beside the pier, while throngs of visitors crowded her decks to wish *bon voyage* to the 1,500 passengers taking this final voyage back to England. Included

Leaving the towers of Manhattan behind, the great British liner picks up speed as accompanying tugs begin to have trouble keeping up with her.

The *Queen Elizabeth* gives her valedictory salute to the Statue of Liberty, so ending two dozen years' service on the North Atlantic.

among them undoubtedly were many who might have been aboard the *Queen Elizabeth* when she sailed as troop ship in World War II.

Our tug tied up at the head of the pier and was soon joined by several others, while our passengers went across to visit the liner. Just before noon, as longshoremen were hustling the final cargo and baggage aboard, stewards were hastening the last of convivial visitors ashore.

"Last call—all ashore that's going ashore!"

Meanwhile, her own passengers re-embarked, the *Doris Moran* backed out into the river to wait while her sisters took their accustomed positions at bow and stern of the liner. They prepared for the dockmaster's walkie-talkie command to exert their thousands of horses, in order to turn the *Queen* promptly at right angles and head her down the river after her enormous bulk had cleared the pier. Slack water was at hand, the gangways were

The *Queen Elizabeth*, surrounded by tugboat escorts, steams down New York Bay heading for the Narrows, October 30, 1968, as an era comes to an end.

hauled ashore, the mooring lines singled up ready to cast off. Only confetti streamers bound her to the land.

The *Queen* announced the moment of her departure with a long, deep-throated blast from her imperious steam whistle, keyed to base A-flat and audible for ten miles. Slowly backing out into the stream on her own power from giant quadruple screws, the Moran tugs immediately snugged their well-padded snouts against the liner's high bows and flanks and began to shove. In a matter of minutes the maneuver was complete, the tugs tooted and fell back and the tinkle of the liner's engine telegraph signaled slow speed ahead.

For an appreciable moment, the *Queen* lay motionless in the middle of the Hudson River, as if reluctant to leave the port which had been her second home since the winter of 1940, when she had concluded her first and secret wartime voyage from the Clyde. For that moment, time stood still, while the picture etched itself in unforgettable memory.

At last the spell was broken as the great ship slowly gathered headway, and an accompanying fleet of tugs and excursion boats took station on either side while picture-taking helicopters hovered overhead. And then, capping the climax to a colorful ceremony, the *Queen Elizabeth's* "homeward bound" pennant was broken out from the mainmast peak. Measuring 280 feet in length—ten feet for every year of service is the formula—this whip-like streak of red, white and blue bunting was swept out in the breeze to port. The venerable *Queen* was finally going home.

Speeding ahead, our tug paced the liner down the Hudson River, past the man-made canyons of lower Manhattan, where fireboats sent up their plume-like sprays in salute, and then coming abreast of the Statue of Liberty. Here the *Queen Elizabeth*, symbol of Britannia's rule of the waves, sounded her final deep-toned salute. The ship had picked up speed by then and, unable to keep pace much longer, one by one, the flotilla of accompanying small craft peeled off and headed back home. Soon the liner was steaming unescorted toward the open sea, where she so truly belonged.

Lowering clouds were gathering overhead as she vanished in the distance.

CHAPTER 19

(1971)

The *Elko Victory* Goes Back to Bed

Having enjoyed a visit on board a Liberty ship laid up in the James River Reserve Fleet Anchorage in the fall of 1965, as recorded in Chapter 17, six years later I made another visit there to look over a Victory ship. This was no mean routine look-see, however, for this time, accompanied by *Daily Press* City Editor Bill Hockstedler, we would witness the procedure of detaching one ship from the anchorage and accepting another for storage—a considerable activity on the part of both the fleet tugs doing the docking and the commercial tugs handling the tows.

Welcomed by Superintendent John Negrotto, we were soon suited in coveralls, equipped with our miners' lights, and set out on a fleet workboat to board the steamship *Santa Clara Victory*, to watch her preparations for departure down river to the Norfolk shipyard. Meanwhile, the *Elko Victory* was being towed from Norfolk and, on arrival, we would climb aboard her to witness her being anchored and put to bed.

It was an unseasonably warm and delightful morning in late February, 1971. It was a pleasure to participate vicariously along with those dedicated men who do business in great waters.

———

The recent arrival of the cargo steamer *Elko Victory*, at the James River Reserve Fleet Anchorage off Mulberry Island, made no more than the usual ripples which accompany movements of the idle ships—disbanded and cold—which live out their final destinies moored side-by-side in the turgid James.

Unlike the luxury liner *United States*, the *Elko Victory* had nothing particularly in her favor, which, had she been a glamor craft, would have made her arrival a noteworthy event. For this 27-year veteran of the high seas was merely another of the hundreds of work horses needed to tote the nation's waterborne commerce in war and peace and, like many another veteran of the recent Vietnam sealift, she was now returning to rest.

The *Elko Victory* had done it before. But this time it was certainly problematical whether her subsequent awakening from a Rip Van Winkle-like sleep would lead to reactivation and duty afloat, or to a trip to the shipbreakers and scrapping. Yet, for the time being at least, the old Victory ship was to be kept in a state of partial readiness with her engine room and one cargo hold—crammed with such equipment as lifeboats, deck winches, cargo booms and other topside equipment—sealed off under a dehumidification program designed to keep them moisture-free and, therefore, less subject to deterioration and more quickly amenable to reactivation.

Another factor which contributed to the seeming anonymity of the *Elko Victory* was that, as a World War II-built Victory ship, she was only one of

The *Elko Victory*, veteran of three wars, is towed up under the James River Bridge to be put to bed in the James River Reserve Fleet Anchorage off Mulberry Island. *Daily Press photograph by Jim Livengood.*

over 500 virtually identical craft, all hastily constructed in the 1940s to further the war effort. As such, she and her sisters were a decided improvement over the nation's initial emergency cargo ship type—the famous Liberty ship of which more than 2,500 were launched before American shipyards could re-tool to handle the more sophisticated Victory class. The Liberties could only make 11 knots with their old-style, slow-moving, up-and-down engines. The Victories, with 6,600 shaft horsepower geared turbines to drive them, could steam at better than 14 knots.

So it was, then, at the end of World War II, there was not much of a market for the lethargic Liberties, but the Victories remained in demand for moving peacetime cargos. However, as newer and more efficient ships made their appearances on the sea lanes, the Victories, too, began to show up in the reserve fleet anchorages maintained by the government around the

The Curtis Bay Towing Company's powerful diesel tug *Sparrows Point* is at the business end of the towline bringing the freighter *Elko Victory* up to join the James River Reserve Fleet. Her consort, the *Sandy Point* is alongside, February 24, 1971.

country—here in the James River, up the Hudson and in lay-up fleets in Gulf and West Coast waters.

The weary old *Elko Victory* may at first seem nondescript and hardly worth giving a second glance, as she was nudged in by the fleet tugs and fastened to a group of half a dozen ships at anchor in the river. But, she does well merit respectful consideration as typifying the nation's might on the Seven Seas, and its readiness to take on a job, no matter how distasteful, such as the Vietnam War. Two hundred years ago, no less an authority than General Washington recognized at Yorktown that this nation's destiny lay in control of the seas. The *Elko Victory's* modest role today is merely an extension of that thought.

Fleet crew hauls in starboard anchor of the *Santa Clara Victory* as they prepare to unmoor the ship prior to its being towed down the river to the Norfolk shipyard, February 24, 1971.

Lifting the *Santa Clara Victory's* mooring chains from the bitts to unmoor the ship.

The *Elko's* career began in 1944 when she was launched at Richmond, California, by the Permanente Metals Corporation's No. One Shipyard. Like her sisters, she measured 455 feet long by 62 feet wide and 28 feet, 6 inches deep. Initially classed VC2-S-AP-2 for operation by the U.S. Navy, she rated 7,608 gross tons and sailed out of San Francisco transporting war cargo on the Pacific fronts.

Some time after World War II, the *Elko Victory* was decommissioned and taken to a lay-up fleet. But the Korean conflict occurred and, with the need once more to transport military cargo, she was reactivated and pressed into service. Korean duty over, she arrived at the James River Reserve Fleet Anchorage September 19, 1952, from operations.

Her period of idleness this time was to last 13 years. But, with the Vietnam conflict underway and again a crying need for ships to carry the material of war, the *Elko Victory* was reactivated December 24, 1965, and left immediately for Southeast Asia.

Meanwhile, the so-called Vietnamization Program had also caught up with the *Elko Victory* and, replaced by more modern and speedier ships on the transpacific sealift and with South Vietnam ports able to handle freighters with a quick turn-around (some American cargo ships had to wait in the stream for months to be unloaded at Saigon), the *Elko Victory* returned to the James River's Idle Fleet on May 27, 1970. Initially she was held in ready status, but on January 28, 1971, it was determined that she would not again be needed in the foreseeable future. Accordingly, she was towed down the James to the Norfolk Shipbuilding and Dry Dock Corporation for the decommissioning program in which, as stated, perishable topside gear was stowed below for safe-keeping and the hatches sealed. So it was, then, that on Wednesday morning, February 24, 1971, from a Reserve Fleet Anchorage tug we watched the *Elko Victory* slowly arriving under tow to be put to bed.

Custodians of the *Elko Victory*, and some 325 similarly inactive vessels anchored in the James, is a little-known but quite remarkable organization brought into being by the U.S. Maritime Administration for the purpose of caring and storing the nation's floating properties to have them available in time of need. Other old and unwanted war-spawned ships are merely held for subsequent scrapping. The James River Idle Fleet, of which former seagoing engineer John S. Negrotto is superintendent, employs over 200 men. They are by no means idle, despite the unofficial name sometimes given the local anchorage facility, stretching along several miles of river near Fort Eustis. Recently, the fleet has handled—in other words activated and then deactivated—45 Victory ships for and from the Vietnam operations, out of the nation's total of more than 150 vessels used on this sealift. The *Elko Victory* is one of the last of this group to return to dead storage. Thus, her arrival marked the termination of an era.

The Curtis Bay Towing Company of Norfolk is one of the local towing concessionaires which handle ship movements for the James River Reserve Fleet. With the diesel tug *Sparrows Point* at the business end of a husky nylon towline and her sister tug, the *Sandy Point*, secured alongside the *Elko's* starboard quarter, the freighter cleared the Norfolk shipyard at 8 a.m., heading for the Reserve Fleet. The cavalcade passed under the draw of the James River Bridge an hour and a half later and, just before noon, arrived off the Anchorage.

James River Reserve Fleet tug *TD-23* approaches the *Elko Victory* to take her over from the commercial tug *Sandy Point*, foreground.

A pair of powerful fleet tugs shove the *Elko Victory* alongside a group of Victory ships for permanent mooring.

Meanwhile, fleet maintenance tugs had been preparing another Victory ship, the *Santa Clara Victory*, for a visit to the Norfolk decommissioning facility and she was ready to be cast off when the *Elko Victory* arrived. The two pairs of tugs then switched their charges, and the Curtis Bay vessels turned around and commenced to tow the *Santa Clara Victory* downstream, while the anchorage tugs attended to the permanent berthing of the decommissioned *Elko*.

The *Elko Victory* was nudged in broadside to a group of five ships—moored bow to stern, stern to bow—at the northern end of the Anchorage. The tugs held her next to the outboard ship while wire breastlines were tightened and secured and chains rigged from the *Elko's* stern to the bow of the adjoining vessel. Final act in this nautical drama consisted of properly placing the *Elko's* two bow anchors. In order that there be a suitable lead in the way the chains were to extend out from the bow of the ship; in turn

A fleet tug hauls out the *Elko Victory's* port anchor to drop some distance from the ship to provide adequate holding power at the end of the mooring operation.

the anchors were lowered down to waterline level. A tug then passed a slip cable through the eye at the head of each shank and then backed away, towing the anchor away from the ship. When at some distance from her, the anchor was dropped by releasing a pelican hook in the slip cable—an intricate maneuver designed to insure that each vessel in the group would assume its rightful share in taking the strain of wind and tide as the ships lay at anchor together.

At length, the mooring process completed and all shipshape and Bristol fashion under the critical eye of Fleet Captain Rodney Adams, we returned to the work boat which had been our grandstand seat for the operation and were taken ashore. We were confident in the assurance that, though their lives may now be devoid of glamor, at least the nation's idle ships are receiving the best of care to insure their immediate availability in the event of an emergency.

The fleet tug returns to haul away and drop the *Elko Victory's* starboard anchor.

The expense of maintaining a ship such as the *Elko Victory* which would cost at least $10,000,000 to replace, sets back the American taxpayer merely $20.00 per day—a remarkable bargain in security in these days of spiraling costs. The U.S. Maritime Administration, and Mr. Negrotto and his men, deserve the country's gratitude for a job well done.

CHAPTER 20

(1972)

A Pilot's-eye View of the New *Queen*

Although the *Queen Elizabeth 2*, the somewhat modest replacement for Cunard's famous transatlantic giants, *Queen Mary* and *Queen Elizabeth* (I), arrived at New York on her maiden voyage on May 7, 1969, after a four-day, 16-hour crossing, she did not get around to visiting Virginia waters until mid-January of 1972. She was then booked to carry local passengers on a pair of fortnightly West Indies cruises. Unlike the two original *Queens*, the *QE2* had been designed as much for tropical cruising as for transatlantic ferry service.

Over the years, I have been privileged to enjoy the most pleasant relations with members of the Virginia Pilot Association. Although the Cunard people would not permit anyone but the pilot to board the ship when she arrived off Cape Henry, Captain Richard Counselman arranged that I should go out on the pilot launch with the pilot assigned to bring the *QE2* in to Hampton Roads. This necessitated the pre-dawn rendezvous with Pilot Captain Robert Holland at Lynnhaven, as described in the following account published in the *New Dominion*, February, 6, 1972.

This story did not describe the most exciting part of the venture, however. Shortly after the new *Queen*, with Pilot Holland at the con, had gone on her proper way down Thimble Shoal Channel, I returned on the launch to the pilot boat to wait a chance to be taken ashore again. Meanwhile, the fresh wintry breeze sweeping down the bay had increased considerably when Captain Douglas Broad, Apprentice Jimmy Stallings and I embarked in one of the 30-foot launches for the return to Lynnhaven Inlet. Waves were now breaking completely across the mouth of the shallow channel leading to the inlet. We had to approach this at an angle and for several anxious moments, while the launch twisted and turned like a hula dancer, we wondered whether she might broach to and be rolled over. At length, though, the worst was over and we moved in under the bridge to tie up.

I had wondered what would have happened if we had suddenly found ourselves in the breakers. I agonized over the fact that the photographs, I had been at such pains to take, would then have been completely ruined. At the time this seemed far worse than mere drowning.

The view of angry North Atlantic seas from the seemingly precarious sanctuary of a wildly bouncing 30-foot launch in mid-winter can be extremely moving to the neophyte mariner. Yet to members of those understandably elite organizations devoted to pilotage, and specifically my hosts, the Virginia Pilot Association, such a sight is merely routine business. Whatever their personal preferences might be at the moment, Virginia pilots must be out there at the point where the mouth of Chesapeake Bay meets the

Virginia Pilot Association Captain Robert L. Holland boards the pilot launch off Cape Henry on the way out to take the conn of arriving Cunard liner *Queen Elizabeth 2*, January 15, 1972.

ocean to provide their vital services. Without pilots, operation of the great ports of Virginia—and the rest of the nation, too—would come to a standstill.

My reason for being on board the pilot launch that blustery winter morning of January 15, 1972, was to witness the arrival of R.M.S. *Queen Elizabeth 2*, making her first visit to Virginia waters to inaugurate West Indies cruises from Norfolk.

Though pilotage in Virginia dates back to colonial days with the official appointment of Capt. William Oewin as "Chief Pylott" in 1661, the present association originated in the trying days following the Civil War when carpet-bagger pilots came from the North to undercut the local mariners, with several shipwrecks and strandings resulting. Capt. Sam Wood called the Virginians together in 1865 and they were able to form the association which now enjoys a monopoly of piloting in the Commonwealth.

Until 1891, the association used sailing vessels exclusively for the offshore pilot boats stationed near Cape Henry. Their first steamer, the *Relief*, an iron-hull screw vessel of 242 gross tons and 510 horsepower, was expressly built as a pilot boat by Neafie and Levy of Philadelphia.

The Virginia pilot boat *Hampton Roads* is mother ship to a brood of pilot launches on duty at the pilot station off Cape Henry and the Chesapeake Bay entrance.

The *Relief* was followed by a series of auxiliary schooners and by a former steam yacht built by the Newport News Shipbuilding and Dry Dock Company in 1925 as the *Pawnee*. She was acquired seven years later and was renamed *Virginia*. Converted to diesel power, the *Virginia* performed yeoman duty for the pilots until finally put out to pasture in the late 1960s, as being too venerable for further duty.

Meanwhile, however, the association had acquired their present vessel, the former U.S. Coast Guard steam cutter *Comanche*, built at Wilmington, Delaware, in 1934. She too, was converted to diesel to make her more economical to operate, since her duties permit her to ride to a mooring buoy with the power plant shut down in periods of limited activity.

Renamed *Hampton Roads*, the former cutter, at 153 feet long by 36 feet beam, powered by 1,400 horsepower diesels, is the largest and most powerful vessel ever owned by the association. Having an ice-breaker's plump, rounded hull, she is a roller, bobbing about even in calm seas. But she is suitable as a year-round station ship for all weathers, as I was to witness on my brief visit off Cape Henry.

This began before dawn on a mid-January Saturday morning when I met Capt. Robert B. Holland. On the basis of regular rotation, he had drawn the assignment to bring in the *Queen Elizabeth 2* on her maiden voyage to Chesapeake Bay. At Lynnhaven Inlet we boarded one of the association's 30-foot, 150-horsepower launches for the five-mile trip out to the pilot boat. Here, with an estimated time of arrival set at 9 a.m., Captain Holland would

The pilot boat *Hampton Roads* almost drops from sight in the trough of the waves on the stormy morning of January 15, 1972 while one of her pilots goes out in the boarding launch to greet an incoming ship.

await the approach from sea of the 963-foot flagship of the Cunard Line. She was due to sail from Norfolk later this same day, with more than 1,000 passengers embarked for the 21st annual 12-day Virginia Cruise to the Caribbean.

Winter, too, was arriving with the *Queen*. The thermometer was falling and freshening winds out of the north bringing occasional snow flurries were already blowing Force 7-8 on the Beaufort scale. Though protected by the land mass of Cape Charles from ocean swells from the northeast, seas, ranging unchecked down the full length of Chesapeake Bay, were short and steep, their breaking crests smothered in white foam. This was scooped off the tops by the wind and flung to leeward in flying scud. The launch pitched violently, often completely burying itself in foam, but shaking free—like a retriever coming out of water—it pressed on and ultimately reached the

Hampton Roads. Here we climbed on board only to be tossed around with a different motion.

Several ships passed nearby on the way to and from sea and their pilots came and went. The *Hampton Roads'* launches plied their busy trade, coming alongside at the foot of Jacob's ladders let down on the ships' lee sides amidships, whence the pilots climbed up or down.

The last pilot safely aboard before the *QE2's* E.T.A., the *Hampton Roads* headed to sea to meet the oncoming *Queen* beyond the Capes. The great liner was a splendid sight as she approached, flags and pennants whipping at her single tall foremast and her jet black hull cradled in white water.

A view of the mighty *Queen Elizabeth 2* moments before the pilot launch came alongside to put a pilot on board the liner to bring her in to Hampton Roads January 15, 1972.

Captain Holland and I climbed down to the launch, tugging at her lines alongside the pilot boat and in a trice we were heading seaward to our rendezvous with royalty. Looking astern between cascades of spray, the *Hampton Roads,* soon small by comparison, would disappear from sight as the scend of the sea sent the launch tobogganing down into the troughs of the waves. Then the sturdy little boat would heave up again to a crest, only to be swept anew by stinging spray.

In a few minutes we were close aboard the liner and Captain Holland assumed his position on the foredeck of the launch, awaiting that moment of truth when he would reach to grasp slippery bottom rungs of the ladder let

down from a side port in the leviathan's hull. The launch rose to the crest of
a wave, caromed off the ship's side as Holland swung across the foaming
chasm and quickly climbed up to the port, turning for a second to wave back
to those of us remaining in the launch. The *Queen's* powerful twin screws bit
hard on the water as we veered off to return to the pilot boat. A knowledgeable hand was now on the bridge to conn Captain William Warwick's $4
million ship safely to port.

Pilot transfer from launch to pilot boat *Hampton Roads* at the mouth of Chesapeake Bay
during heavy winter weather off the Capes.

Routine work? Well, not quite really, for as famed Nathaniel Bowditch
had said almost two centuries earlier: "Piloting is the most important part of
navigation and the part requiring the most experience and nicest judgment."
I was sure that *QE2* was receiving exactly that.

CHAPTER 21

Inferno on the *Yarmouth Castle*

A somewhat shortened version of the ensuing story on the *Yarmouth Castle* holocaust was published in the January, 1976, issue of *The American Neptune* commemorating the tenth anniversary of this terrible disaster in which 90 people died. Owing to space limitations, it omitted an account of the voyage which my family and I had made on the ancient vessel only five months before catastrophe struck. This is covered in the first part of the unabridged narrative following. Assistance in the preparation of the story was graciously extended by Lt. George F. Johnson, USCG, Public Affairs Officer, 7th Coast Guard District; Prof. Arthur L. Johnson, State University College, Potsdam, New York; Capt. Carl R. Brown, Coral Gables, Florida; John L. Lochhead, The Mariners Museum, Newport News, Virginia; and the Honorable Thomas N. Downing, Washington, D.C.

Even without benefit of 20-20 hindsight, it is safe to say from our June, 1965, observations that the disaster which overwhelmed the badly-run *Yarmouth Castle* on November 13, 1965, was not unexpected. We were, of course, only too thankful that fire had not broken out while we were on board. How ghastly it was for those who were embarked on her last ill-fated voyage!

On the morning of the day we planned to take the boat back home from Nassau, Johanna arose and announced that her throat hurt and her neck was swollen. Johanna was almost seven and, since several of her chums at Saint Andrew's had come down with mumps shortly before the school term ended a couple of weeks earlier, our suspicions, aroused the day before when she did not seem to act quite right, were now realized. We did not feel happy about it.

Johanna, her mother, her 12-year-old sister, Suzanne, and I were then on the last lap of a long-anticipated two-weeks' excursion to the Bahamas which had included a trip to the New York World's Fair, a three-day cruise on the new and elegant Italian-built luxury liner *Oceanic*, then several days' stay at the commodious British Colonial Hotel in Nassau. I might state, parenthetically, that I had entertained the nebulous hope that the change might benefit my vocal chords, one set of which, curiously enough to my doctor and me, had become paralyzed a couple of months before, making it difficult to communicate except in a raspy whisper. I mean no snide remark in stating that, of necessity, my wife then did all the talking, which she is good at anyway. I might add that my vocal chords remained inoperative for several more months and, as inexplicably, suddenly began to work again when, in a moment of preternatural annoyance, amazingly I found myself shouting.

But, back to Nassau. Following our exotic tropical holiday, getting home was merely a necessary anticlimax and, since the girls did not fancy air travel, we had opted for an overnight boat from New Providence Island to Miami. There, we were to connect with the Seaboard Railroad's *Silver Comet* up to Richmond to catch the morning Chesapeake and Ohio train (they were in operation then) back down the Peninsula to Newport News.

After cruising on the lordly 782-foot *Oceanic*, we had not expected a ship of any great size or magnificence, but we were hardly prepared for the superannuated nautical conveyance that fate had dealt us. Though particulars were not uncovered until later, this proved to be the 38-year-old Canadian-owned coastwise liner *Yarmouth Castle*. She was held together by

The *Evangeline*, built in 1927 for Eastern Steamship Lines, to be used with sister ship *Yarmouth* on Boston to Yarmouth, N.S. service. *Photograph from the William B. Taylor Collection, courtesy of The Mariners Museum.*

paint and bravely eking out her final employment under the flag of Panama as a B-Class cruise ship with a multi-national crew, serving under a Greek captain. Other countries represented on the manifest were Austria, the Bahamas, Canada, Colombia, Cuba, the Dominican Republic, Haiti, Honduras, Jamaica, Spain and the United States. Curiously, there were no Panamanians—maybe they knew something! Along with several similarly aged sisters, the *Yarmouth Castle's* clientele consisted of economy-minded Americans embarked on what were touted as carefree, three-day, all-expense paid Caribbean cruises from Florida to Nassau at $59.00, complete.

The *Yarmouth Castle's* running mate on this twice-weekly service was the *Yarmouth* ("two great fun ships," the advertising copy read). They were identical vessels designed by Theodore E. Ferris and built at the William Cramp and Sons Ship and Engine Building Company in Philadelphia in 1927.

As neat little twin-screw, 18-knot turbo liners, they plied between New York or Boston and Canada's Maritime Provinces in the heyday of America's Eastern Steamship Lines. Christened *Evangeline*, the renamed *Yarmouth Castle* had been kicked around considerably before she finally settled on the 186-mile Miami-Nassau shuttle. However, no one knew how rapidly her sands were running out, for actually she had only five more months to live. On that fatal predawn morning of November 13, 1965, the old ship turned into a raging funeral pyre for more than four score innocent passengers, such as ourselves, and on just such a trip as we were to make.

However, in June of 1965, since by advance booking the *Yarmouth Castle's* schedule fitted our own, we were only too happy to avail ourselves of the transportation she provided. After all, it was to be for only one night. But Johanna's mumps were something else again. Naturally, we did not want her to be spreading any germs, about which, no doubt, the law had its opinions. But when you are sick, the best place to be is in your own bed at home and that is just what we had in mind for her. There were decided problems, however.

Our last day in Nassau was by no means fun-filled. Never one to do things halfway, Johanna had really come down with a fine case; her temperature was up and the glands in her neck were badly swollen and extremely painful. Her mother tried to keep things under control by liberal doses of a children's aspirin and cold compresses. But the poor little thing was fretful, dizzy and in considerable pain.

What should we do?

Despite the fact that my vacation ended two days hence, I wondered if I should try to extend it, and all four of us plan to stay on at the British Colonial until the storm passed—if they would keep us. Or, perhaps, should Johanna and her mother remain shut in at Nassau while Suzanne and I carried out our original schedule? Or should we all take the boat as planned, and, if the next day Johanna became any worse, at least we would be on home soil in the good old U.S.A.? However, if her condition were detected on the boat, would Johanna be seized by the U.S. quarantine officials when we reached Miami, and then whisked off to some pesthouse while I went to jail? To make inquiries about these grim possibilities would only expose our situation. All in all, whatever we had to do did not sound pleasant, and we had to decide upon a course of action very shortly. Then there would be no turning back.

Although she was unable to eat anything, Johanna felt a little better at noontime. At length, and with some trepidation, we decided that all of us would go ahead as originally arranged, take the boat that afternoon, and hope for the best. For the moment the aspirin and ice seemed to be keeping things under control. But, there were a couple of anxious hours after we gave up our hotel rooms and before we could go aboard ship. Eschewing the more exotic conveyance of a horse-drawn carriage (the horses in Nassau wear straw hats) to take us to the Prince George Wharf, we took an ordinary taxi and soon arrived at pier side. Our cabins were located on the boat deck, starboard side forward, Numbers 817 and 823. Unfortunately, these were not outside cabins, but they faced each other across a narrow passageway leading directly out on deck in one direction, and, in the other, in line with the ladies' washroom. I might remark that the occupants of both these cabins were among the missing and presumed dead in the subsequent tragedy.

Our accommodations seemed small compared to the *Oceanic*, with narrow upper and lower bunks running fore and aft on the inboard side, and hardly enough space for two people to turn around in front of them. However, they were undoubtedly more commodious than the "preposterous box" that Charles Dickens had complained so bitterly about when he made his classic transatlantic crossing on the pioneer Cunarder *Britannia*, more than a century earlier. He stated that a giraffe could more easily "be persuaded into a flower pot" than his wife's portmanteau could be fitted into the cabin.

Later, we liked our quarters even less as long night hours dragged. For the moment, though, we were happy to find them. There was a short delay while a steward could be located and persuaded into the cabins to clean them after the previous occupants. Obviously the *Yarmouth Castle* was not a taut ship and this little detail had been neglected. Johanna was immediately put to bed in the lower berth of Number 817 while I explored the boat until the 5:00 p.m. sailing time, still an hour or so thence.

Both *Yarmouth* and *Yarmouth Castle* were small ships, only 379 feet long. Originally painted black with a white superstructure, by the time they began making tropical cruises in the Caribbean for the Chadade Steamship Company, their original black hulls had been covered by numerous coats of white. Also, to attract a cruise clientele, some minor structural changes had been made to the decks overhanging the fantails, providing miniscule half-moon-shaped swimming pools filled during the hours the vessels were in port. This permitted their owners to proudly proclaim that they were "the only regularly-scheduled ships from Miami to Nassau and Freeport with swimming pools." Other modifications included small, individual air-conditioning units installed in the majority of the cabins and, since such gadgets as electric curlers and razors were not common in 1927, a variety of electric outlets were also added to the staterooms. To effect this modernization, hot wires were simply tacked along the wooden bulkheads and painted over.

On the *Yarmouth Castle*, the main deck forward was devoted to the pantry and a dining saloon, sporting gilded columns and capable of seating about 150 people. As the passenger capacity of the ship was in the neighborhood of 400, there were generally at least two sittings. The rest of the main deck was mostly passenger cabins, both inside ones and those with portholes. Decks above the main deck were made of wood and virtually all of the promenade deck, next higher, was also taken up by passenger quarters, with the outside cabin windows overlooking a narrow open deck running completely around the vessel. The boat deck was the highest one which carried staterooms. It accommodated the ship's officers forward, then a bank of cabins clustered around the fore stairwell, the vent from the galley range and the funnel trunk. This group included our cabins and extended to the ship's mid-length. The "fun" departments were located beyond—the Blue Lounge, the dimly-lit Neptune Bar, and the Neptune Ballroom with its calypso band. The main stairway was located around a small saloon between the Blue Lounge and the bar. The ballroom continued aft to a sort of patio, with tables overlooking the glorified blue bathtub which passed as the swimming pool. Nothing was very expansive or extravagant for, being designed merely as an overnight boat, all available space had been used to increase the passenger load, and there were no open decks topside as on the *Oceanic*. Passengers were expected to find their principal diversions ashore during the two full days provided while the ship was docked in Nassau. It served for the night merely as a place to sleep—"your floating hotel" for "the gayest, most carefree days and nights of your life," the inspired copy read.

All in all, the *Yarmouth Castle* had a brave, but specious baby-doll elegance, provided in part by the fish-net decor of the bar, the gilding and the many coats of gay paint intended to conceal the fact that the ship in actuality was a tired, sagging old dowager. But, as we said, we were not taking a glorious fun-filled three-day cruise, but merely an overnight boat ride home —and the sooner over the better.

One may well wonder why an antiquated firetrap, such as the soon-to-become infamous *Yarmouth Castle*, was permitted to operate at all—let alone for the virtually exclusive patronage of American tourists sailing out of an American port. Simply stated, there were loopholes or escape clauses in the maritime laws applying to vessels of foreign registry and they permitted entire fleets, unsafe by American standards, to get by in an area where American ships would be debarred. Though this annoyed the U.S. maritime unions, naturally the American public that patronized the boats were none the wiser, for they were enthusiastically endorsed by American travel agents whose business was to sell tickets—*caveat emptor*. However, a former captain of the Yarmouth Lines reported after the disaster that "anyone booking passage was taking a calculated risk."

Only two years earlier a glaring example of such hazard had been amply given in the case of the 1930 Dutch-built liner, *Johan Van Oldenbarnevelt*. In 1960, 30 years later, this venerable ship was sold to Greek interests and renamed *Lakonia*—a nice, substantial Cunard Line-sounding name. Though pronounced modern and seaworthy, the *Lakonia* met disaster in mid-Atlantic only 25 months before the *Yarmouth Castle* encountered a similar fate. On December 22, 1963, the old Dutch vessel was ravaged by fire at a cost of 125 lives. Obviously, she suffered serious deficiencies in fireproofing, in addition to irresponsible management, causing eight Greek officers to be charged with negligence.

The United States, of all countries, has enjoyed the strictest regulations for vessels flying our nation's flag. However, ship construction materials and arrangements considered safe in the 1920s and early 1930s, particularly connected with lifeboats and watertight bulkheads and doors, following the *Titanic*, experienced another rude awakening on the morning of September 5, 1934. This was when the four-year-old liner *Morro Castle* caught fire off the New Jersey coast while returning from a Havana cruise. Built at Newport News, Virginia, in 1930—only three years after the *Yarmouth Castle*—this fine, medium-size liner was strictly an A-1 Class ship enjoying all the life-saving and fire-warning devices then currently approved and adopted. But panic set in when the predawn fire broke out. A storm was raging, the ship was badly handled, communications broke down, some of the crew deserted their posts and, as a result, 134 people were burned to death or drowned (Chapter 9).

Expectedly, Newport News shipbuilders were gravely concerned, lest it be discovered that defective design or workmanship had caused the *Morro Castle* disaster. Initially, one widely-held theory was that improper maintenance of the oil-fired burners in the boiler room had caused overheating in the stacks, which turned them cherry-red. This, in turn, ignited plywood partitions in an adjacent writing room located just behind the uptakes. At length, however, it was circumstantially proven, by his subsequent behavior, that the fire on the *Morro Castle* was caused by a psychopathic arsonist who used an intricate and lethally effective infernal device for the purpose.

Meanwhile, after 1934, the U.S. government took a long, hard look at the various combustibles used in the construction of existing passenger ships and announced revised safety measures which, for new vessels, debarred the employment of wooden decks, partitions and paneling on all craft built for, or transferring into, United States registry. Greater emphasis was also put on fire screens, efficient sprinkler systems throughout all compartments, automatic fire alarms and other measures. These new fireproofing requirements were legalized by Congress on May 27, 1936, by the time that the Newport News Shipbuilding and Dry Dock Company began work on the liner *America*. As the largest and finest passenger ship to fly the American flag, when this vessel came out in the early summer of 1940, she reflected all the technological improvements available and used tested fire-resistant and fire-retardant materials throughout, even glass-fiber curtains. She was, however, criticized by many travelers for her drab gray marinite paneling, her spartan decor, absence of grand stairways (always excellent chimneys for a burning ship!), and general lack of fanciness throughout.

Following the *Morro Castle* tragedy, existing American vessels were allowed to continue to operate for a transition period under U.S. registry, despite the burnable materials in their construction. For this they were granted waivers by the U.S. Coast Guard. But what are familiarly termed "grandfather clauses" were designed ultimately to get rid of them all. When their times ran out, however, unless further waivers could be secured (as was perennially done for the venerable Mississippi River stern-wheel steamer *Delta Queen*) they could no longer fly the American flag. Since foreign vessels were operated less expensively on their own, less demanding regulations, there was, expectedly, a general exodus of the old American ships to these "runaway flags," or "flags of convenience." Unreasonable demands by crewmen and the capricious behavior of U.S. maritime unions were beginning to make the passenger carrying business unattractive to shipowners anyway. This, coupled with increasing transoceanic air travel, marked the progressive decline and present extinction of the American-owned and operated passenger ship, now unfortunately as dead as the dodo.

Both the *Yarmouth* and *Evangeline*, with exceptions allowed for their wooden decks, continued to operate for the Eastern Steamship Lines until the advent of World War II when the government took them over on January 6, 1942, for use as transports, for which they gave good service. Following the war, in 1946 and 1947 when they were being readied for civilian use again, the question of fireproofing their stairwells and replacing wooden decks with steel ones arose. The War Shipping Administration determined that this addition to topside weight would make them unseaworthy unless compensated by additional ballast. It was estimated that all this would bring about a total loss in deadweight capacity of some 450 tons, plus increasing the ship's draft—originally 18 feet—beyond acceptable limits. In the end, then, as the lesser of two evils, they returned to service under the same old "grandfather clause" waivers. But Eastern's coastwise service never properly came back after the war, and the *Evangeline* was laid up between 1948 and 1953 except for two and a half months in 1950 when she was reactivated to make ten trips to Nassau. So it was that in April, 1954, the two ships were "sold foreign" to assume Liberian registry, taking Monrovia as hailing port. Soon afterward, Eastern quietly went out of business for good.

During the ensuing decade, both *Yarmouth* and *Evangeline* went through several changes of ownership. Having adopted the flag of Panama in 1958, on April 16, 1964, half a dozen years later, the boats were acquired by the Chadade Steamship Company, chartered in Panama, but owned by a concern entitled Commander Investments, Ltd., of Nassau. It, in turn, was wholly owned by Jules Sokoloff, a Canadian shipping magnate. Prior to this, for unexplained reasons, previous owners had renamed the *Yarmouth*, the *Yarmouth Castle* in 1954, then renamed her *Queen of Nassau* in 1956. Curiously enough, she was again called the *Yarmouth Castle* later the same year. By 1958, however, the ship had returned to her original name of *Yarmouth* and, when he acquired both vessels in 1964, Sokoloff left the *Yarmouth's* name as it was, but christened the *Evangeline*, the *Yarmouth Castle*. These shenanigans have been the despair of steamship buffs, trying to keep the identities of the vessels straight at this stage in their careers.

From a legal point of view, the now called *Yarmouth* and *Yarmouth Castle* were operating in accordance with standards established during the 1960 International Convention on Safety of Life at Sea, to which the United States was a signatory. Though striving for vessels to be reliable in every respect, "SOLAS," first convened in 1914 following the *Titanic* disaster, and again convened in 1929 and 1948, permitted several major departures from restrictions required for the U.S. Merchant Marine. These, necessarily, we had to honor. They included the use of wood for decks and partitions, the "nesting" of lifeboats, with two boats using the same sets of davits, and such interior watertight compartmentation as provided floatation in case one compartment was flooded. American requirements were for floatation even if two compartments were full. Foreign ships could also operate with only one radioman on such short runs as the *Yarmouth* and *Yarmouth Castle* later assumed. Obviously, this would not permit a continuous listening watch as required by the United States and, on the *Yarmouth Castle*, it was customary for the radio operator, having stood his eight-hour watch, to go off duty at midnight.

Since the holding of diplomatic conferences to handle maritime safety was now considered insufficient to deal adequately with continuing problems (giant tankers were coming down the ways with increasing frequency and the wreck of the *Torrey Canyon* on March 18, 1967, with subsequent mass pollution of English waters, was just around the corner), SOLAS was being assisted continuously by a new specialized agency of the United Nations. This was titled the Intergovernmental Maritime Consultative Organization, or IMCO. Curiously, though seaworthiness was stressed, fireproofing of passenger vessels had then been limited merely to formation of a committee to study it.

Sokoloff first chartered the two *Yarmouths* to run between New York or Baltimore and the Bahamas, but the machinery being old and not properly maintained, was subject to breakdowns and the operators were unable to maintain even the modest promised speed of 15 knots. This was attributed to the occasional use of salt water to fill the boilers. The *Yarmouth Castle* came in 15 hours late on four sailings. This displeased her passengers mightily, as did leaks in the rotting, canvas-covered, boat deck roof, but it was nothing compared to later performances in which two whole shiploads were stranded on the dock in New York under circumstances that strongly suggested a swindle. This caused the bankruptcy of the operating agency of Caribbean Cruise Lines, Inc., which had chartered the ship. Sokoloff then

Yarmouth Castle docked at Prince George Wharf, Nassau, Bahama, on June 25, 1965, preparing for departure to Miami.

switched his vessels to the more leisurely, 186-mile, 15-hour Miami to Nassau run under his newly found subsidiary, Yarmouth Cruise Lines of Miami. And there they were, in June of 1965, when it came time for us to try to smuggle Johanna back home on board the *Yarmouth Castle*.

It was close to sailing time now and I was delighted that Johanna felt well enough to join me on deck to watch the traditional throwing of streamers and general hoopla attendant on departure. At length the ship's steam whistle gave its imperious blast, mooring lines were removed from the bollards, slithered off the side of the dock, splashing into the water as winches reeled them into the ship. The *Yarmouth Castle* was under way. I looked at Johanna with her scarf tied around her neck to hide the swelling, and uttered a little orison for the Lord's protection, not only for those in peril on the sea, but also with the mumps. We needed it on both counts. I also prayed that no emergency should arise which demanded the impossibility of my trying to call out to anyone in a loud voice.

Soon the harbor fell behind and the silhouette of our erstwhile home, the British Colonial, faded in the evening mists. In quest of a little Dutch courage for ourselves and ginger ale for the girls, we now moseyed on into the bar which by this time had filled up with enthusiastic cruise passengers. From the noise and conviviality it was obvious that there were many who were not going to pass up the opportunity for a last fling aboard. Some were badly sunburned, some were obviously bushed and some were already pretty drunk. They were the ones who, bent on getting their money's worth, we were to hear later on that night noisily roaming the passageways. I would be a feckless reporter if I did not chronicle the fact that, by and large, our fellow shipmates were a scruffy lot. One of them, an enormous, muscular woman whose bare arms were bedecked with tattoos, was truly a frightening creature.

Since we did not plan to leave Johanna by herself even for a moment, as soon as the first seating for dinner was announced, I descended the two decks to the dining room, quickly gobbled the meal and ordered ice cream for dessert. This I took back up to our cabin, hoping that Johanna would be able to eat a little. The *Yarmouth Castle* provided no such pampering as room service. Suzanne and her mother then repeated the process while I stood guard.

Fairly early in the evening the girls were bedded down in their respective berths. Johanna's temperature had now begun to shoot up to alarming proportions, and my wife thought we ought to tell the captain about her. I vetoed the suggestion on the grounds that, being Greek, he undoubtedly would not fully understand our predicament, could do nothing about it anyway, and would only report it to the ship's doctor. The doctor, in turn, could do no more than Johanna's mother was already doing and, in this case, the "cat would be out of the bag" as far as any attempt to unobtrusively slip her past the quarantine officials the next morning. Reluctantly this council of desperation prevailed and we sat tight.

Johanna was delirious and hot enough to set the stateroom on fire herself, even though her mother kept trying to cool her down with cold compresses. Outside on deck, it was a beautiful night with a bit of moonlight to silver the calm waters of Northeast Providence Channel. I am ashamed to say that I could not help enjoying it as the old ship trundled comfortably along at her leisurely 13- to 14-knot pace. Phosphorescence gleamed in her curling bow waves as she slowly ate up the miles toward the now-visible flash of Great Stirrup Cay Lighthouse, whence she would take a more westerly course aiming for the Florida peninsula.

By contrast, however, it was a long and agonizing vigil in the stuffy cabin watching the fretful little sleeper. The only diversion was to trace and retrace the electric wires coursing the bulkheads and wonder, almost mesmerized, if the ship suddenly might not spontaneously burst into flames, or at least be set afire by some drunk smoking in bed in the next cabin. Incredibly, the time somehow passed and dawn came at length. Fortunately, when she woke, Johanna felt somewhat better and we bestirred ourselves about getting

Yarmouth Castle approaching Miami after an overnight run from Nassau, June 1965.
Quarantine officials are being picked up from launch.

up. I abandoned the idea of taking a shower on the strength of the fact that, in addition to the washroom being insufferably hot, only hot water came out of the cold faucet and the hot one produced practically live steam. No wonder, the boiler was located directly below.

It was a lovely bright morning, and on deck we watched fascinated at what seemed an untidy stubble on the western horizon slowly materialize into Miami Beach skyscrapers gleaming in the sun. Journey's end was in sight at least. We took turns breakfasting, beginning at 7:30, an hour before the scheduled time of arrival at Yarmouth Lines Pier Three, Biscayne Boulevard and 12th Street. As we steamed up Biscayne Bay Channel, I watched with some trepidation as the port doctor and quarantine officials boarded the steamer from a launch that put out from shore to intercept her.

Johanna was carefully coached for her ensuing role in running the health department gauntlet. We decided, however, to wait until the majority of the passengers had made their ways through the lines set up in the ship's lounge. Our papers were in good order and I went first and handed them in. Then came Johanna, closely followed by her mother, to lend support if necessary. Suzanne brought up the rear. Following instructions, Johanna said nothing and looked like the shy child which we knew she was not. The silk scarf was closely tied around her neck and hid the swelling nicely. Then the moment of truth arrived, but no questions were asked and we went on through without a hitch. Apparently the officials were more interested in seeing how the papers looked than the passengers. Now authorized for entry, there was only a brief delay while we hauled our luggage ashore to go through customs. Fortunately, this was a detail I could attend to myself. Meanwhile the girls found a place to sit down in the big pier shed, away from the long tables where the *Yarmouth Castle's* passengers displayed their newly found possessions. It seemed an unconscionably long time before all tourists had their one gallon each of duty free liquor certified, their purchases of straw hats, bags and whatnots checked off and their luggage examined for contraband. But, at last it was over, and we were now free and clear Americans back in our native land again. In due coarse a taxi was hailed, our belongings and ourselves packed in, and we were off for the railway station.

Freed at length from her enjoinment to silence, Johanna's first remark to the taxi driver was, "Guess what! I've got the mumps!" Fortunately he thought this so preposterous as to be mere childish babble, and he laughed. But, by then, we hardly cared.

Apparently the night on the boat had seen the crisis in Johanna's condition and from then on, it was more or less plain sailing. The railroad station had a large air-conditioned waiting room and though we had some hours to kill until the train departed, the time passed swiftly enough. Finally, we were safely ensconced in our compartment and clickety-clicking on our way north to Virginia behind a pair of powerful, if asthmatic-sounding, diesel locomotives.

But it was a never-to-be-forgotten voyage that we had made on board the *Yarmouth Castle,* and we shall always remember the anxiety and dread of the experience. It was, then, with an almost I-told-you-so attitude that my wife listened to the early morning news of Saturday, November 13, 1965. The shocking story was disclosed that the *Yarmouth Castle* had caught fire on her way to Nassau, and that scores of people were missing and presumed burned to death or drowned—all this on a routine trip which might well have been our own!

———————

Of all the disasters to which mankind is prone, none perhaps can equal the horror of fire at sea at night. Expectedly, there is a morbid fascination in witnessing such a story unfold in the newsroom of a large daily paper and, since I worked on one, I hurried down to the Newport News *Daily Press* Building right after my wife told me what she had heard on the radio. I armed myself with a photograph of the *Yarmouth Castle* taken five months before, when we were about to make our own uncomfortable trip on the venerable "fun ship." But what a contrast! Our penultimate voyage had been filled with forebodings. But for the people on the *Yarmouth Castle* on this final one, it must have been sheer agony, desperation and terror.

The main facts of what happened were already known by midmorning, Saturday, November 13. Succeeding stories, follow-ups, interviews with survivors and rescuers, and updating the "missing and presumed dead" lists kept the *Daily Press* teletype machines busily clicking away throughout that day. First to be interviewed were the badly burned passengers, who had been picked up by U.S. Coast Guard helicopters and taken to Nassau from the principal rescue ship, the *Bahama Star*. Too late for that afternoon's *Times-Herald*, but useful for Page Ones all over the country the next day, were views of the *Bahama Star* upon her arrival at Prince George Wharf loaded with survivors, helicopters evacuating badly burned passengers from shipboard, and views of empty *Yarmouth Castle* lifeboats bobbing about the ocean, one upside down.

Since at first the wirephoto services had only stock pictures to offer of the *Yarmouth Castle* when she was the *Evangeline*, my just five-month-old print of the steamer came in handy right away for a local identification "side-bar" story. Apparently no Virginia Peninsula residents had been on board for that last voyage, but some were turned up who had traveled on the boat comparatively recently. John L. Lochhead, librarian at The Mariners Museum, contributed impressions gained years before, when he had been an Eastern Steamship Lines purser and regularly sailed the *Evangeline*.

Before that Saturday was over, it had been confirmed that 87 people were unaccounted for and presumed to have burned to death and gone down with the ship. In the ensuing days, three badly burned passengers died in hospitals in Nassau and Miami, bringing the grisly toll to 90 persons. Of this number there were 79 American tourists, nine passengers from other countries, and two *Yarmouth Castle* crew members—Phyllis Hall, a Jamaican stewardess, and the ship's surgeon, Dr. Lisardo Diaz-Torrens, a Cuban national, the person to whom Johanna's mumps were never reported.

Expectedly, there was considerable conflict of testimony as to the events of this terrible drama, and many disagreed over the sequence of events, and of just who did what, and when. There was also both praise and censure for the behavior of the officers and crew. This would be expected in such times of stress and anguish. The following gives a reasonably reconstructed account of what occurred during that fateful voyage ten years ago. Taken from contemporary news stories and interviews and, most importantly, from "Findings of Fact" derived from a formal Marine Board of Investigation convened November 22, 1965, a little more than a week after the disaster. This was ultimately issued by the U.S. Coast Guard on February 23, 1966.

Friday, November 12, 1965, was a lovely, warm, autumn day when 33-year-old Captain Byron Voutsinas mounted to the bridge of his 38-year-old command, the *Yarmouth Castle*, and gave the order to cast off. And so, with a complement of 176 crew and 379 passengers, the old ship steamed confidently out of Biscayne Bay on the second of her customary biweekly voyages to "exotic, glamorous Nassau." In addition to the usual shipload of expectant tourists making their $59-and-up poor man's Caribbean cruise, there were 60 members of the North Broward Senior Citizens Club from the Pompano Beach-Fort Lauderdale area.

Despite the *Yarmouth Castle's* age, decrepitude and lack of fire resistance, unsuspected by all but knowledgeable travelers, Captain Voutsinas was proud of his ship, subsequently claiming his first command was "the finest." She sailed with the full blessing of a U.S. Coast Guard inspection which had been made only the month before when the vessel was dry docked in Tampa, Florida, subsequent to a minor collision she had sustained with her sister ship, the *Yarmouth*, during Hurricane Betsy in mid-September. She was cleared, then, as on countless previous occasions, in accordance with standards—although not up to our own—admitted by the 1960 Convention on Safety of Life at Sea.

The weather was fine that night. The sea was smooth, the sky clear and a light southeasterly breeze hardly ruffled the water. After dinner—on the menu were Jamaican Red Bean Soup or Nassau Conch Chowder, followed by Florida Red Snapper a la Yarmouth, or Fresh Nassau Grouper Bahama Style, or Shrimp Creole, Roast Duckling, Veal Curry, or steak—the passengers disported themselves in ways wont of passengers since time immemorial. The drinkers drank, the dancers danced, the gamblers gamed, the lovers disappeared and the conversationalists chatted in the bar or lounges. However, with a long day's activity looming on the morrow, most of them had bedded down early, leaving, by midnight, the die-hards and the graveyard watch the ship all to themselves. Shortly thereafter, Alfonzo Martinez, the radio officer, switched his receiver to automatic alarm and quit the radio shack, located above the boat deck cabin roof aft of the chart house, and directly over the three-story forward stairwell. Not much later, when he tried to return to it to send out an SOS, the place was in flames and no distress call ever left the *Yarmouth Castle*.

Shortly after midnight on the thirteenth, with Cuban Second Mate Jose Rams de Leon, the helmsman, and two watchmen on the bridge, the *Yarmouth Castle* was steaming 14 knots, steady on course 101° true. At that point she was leaving Northwest Providence Channel passing between Great Isaac Light and Great Stirrup Cay, with New Providence Island then in the neighborhood of 60 miles away. Proceeding on a similar course about eight miles ahead was the 1953-built motor ship *Finnpulp*, a 413-foot freighter also bound for Nassau where she planned to pick up a partial cargo of rum. The freighter's name, of course, clearly gives away both her nationality, Finland, and one of her principal cargoes—wood pulp.

Behind the *Yarmouth Castle*, about a dozen miles and also headed for Nassau on the same course, was a competitor, the cruise liner *Bahama Star*, which, like the *Yarmouth Castle*, was a venerable American-built ship that had had other names, services and flags of convenience before settling down to the Bahama trade in her twilight years. Originally the New York and Puerto Rico liner *Borinquen* built at Quincy, Massachusetts, in 1931, the 7,000-ton *Bahama Star*, only four years younger than the 5,000-ton *Yarmouth Castle*, was at this moment owned by the Eastern Steamship Lines, Inc. This was a new Panamanian concern and had no connection with the long-defunct American Eastern Steamship Lines that originally built and owned the *Yarmouth* and *Evangeline*. It was obviously trading on that good name, however. Alas, the *Bahama Star* also came to a dramatic end only four and a half years later. She had made her last passenger trip to Nassau early in November, 1968, and then renamed *La Jenelle*, she was unfortunate enough to break her anchor chain and come ashore on Silver Strand Beach, California, on April 13, 1970. This was the eve of her planned conversion to the ignominious role of floating motel in Ventura County. A 60-mile wind was blowing, and a thousand spectators who lined the shore watched spellbound, as a daring helicopter pilot plucked two seamen from her collapsing bridge. This maneuver was far more difficult than the removal of *Yarmouth Castle* casualties had been during her earlier service as rescue, rather than smitten craft.

It was indeed fortunate that the *Yarmouth Castle* should have been in close proximity to two well-run ships whose lookouts, on reporting their first sight of flames, immediately sent them to aid the stricken cruiser. Without their seamanly assistance, the death toll would undoubtedly have been appalling. There had been no SOS, and vessels beyond visual distance would never have known that the *Yarmouth Castle* was in distress until too late.

First knowledge that something was amiss aboard the *Yarmouth Castle* came shortly after midnight, when several people simultaneously began smelling smoke in different locations throughout the ship. Apparently the first report was around 12:30 a.m., when one of the engine room watch called Chief Engineer George Vazeos to let him know that smoke was coming into the engine room through the natural draft ventilating system. The chief immediately set out on a search of the main deck pantry-galley-bake-shop area, but with negative results. Thus, no report was immediately made to the bridge. Going on to the ship's main entrance lobby, also on the main deck, the chief then ran into a night cleaner named Whyley, who reported that he had just encountered smoke coming in the ventilators in the men's toilet on the next higher promenade deck. More people joined what was beginning to become a desperate search for the source of the fire, as Whyley proceeded aft to start awakening the crew. The gift shop operator, Charlie Agero, fixed the time by his wrist watch at 12:45 a.m.

The search party now included aroused Captain Voutsinas, the cruise director, Jose Martinez, first mate, Francisco Argilagos Guerra, the switchboard operator, as well as other crewmen and a few passengers who had not yet gone to bed. There was considerable confusion and backing and filling as the search went on, but at length both fire and smoke were pinpointed as coming from Room Number 610, on the main deck close by the forward stairs, and from the men's toilet directly above it. This was an ominous discovery, for it meant that containing a fire already on two decks would be difficult if not impossible. Obviously, it must have gained considerable headway. Fire had spread out both vertically and horizontally through various void spaces between floors and ceilings, as well as in the ventilation ducts, many of which had been banked off when she was being air-conditioned. One of the passengers engaged in the search was Lloyd Lamm, a volunteer fireman from Pompano Beach. He had passed Number 610 and, as he went up the stairs to the promenade deck, he put his ear to the wall and could hear flames crackling inside what was identified at the subsequent hearings as the main galley ventilator trunk. This focused suspicion on a flue fire fed by grease, which had become hot enough to ignite adjacent wood paneling.

By the time fire hoses had been run out—one, for ominous reasons never revealed, had been completely severed at the point of connection with the fire main—and the engine room notified to start the fire pump, the blaze in Number 610 appeared to be well advanced. When, moments later, the door was either opened, pushed in, or fell in, flames burst out into the passageway and quickly mushroomed up the fore staircase, and aft through the port side main deck passageway. The fire was now obviously out of control, and hoses and extinguishers made no impression as it ravenously licked its way out in all directions feeding on the inflammable decks and bulkheads with their many, many coats of paint.

Leaving the Chief Engineer in charge, Captain Voutsinas hurried up the stairs to the bridge, one jump ahead of the flames. Word of trouble had come there around ten minutes past one. As soon as he arrived, the captain ordered the general alarm to be sounded. Although he and some other officers testified that this was in fact done, it was not corroborated by any passengers, many of whose first word of catastrophe came when someone—and they first thought they might be playful drunks—banged on their cabin doors. Apparently the ship's public address system was never used either. In any event, the signal to stop the engines was given from the bridge at 1:20 and, a minute later, the engine room watertight doors were closed by remote control. At the same time the helmsman was ordered to turn the ship to port, and the *Yarmouth Castle* slowly came to a stop, drifting broadside to the wind. The captain now belatedly asked his radio officer to send a distress signal, but flames mounting the fore stairwell by this time had burst through the overhead and ignited the radio shack. Thus, all that Martinez could do was attempt to transmit a message to the approaching rescue ships by a hand-held blinker light. The chart room aft of the bridge was now also on fire, and shortly thereafter bridge personnel were forced by smoke and flame to the narrow open deck in front of the wheelhouse.

Realizing that all was lost, at 1:25 Captain Voutsinas ordered the abandon-ship signal and the second mate broke one of the pilothouse windows and reached in to start the whistle by electrical control. But, by then it was impossible to remain even near the bridge, and apparently the complete signal of seven short and one long blast was never sounded.

Right after that, all those on the bridge deck climbed down to the boat deck and attempted to launch lifeboat Number Three on the starboard side, opposite the passageway leading past the cabins that our family had occupied five months earlier. Number Three was the ship's only motor lifeboat equipped with an emergency radio transmitter. The launching attempt was too late, however, as flames shooting out of the passage had already begun to work on it. The men then switched their efforts to lifeboat Number One, the next boat forward, also on the starboard side. After considerable difficulty, owing to the proximity of the fire, this boat was in fact lowered to the water. Captain Voutsinas immediately slid down a rope and got aboard along with the chief boatswain, Ines Gozan-Pinder, the staff captain, Pentagiotis Menegatos, and some others of the crew. By best estimate, the time was now 1:45 a.m.

Meanwhile, the chief mate and others had hurried aft in an attempt to aid stricken passengers now becoming trapped in their cabins by flames coursing the length of the passageways. Those occupying inside cabins were, of course, sealed in and soon incinerated. With flames licking their heels, others in the nick of time climbed, or were hauled, out of their stateroom windows by crew members. Alas, many of the senior citizens were too feeble or stout to make it. And, dreadfully enough, many windows, having been painted over, refused to open. They had to be broken in, thus adding to the hazard of frantic passengers, badly cut climbing through them.

The fire now extended across the full width of the ship, making it impossible to get from one end to the other except deep in the holds below the steel main deck. Burned and lacerated passengers had congregated in the bow, and ladders and ropes were lowered over the side. Number One lifeboat was in the water by this time and some of the people from the foredeck were able to swim over and climb aboard. However, after shooting off some flares, Captain Voutsinas suddenly ordered the boat to head for the approaching freighter *Finnpulp*. Remaining passengers and crew in the bow area, terror-stricken at apparently being abandoned, called to those in the lifeboat to stop and pick them up. And, as the boat rowed away, Second Mate Rams de Leon was heard to yell to the captain to come back, or he would rue the day he ever went off and abandoned his ship in what appeared an effort to save himself. One passenger, Mrs. Thomas Kneeland, corroborated this fact, quoting the mate as calling out to the captain, "I've got your number. You'll never sail again!" Voutsinas denied ever being given such an ominous warning. He later testified that he felt it absolutely necessary for him to reach the *Finnpulp* as soon as possible, to ask its captain to send out the SOS that they had been unable to get off from the *Yarmouth Castle*.

Seemingly, this was a tortured explanation, thought up after the event. Certainly, it was an offense to the intelligence of the master of the *Finnpulp* to assume that he would not have had sense enough to notify the authorities without being told. By then, naturally, the *Finnpulp* had routinely reported a ship on fire as soon as it was detected through binoculars. Immediately the Coast Guard prepared a massive search and rescue endeavor by sea and air, which ultimately included the dispatch of three airplanes, two helicopters and two 95-foot cutters. Human behavior is unpredictable in such time of stress, however, and as soon as he had off-loaded the injured passengers and some of his crew on the approaching freighter, Voutsinas returned to the *Yarmouth Castle* in the same lifeboat. He reboarded his ship by a ladder astern, and subsequently was enabled to make the claim that, although he had been the first person to leave the vessel, he was also the last.

Meanwhile, confusion and terror reigned aboard the stricken vessel. Though there were countless acts of heroism and dedication on the part of the crew, communication was nonexistent and apparently there was never any direction. Naturally an aura of *sauve qui peut* prevailed as, for example, when three crewmen, guided by their knowledge of the ship's layout, quietly went below through the forward hold to D Deck. Here they opened a port cargo sideport, then conveniently went overboard in a small boat that had been stowed there, for occasional use in painting the ship while in port.

Aft on the *Yarmouth Castle* it was now a race against time to get the remaining living passengers out of their cabins before fire sealed them off forever. Ship's hostess, Ruth Wright, a tower of strength, reported seeing crewmen breaking windows with their bare hands in their haste to free people trapped by flames in the passageways.

First indication that the ship was in trouble had come to the Neptune Bar and ballroom area on the boat deck just after one o'clock, when a passenger, Miss Erna Groener from Stateroom 832, burst in screaming, "Fire!" Shortly after, other passengers who were fleeing the mounting holocaust amidships began to arrive at the stern of the ship, mingling with crew members who had come up from the after crew's quarters. The crew helped passengers find life jackets—some even giving away their own—and helped them into them properly. Others manned the fire hoses. Low pressure was recorded at some stations by the fact that, inexplicably, the water main used to fill the swimming pool was discovered, too late, to have been left wide open.

The after lifeboats were also readied for lowering, but difficulties were encountered in the dark and confusion, and one boat davit winch refused to work. Ultimately five boats took to the water—Numbers 7, 9, 9A, 10 and 10A. Some people went down in the boats themselves and others left the *Yarmouth Castle* via lines, ladders, or by jumping overboard. Some slender main deck passengers made their escape through portholes, while various members of the crew left the vessel through the side cargo doors on the lower deck. By this time Captain Voutsinas had returned to the *Yarmouth Castle* in his lifeboat, had reboarded the ship and was assisting people off and into the boats clustered around the stern. By now, his former white uniform was blackened from head to toe.

While fire was raging through the upper decks, it remained comparatively calm below in the engine room spaces for the entire three and a half hours between the time smoke was first detected, and when the last of the "Black Gang" got out around four o'clock. It had been shortly after the routine blowing of boiler tubes that about 12:30 a.m. smoke was noticed coming through the topside ventilators. Notification of this situation was immediately made to Chief Vazeos and the bridge was called at 1:10. First Assistant Ataunasiosk Satama Topuios came down five minutes later to start the fire pump, followed by the sprinkler pump. Then the chief showed up and closed down all power ventilation blowers to check the spread of smoke throughout the ship. Moments later, at 1:20, the engine order telegraph from the bridge signaled all engines stop. To compensate for the fact that full steam was no longer needed on the main turbines, the firemen immediately cut out three of the four burners on each of the boilers then on line. Subsequently one burner each was restored to insure sufficient steam for all pumps to operate. From that time on, engine auxiliaries continued to work normally, with the ship's bilge pump also cut in around 3:00.

While the harrowing drama was being played out topside, for another hour Third Assistant Anargyros Dourabeis and one oiler remained quietly at their posts, the other members of the watch having departed when the main engines were stopped. However, realizing by then that the ship was doomed, and not relishing going to the bottom with her, as there was nothing more they could do, around 4:00 they, too, left the engine room and were among the last to climb out of a midships side port on D Deck.

Presumably some of the various pumps were still running normally when the abandoned *Yarmouth Castle* took her final plunge two hours later.

The *Yarmouth Castle's* fate was already sealed when at 1:30 a.m., the watch officer on the motor freighter *Finnpulp*, who had been tracking the cruise liner on radar and observing that she had been slowly gaining on his vessel, noted that the almost eight-mile range had suddenly begun to open, indicating that the other ship must have stopped. Seconds later, when he made a visual check and saw a bright glow coming from the ship astern, he notified the captain. Immediately the *Finnpulp* was turned around and headed back. The *Finnpulp* radio officer then tried to raise Nassau to report a vessel on fire, but failing to establish contact, he made his report to U.S. Coast Guard Radio, Miami, precisely at 1:54. Meanwhile *Finnpulp's* Captain Johan Lehto had called for all the turns he could get as the ship's speed increased from a leisurely 13 knots to about 16 or 17.

As she approached, towering flames were seen rising from the *Yarmouth Castle* midships. When she was about a third of a mile away, the freighter hove to and commenced putting down gangways and lowering lifeboats. Meanwhile, the *Yarmouth Castle's* lifeboat Number One arrived alongside. After he had taken four injured passengers and most of the 15 or 20 crew members on board his ship, Captain Lehto summarily ordered the *Yarmouth Castle* boat back to help its own ship. The *Finnpulp* had a power lifeboat and it was soon performing prodigies of rescue work, picking up people from the water and towing other oar-powered boats to the side of the rescue vessels.

"The Finnish people did a terrific job," was the appreciative comment of Captain Carl R. Brown, American shipmaster of the *Bahama Star*, whose own crew behaved in an inspired manner. The Finns now gave a further demonstration of their bravery. Taking a calculated risk, Captain Lehto nosed his ship in to the port bow of the *Yarmouth Castle* and thus, a number of stranded people were able to jump directly from one vessel to the other. Soon the *Finnpulp's* paint began to sizzle, and Captain Lehto backed her away lest she also catch fire.

The watch on *Bahama Star* observed flames coming from the vessel a dozen miles ahead of them at about the same time the *Yarmouth Castle's* predicament came to the attention of *Finnpulp*. Summoned immediately, for a second, Captain Brown thought that he was looking at a distant Cunard liner with spotlights illuminating an orange-red funnel, for so the color of the flames from the rival cruise ship first appeared at that distance. But it did not take him long to realize what was the trouble and he ordered the helmsman to "come left and steer for that ship."

The *Yarmouth Castle's* blinker light was soon observed, but no actual message was read or understood—not that one was needed, for by this time the midships section of the ship was seen wreathed in flame from the stack forward, including the bridge and radio shack. Cabins were brilliantly illuminated through portholes on all the decks down to the main. Light even shown through the hawse pipes.

As on the *Finnpulp*, the *Bahama Star* readied her boats for launching, and at about 2:25 a.m., when she came close aboard the *Yarmouth Castle* to starboard, all 14 were put in the water and started their rescue work. En route to the *Yarmouth Castle*, the *Bahama Star* passed three of the former vessel's own boats full of people, but Captain Brown did not stop, calling out that he would be back for them later. One of the boats caused its occupants considerable concern when it began to leak. Since it was not picked up until about two and a half hours later, it was fortunate that a pump was found on board that would work.

The situation on the after decks of the *Yarmouth Castle* was now desperate. People were screaming for help, and fear that at any moment the ship itself might explode, provided added terror. Immediately on arrival, Captain Brown, speaking in a calm, reasurring voice, used his bullhorn to plead with the *Yarmouth Castle's* people to get themselves overboard without delay by whatever means possible and that they would be saved. Many hesitated, however, for fear of sharks, but even they soon seemed less terrible than the searing flames. Every person who jumped was immediately retrieved and fortunately no sharks materialized. But some who could have survived, never made it over the rail.

Not long after four o'clock, apparently all living persons from the *Yarmouth Castle* had been pulled from the water and were either in the lifeboats or on board the rescue vessels. Already noted was Captain Voutsinas' firm claim that he was the last to leave the ship. There is no doubt that the *Yarmouth Castle's* master did remain on board until the end. However, Bill Gadner, chief engineer of the *Bahama Star*, who commanded one of that ship's lifeboats, had boarded the stricken liner to lend a hand in getting the passengers off. He reported to Captain Brown that he was confident when he came down a stern line into his boat that he had been the last man off the *Yarmouth Castle* alive. Actually, it makes little difference, and possibly crewmen leaving the liner via the D Deck ports were actually the last to go.

At the final tally, MV *Finnpulp* received 51 passengers, some badly burned, and 41 crew. She also picked up two *Yarmouth Castle* lifeboats, subsequently putting them ashore at Savannah when she called there for cargo on November 16. The *Bahama Star* took on board 240 passengers, also many dangerously injured, as well as 133 *Yarmouth Castle* crew, for a total saved by both ships of 465 people.

Meanwhile, U.S. Coast Guard aircraft had arrived on the scene in response to the *Finnpulp's* message. Beginning at exactly 5:13, the first of a dozen badly burned passengers from the *Bahama Star* and one from the *Finnpulp* were transported by helicopter to Nassau's Princess Margaret Hospital, whose staff had already been alerted for the grim work ahead. About this time the

361-foot American container ship *Floridian* had arrived in the area to offer assistance. But, by then all those able to be rescued had been taken care of. All three craft remained in the vicinity until dawn while lifeboats coursed back and forth making a thorough search of adjacent seas.

While fire was raging through the superstructure of the *Yarmouth Castle*, she lay hove-to with the wind over her starboard beam, gradually assuming a port list and going down slightly by the head. She had, of course, pumped gallons of water into her own vitals and had sunk low enough by four a.m., when the last people left, to let sea water enter the open cargo side port forward as she listed some seven to eight degrees. As the ship settled more,

Yarmouth Castle afire, November 13, 1965. *Photograph by John Masterson of Miami, passenger on the* Bahama Star. *Distributed by the Associated Press Wire Service. Courtesy of the Daily Press, Inc.*

the port list gradually increased until the port rail went underwater. She then began to settle rapidly, and at precisely 6:03 a.m. the still blazing hulk quickly rolled over, turned bottom up and sank bow first in a cloud of steam. Her position was approximately 25° 55' north latitude by 78° 06' west longitude.

Seconds before the *Yarmouth Castle* disappeared for the ocean depths some 1,710 feet below, air trapped within the hull made its escape through the funnel and ventilators with an eerie sound, described by several witnesses as resembling the moan of a child. Captain Lehto of the *Finnpulp* stated that it was "a noise I want to forget . . . the end of a nightmare." *Bahama Star's* Captain Brown stated that the "ship was making a sound like someone wailing," further likening it to "the wind moaning through the rigging of a sailing ship." "It was all over in less than a minute," he said. "And then there was a glorious sunrise."

Coast Guard planes circling overhead had a grandstand view of the death throes of the *Yarmouth Castle*. A newsman accompanying them, Gene Miller of the Miami *Herald*, cited flames rising an awesome 200 feet into the air, and Lieutenant Allen Dehmas remarked on the "great pall of smoke" 4,000 feet high floating above the blazing liner. "It was a terrible sight," confirmed helicopter pilot W.R. Cooper.

Shortly after the *Yarmouth Castle* disappeared, the Coast Guard dropped a dye marker in the water to locate the spot, and both *Finnpulp* and *Bahama Star* then made all speed for Nassau and the final accounting of the disaster. Their cargoes of blackened, bone-weary castaways, many in makeshift garb, had lined the rails to watch their former holiday ship sink beneath the waves. Behind was left an untidy sea with all manner of flotsam bobbing about amid the bubbles which continued to come up from the depths. No bodies were to be seen, but 87 of them now forever lay buried in storied Davy Jones' Locker. The *Yarmouth Castle* was gone, but certainly not forgotten. Nor apparently will she ever be, having joined that select company of infamous immortals including the steamers *Arctic*, *General Slocum*, *Titanic*, *Lusitania*, *Eastland*, *Morro Castle*, *Andrea Doria*, *Lakonia* and others.

As soon as the gangplanks of *Finnpulp* and *Bahama Star* were down at Prince George Wharf, crew and passengers who were able swarmed ashore into the waiting arms of an army of friends, relatives, Red Cross workers, steamship line agents, hospital corpsmen and newshawks who descended on them to grab up whatever scraps of information they could. *Life* magazine alone sent a team of ten reporters to the island. Expectedly Captain Voutsinas was nowhere to be seen. He did not show up until three days later at Miami when the preliminary U.S. Coast Guard investigation, headed by Captain V.C. Niebergall, in charge of the Seventh Coast Guard District's merchant marine safety division, began its sessions on November 15. But the Coast Guard had gotten a start even before then. Three officers were flown out by helicopter and lowered on board the rescue ships and were interviewing people and gathering facts even before they made port.

But if *Yarmouth Castle*'s skipper proved elusive, Captain Brown of the *Bahama Star* gladly held court for reporters, explaining that as far as the *Yarmouth Castle* officers were concerned, "they were following an old rule of the sea: talk to your lawyers first before giving out information." The 32-year-old master of the rescue ship, refraining from passing judgment, provided newsmen with a thorough and reasoned account of the catastrophe. He modestly cited his own efforts in pleading with "dazed and helpless" passengers to save them. No doubt he privately admitted: "There, but for the grace of God, goeth I."

Captain Brown's interview was published in full in the newspapers beginning November 15. Survivors consulted, however, were considerably more critical in their recital of events of the last cruise of the *Yarmouth Castle* and of the behavior of officers and crew. "It was a poorly run ship," summarized passenger Gerald McDonald. But he said he had "no quarrel with the crewmen—they did a very fine job."

Arrangements were quickly made for all who wanted to leave the island as soon as possible—for most, a tropical holiday was now out of the question anyway—and British Overseas Airways Corporation provided shuttle flights to the mainland. But, on arrival at Nassau on the morning of November 13, some 32 people were sufficiently injured to require hospitalization. One of them, Nathan Lehr, died the next day. Five others, Mr. and Mrs. Nathan Barkin, Anne M. Jackson, Peter Reich and Harvey W. Barton, were subsequently removed by air ambulance to the special burns clinic at Miami's Jackson Memorial Hospital. But, of this group, death soon took further toll. Mr. Barkin died November 20 and Miss Jackson on December 5.

For some, arrival at Nassau brought a happy ending when frantic families, who had become separated and brought ashore on different rescue ships, were reunited. Others, however, had their hopes dashed to the depths when loved ones could not be found. A particularly heart-rending case was that of two hysterical mothers, Mrs. Frank Wright and recently-widowed Mrs. Mary Hamilton, both of whom were to discover that their fourteen-year-old sons, Stephen Wright and Jonathan Hamilton, cabin mates on the boat, were among the missing. Courageous Mrs. Hamilton was badly burned herself and subsequently had to have a leg amputated. She was to spend the better part of the next two years in hospitals recuperating.

Mrs. Margaret Farrell told a frightening tale of becoming separated from her husband as they blindly groped their way along a smoke-filled passageway leading to the main stairs, burning her feet in the process, for she had forgotten her shoes, only to be shoved down and trampled in the panicky rush. A crewman found her and led her to a lifeboat. Ultimately she was taken to the *Bahama Star* where her husband had already arrived. Separation and reunion also happened to the Russell Moodys and the Francis Middletons. Others were not so fortunate, and even told of watching loved ones consumed in flame before their very eyes.

Especially harrowing was the account given by the survivor of a pair of New York widows, Adele Simister and Mabel Straub. Sealed off by flames in Cabin Number 615, which they shared on the main deck almost next door to the room where the fire started, the two ladies put on their life preservers. Mrs. Simister then climbed up on her suitcase and started to blow the whistle attached to her life jacket through the porthole. Just in time, Winton Roy Drysdale, a Jamaican waiter who also doubled as a singing entertainer, heard the whistle and swung himself down over the promenade deck rail, calling, "Lady, Lady, give me your hand." Mrs. Simister dropped her purse, watching it burst into flame on the floor behind her, then reached out to her rescuer. Drysdale managed to haul her out of the porthole while other crewmen grabbed her and drew her up to the promenade deck above. Told that there was another woman in the cabin, Drysdale then went down again—head first this time—for Mrs. Straub, also standing on the suitcase but with her clothing already ignited. She leaned out through the port and Drysdale made a grab for her outstretched arms, but the flames gushed up around her and she fell back never to rise again.

Expectedly, the North Broward Senior Citizens Club sustained a dreadful toll (almost half were missing), 27 of the 60 that had happily set out on their long-anticipated annual excursion on that fateful November 12. Every year since, they have held memorial services at Pompano Beach Cemetery for the

Yarmouth Castle dead. A honeymooning couple from Guatemala, Castillo and Mercedes Hurtarte, may well have died in each other's arms in Cabin N-1 at the forward end of the promenade deck—one of the *Yarmouth Castle's* cabins-de-luxe.

Mr. and Mrs. Nathan Barkin were sealed off in their cabin, Number 820 on the boat deck, by smoke and flame, but Barkin broke a window with his fist and they both managed to reach the deck. Nevertheless his wife was burned on both hands and legs and had her hair badly singed, while her husband sustained the injuries which later proved fatal. "It was horrible, just horrible," Mrs. Barkin said after they reached a lifeboat and temporary haven aboard the *Bahama Star.*

Arthur Gordon and his wife were awakened from a sound sleep by the commotion outside their cabin. When Gordon opened the door he found himself surrounded in flames. Quickly pulling back and slamming the door, he returned to the cabin, and they both crawled out of their narrow bathroom window to the deck. Gordon was badly burned, however, and was one of those picked up by helicopter and taken to the hospital at Nassau. While being X-rayed and treated for shock, Gordon was interviewed by a reporter. He summed it all up for virtually every passenger on the ill-fated liner, when he also said it was a "very, very horrible experience."

Expectedly, the bubbles had hardly stopped rising from the bottom before the owners of the *Yarmouth Castle* received summons to account in the courts, and by Tuesday, November 17, two damage suits had already been instituted. This tide would ultimately swell to some 440 claimants seeking a grand total of $59 million. The first suit was filed in the State Supreme Court of New York for two and a quarter million in behalf of Harry Ebner for his wife Sylvana, listed among the missing. The second, for one million, was by critically burned Anne Martin Jackson for her deceased mother, Louise Jackson. Nineteen days later, however, Miss Jackson joined her mother in death. Both these suits charged that the officers and crew of the *Yarmouth Castle* were "wholly inadequate" to operate the vessel safely, and that the owners had expressly registered the ship under a "flag of convenience" to escape United States safety regulations.

Similar litigation quickly followed. While the official Coast Guard investigation progressed, attorneys for the Chadade Steamship Company on December 9, 1965, petitioned the U.S. District Court in Miami to have its liability restricted to the paid-in passenger fares and the present value of the ship. Inasmuch as tangible remains now amounted only to the six lifeboats that escaped—at best, worth not much more than a thousand dollars apiece —and with the *Yarmouth Castle* herself patently valueless lying some 285 fathoms under the sea, the petition was denied. They then sought to have the damages assessed under the more lenient United States laws by which, unless fault or "privity" is demonstrated, the ship owner's liability is limited to $60 a ton. In the case of the *Yarmouth Castle*, this amounted to only about $350,000. However, claimants filed a motion asking the court to rule that Panamanian liability laws applied. This was a logical decision since the ship flew the flag of Panama and sank on the high seas. United States District Judge William O. Mehrtens handed down an order on April 6, 1966, stating that the territory of the damage under those circumstances is established by the nation of registry. He explained that the United States limitation of liability act was passed primarily to encourage American shipping, and to put it on an equal footing with foreign craft. Since the *Yarmouth Castle* had deliberately sought a "runaway flag" he stated that "there seems no basis in equity and justice upon which the foreign ship owner should be enabled to receive those benefits and yet evade the burdens that may accompany them."

Touché.

At length, however, the Chadade Steamship Company was assessed the relatively modest cost of $3,000 per life lost.

While waiting official authorization from the Republic of Panama to conduct a formal inquiry into the disaster to the Panamanian ship, the U.S. Coast Guard continued its preliminary investigation, started on board the rescue ships themselves. The Bahama government, too, was apparently only too happy for the United States to take over this responsibility, since it was determined the sinking took place outside their territorial waters.

From the first, the location where the fire seemed to have started, Room Number 610, was generally agreed upon and so testified to by Chief Engineer Vazeos. The actual cause was never conclusively established, however, an obvious impossibility with the *Yarmouth Castle* now at the bottom of the sea. Arson was suggested and as late as December 17, shipowner Sokoloff reported from Toronto that there was "no doubt in the world" that a firebug, disgruntled seaman, or even a professional arsonist had set the blaze. But he provided no proof.

One unfortunate former passenger, described as a 36-year-old "problem child," but not further identified, who had a history of mental illness and had been in institutions following fires of undetermined origin in his hometown, was scrutinized with particular care. But in the end, arson was dismissed in view of the preponderance of other, more logical reasons for fire to have broken out.

The condition of Room Number 610 and the equipment stored in it gave indication that either spontaneous combustion, defective electrical equipment, sparks from blowing the boiler tubes finding their way in through the ship's void spaces or ventilation ducts, carelessness with matches or cigarettes, or other personnel negligence had been the responsible factor. Originally intended as a washroom, Number 610 at one time had been finished off as a cabin for the ship's hostess. As such, however, the overheated room proved virtually untenable, being directly over the boilers and with the galley stovepipe located behind one of its walls. Fortunately for them, the hostesses were given better quarters thereafter. Under Chadade ownership, the cabin had then been stripped of its wood paneling, ceiling and all fixtures and was used as a storeroom for such miscellaneous items as cleaning materials, vacuum equipment, pieces of joiner work, broken furniture and spare bedding. Illumination came from a single naked light bulb with bare wire connections stretched across the room. There was no sprinkler head. Ventilation via the ship's blower system was provided by a vertical duct connecting with the toilets on both superior decks. Since the room had neither walls nor ceiling, being merely a metal shell, direct connection with the void spaces overhead could explain the ease with which the fire, once started, was enabled to spread out in all directions. As an example of good housekeeping the room was the very disaster which it so proved.

The fact that mattresses were stored in Number 610 was brought out when gift shop operator Charles Agero stated that earlier on the fateful evening of November 12, he had requested, and was brought, a spare mattress from that very room. One of the stewards delivered it to his cabin some time before midnight. This act proved that at the time the steward entered Number 610 everything was still normal. But he might well have been the one who triggered the disaster by cigarette carelessness, piling other mattresses against a worn electric cord or some other unintentional act.

At the official investigation convened at Miami on November 22, with Rear Admiral Louis M. Thayer, USCG, as chairman, an initial highlight was the showing of a 15-minute color movie taken by *Bahama Star* passenger John Johnson of Worthington, Ohio, a soft drink bottler. Typical of amateur movies, this started with the customary dockside farewells as Johnson sailed out on his weekend cruise to Nassau. Then in a flash, the scene shifted to a frightening night view of the *Yarmouth Castle* aflame, taken from the *Bahama Star* at a distance of about 250 yards. Johnson panned the full length of the burning ship, but most of his footage showed the forward part of the vessel between the pilothouse and funnel, where the fire was the most intense. For a ghastly second, three crouched figures could be seen running forward past a door, silhouetted against the flames ravaging the interior and showing through all windows and doorways. But, then the unfortunates had nowhere to go. Lifeboats burning at their davits and steel superstructure turned cherry red were also clearly delineated. Final daylight shots showed helicopters hoisting the injured off the deck of the *Bahama Star* in litter baskets and, on arrival at Nassau, nurses and corpsmen helping the injured ashore and into ambulances. The frequently mentioned "incredible speed" with which fire consumed the ship was fearfully depicted in Johnson's unforgettable film, which was televised in part on the CBS evening news. Stills made from individual frames were sent out by the Associated Press Wirephoto Services and, as a two-page spread, one appeared in full color in the November 26 issue of *Life*.

After the movie showing, plans of the ship, passenger and crew manifests and other documents were introduced at the inquest, as Captain Niebergall first took the witness stand to relate the long and latterly troubled history of the ill-fated cruise ship. A parade of witnesses was then progressively summoned. Captain Voutsinas was called on November 24. The board listened attentively to his seemingly lame explanation as to why he felt compelled to leave his ship in the first lifeboat, despite the second mate's warning that his career would be at stake if he did. This, Voutsinas claimed anew he had never heard. He also testified that he had only been absent from the *Yarmouth Castle* for a matter of ten minutes anyway. Nevertheless, Commander William Kesler, Jr., USCG, the Board of Inquiry's recorder, found it extraordinary that Voutsinas could have rowed 300 yards to the *Finnpulp*, unloaded a number of people and gotten back in that short time. "Maybe it was 15 minutes," the Greek captain then admitted, but subsequently said he must have been gone for more than half an hour. He also testified that he had later pleaded with Captain Brown for another lifeboat, but that the *Bahama Star* skipper had warned him away, lest the *Yarmouth Castle* should explode. Brown said, on the contrary, he had ordered his boats in as close to the flaming ship as possible for he knew that it would not explode, and he wanted to reduce to a minimum the distance the lifeboats must travel.

Other discrepancies occurred and Voutsinas did not come through as an entirely credible witness. The board appraised his behavior as a demonstration of negligence, "abandonment of command responsibility, and an overall failure to approach and cope with the difficulties attending the accomplishment of a task of this order of magnitude." Undoubtedly, his return to his ship after the *Finnpulp* caper was all that saved him from criminal action.

As with most of the other crewmen of the *Yarmouth Castle*, loss of the ship meant loss of their jobs as well. It was almost a year later, on September 7, 1966, that Voutsinas was granted United States citizenship. However, before he took the oath of allegiance, he expressly had read into the record his defense for having left his burning command. As a citizen of Greece, he had been unable to get work, but now, as a new American, he said he planned to ship out as captain of a freighter of U.S. registry. There is no record, however, of his ever having been granted a Coast Guard license and apparently he never got a command. Miami *Herald* staff writer Frank Greve reported in a 10-year anniversary story about the disaster published November 9, 1975, that Voutsinas, after briefly returning to Greece, shipped out as a crewman on a vessel plying between Houston, Texas, and Venezuela. Following this, he became a restaurateur at Hempstead, Long Island. But this did not work out and he sold his establishment in 1973. When last heard of, Greve reported, he was bound for Venezuela again.

In order to obtain a better picture of the *Yarmouth Castle*, her sister ship, *Yarmouth*, was held over in port at Miami on November 26, pending a safety check that one may be well assured on this occasion was by no means perfunctory. This gave the investigating team opportunity to hold one of its sessions on board the almost identical vessel, thus examining comparable layout and facilities.

In all, during the first three weeks, the board heard from 45 witnesses and produced some 1,507 pages of testimony. It then went into recess on December 13 to digest the material received. It determined that the mushroom effect of the fire was proven by the fact that, on the main deck amidships where it started, some 14 persons assigned cabins on that deck had perished. But 22 persons were missing from cabins on the next higher promenade deck just above, and 54 persons lost their lives on the still higher boat deck where the flames fanned out under the cabin roof. All occupants of these staterooms were passengers. The doctor and a stewardess were the two crew members lost, but under circumstances and in locations unknown to any witnesses. For what it is worth, the doctor's office was located at the extreme stern of the ship on the main deck. But the chances are that his end must have come elsewhere, possibly while ministering to an unfortunate passenger.

At length the Coast Guard issued its carefully considered report dated February 23, 1966. A 27-page document, it presented its findings of fact commencing with the names, addresses and cabin numbers assigned to all persons missing or dead. Then it gave a history of the ship from cradle to grave and, as best could be pieced together, a chronological recital of events leading up to and during the fire and rescue. Finally came some 22 closely-written paragraphs of conclusions, followed by two pages of recommendations.

Construction, physical condition, operation and management of the liner were all severely criticized. Specific items highlighted were failure to sound the general alarm; to use the radio while it was still possible; to use a public address system to alert passengers together with the unconscionable delay in informing them of danger. Also listed were: failure to maintain cabin windows and shutters so that they might be easily opened; failure of the master and officers "to take firm and positive action," negligence of the master in leaving the ship "alledgedly to go to the rescue vessel to assure the sending of the distress signal"; and the lack of organization of the ship for fire fighting or abandoning ship. A breakdown of communication between officers and crew was suggested by the many nationalities represented with a "Tower of Babel" effect militating against effective ship organization and comprehension of the problem.

About the only note of approval in the whole report was the statement that the rescue efforts of the *Bahama Star* and *Finnpulp* were "performed in an exemplary manner and in keeping with the highest traditions of the sea," and the board recommended that letters of commendation go out to them forthwith. Belatedly, about two years after the sinking, Captain Brown recalls, framed letters of commendation, signed by the Coast Guard Commandant, were presented.

Naturally, the Coast Guard was not the only agency concerned with the disaster of the *Yarmouth Castle*. The American public, judging by press coverage and editorial comment, which had not previously paid much attention to such things as flags of convenience flying from antiquated firetraps, was now up in arms demanding a scapegoat. It did not become similarly exercised, however, by the total of 166 people who had then only recently lost their lives in aircraft accidents—68 Argentine cadets near Panama on November 3; 58 passengers near Cincinnati on November 8; and 40 at Salt Lake City on November 11—or by the more than 500 persons alone who died on the nation's highways merely during the 1965 Thanksgiving holiday weekend occurring later the same month—such is the dramatic impact of disaster at sea compared to less glamorous means of losing one's life elsewhere.

As spokesman for an aroused citizenry, on December 11, 1965, the late syndicated columnist Drew Pearson listed in his popular *Washington Merry-go-Round* a roll call of more than 30 venerable foreign-registered ships which regularly called at American ports. These ships, although certified by the U.S. Coast Guard to pick up American passengers, did not meet even the 1960 SOLAS standards. This was Pearson's second nationally distributed column inspired by the *Yarmouth Castle*. The first, November 20, discussed the mystery of the ship's "tangled corporate network" ownership through a variety of apparently dummy corporations (Panamanian, Bahaman, Floridian and, curiously, Washington State) set up by Jules Sokoloff to gain tax advantages and avoidance of strict safety standards. Pearson was curious to learn who cashed in on the ship's insurance money. But this hardly proved a bonanza for Sokoloff. *Herald* writer Greve cited the Canadian's trail of bankrupt assets pledged to acquire not only the two antique cruise liners, but a

Miami Beach bank and a Florida apartment complex, all of which went down with the *Yarmouth Castle*. Greve also reported that Sokoloff now lives in a Los Angeles suburb, full of bitterness and still claiming that his ship had been sabotaged. His life since 1965 has been, he was quoted, "a series of deals that didn't pan out."

Eleven shipowning nations were cited in Pearson's roll call of antique liners with Panama providing not only the *Yarmouth* and *Bahama Star*, but also the 1931-built *Homeric* of the Home Lines, the new *Oceanic's* running mate on West Indies cruises. Most of the regular Caribbean tour boats— *Yarmouth* (1927), *Florida* (1931), *Bahama Star* (1931), *Viking Princess* (1950), *Ariadne* (1951), and so forth—Columnist Pearson rightfully concluded, "are creaky old vessels filled with combustible bulkheads and furnishings." Pearson's prophecy certainly came true as far as one of them was concerned. On April 8, 1966, only five months after the loss of the *Yarmouth Castle*, the Norwegian cruise ship *Viking Princess* was also destroyed by fire. Of a total of 496 persons on board, only two died—as the result of heart attack—when, on the last day of a Caribbean cruise, the ship was badly burned returning through the Windward Passage. The hulk was towed to Jamaica. Despite Pearson's emphasis on the ships' antiquity, it should be pointed out that age in itself is not necessarily a damning consideration. However, substandard maintenance over long periods, coupled with indifferent operation and command, can make the best built ship in the world a navigational hazard. Conversely, an old vessel, even if built of burnable materials, may well be reliable and seaworthy if properly cared for and operated, which the *Yarmouth Castle* was not.

All vessels on Pearson's roster squeezed by minimum safety regulations. The United States had but limited authority over ships flying the flags of the nations which had signed the SOLAS conventions. Thus, failure to grant them permission to load at American ports, by trying to enforce United States standards, would have become the cause of incidents of diplomatic consequence, subject to reprisals taken against U.S. vessels abroad.

Pearson commented upon the *Yarmouth Castle's* history of erratic behavior. He mentioned that for a brief period in 1954, when she was operating out of New York, the Coast Guard, complaining to the Panamanian consul there, actually had temporarily revoked her loading certificate. The reason given was that the crew obviously was not properly trained for fire and lifeboat drills. The owners rectified this in part by sending the *Yarmouth Castle* to Miami empty, then hiring a few trained crewmen and staging a satisfactory drill.

Late in 1954, however, when her tottery machinery finally broke down, stranding the passengers in New York, the ship was laid up several weeks for repairs. Before Sokoloff put her on the short Miami-Nassau run, Congressman William Mailliard, ranking Republican in the House Merchant Marine Committee, made the prophetic comment: "The *Yarmouth Castle* is certainly a shining example of a ship that was not in proper condition to engage in cruise trade."

But few listened to his warning.

Still another member of Congress, Representative Edward A. Garmatz, chairman of the Committee on Merchant Marine and Fisheries, had had prior occasion to become mightily displeased with the management of the *Yarmouth Castle* by what he felt were unscrupulous operators. Garmatz first entered the lists against fly-by-night, quick profit cruise ships following the stranding of the *Yarmouth Castle's* passengers in New York prior to her assuming Miami-Nassau service. His Bill (HR 10327) dated September 23, 1965, was to require operators of ocean cruises sailing from American ports, to file evidence of financial security and to post bonds sufficient to cover indemnification of passengers for nonperformance.

Report Number 1089 of the 89th Congress, First Session, cited the crying need for such legislation, citing in detail instances of passenger strandings by the MV *Riviera Prima* (soon to be renamed *Viking Princess*) and *Yarmouth Castle* in the summer of 1964. It then went on to report the "unfortunate fate" of the 1963 Christmas cruise of the 33-year-old *Lakonia*. Prophetically, it observed that "a similar fate might well lie in waiting for unwary citizens of the United States patronizing like ocean cruises." As with the warning of Congressman Mailliard, Garmatz's dire prediction also had no appreciable number of listeners. Yet less than two months later, the *Yarmouth Castle* all too tellingly made his prophecy come true and the *Viking Princess* followed suit five months later.

Garmatz then swung into high gear, announcing as early as November 21, 1965, that his committee would begin an in-depth investigation in January when Congress reconvened. In order to obtain the best possible professional advice, he assigned Emeritus Professor H.L. Seward of Yale, retired Coast Guard Rear Admiral H.C. Shepherd, and Commodore E.M. Webster, USCG, to the task. These men, plus recently deceased Vice Admiral E.L. Cochrane, USN, had served on an investigation board looking into the disastrous collision off Nantucket of the *Andrea Doria* and the *Stockholm* July 25, 1963. Their 28-page document on the *Yarmouth Castle*, dated April 11, 1966, was issued as House Report Number 1445 on April 20. Paralleling, but also going beyond the scope of the earlier Coast Guard investigation, it proceeded to attack the problem of safety at sea from the diplomatic angle as the Coast Guard board members had urged. Perhaps its strongest recommendation, following the insistence that all future passenger ships be fireproofed, was for the elimination of the all-too-convenient "escape" provisions available under the 1960 SOLAS regulations.

The committee also excoriated the operators of the *Yarmouth Castle* for their poor housekeeping, substandard operation under previously allowed immunity from safety standards, ineffective radio performance, and lack of "reasonable intercommunication between the responsible officers and members of the crew for purposes of effective ship organization."

"There is little evidence the *Yarmouth Castle* was efficiently manned and operated when it met with disaster" was the scathing summary.

But, after all, the *Yarmouth Castle* had been a Panamanian ship, operated in accordance with that nation's laws. Obviously, rectification would have to be made on an international front. While Congress was deliberating upon Mr. Garmatz's remarks, the U.S. State Department triggered action leading to an extraordinary session of the Maritime Safety Committee of IMCO held in London May 2, 1966. This was to consider amendments to existing SOLAS requirements in the realm of improved fire resistance of new and existing passenger craft.

Following Garmatz's strongly and reasonably presented report, at length on November 6, 1966—almost a full year after the disaster—Bill HR 10327 was signed into law. Stricter safety standards were now to require adherence, and foreign carriers were to demonstrate fiscal responsibility when they traded in this country. The law was to take effect November 1, 1968, after which noncomplying ships might be excluded from doing business in the United States.

Curiously, when IMCO met in the autumn of 1966 to pass the new safety rules discussed earlier in the year (which included the U.S. demand for the elimination of the "grandfather clause") both Spain and Greece, notorious operators of obsolete vessels, dissented and the Soviet Union and its satellites abstained, voicing opposition. In the end, though IMCO's new rules were still by no means as strict as the United States would have wished, the Senate ratified the new convention which President Johnson duly signed in March, 1967.

Even though it took considerable time for the legal aspects spurred by the *Yarmouth Castle* to come into effect, popular sentiment immediately began to raise havoc with the existing foreign operators' Caribbean cruises. Without the *Yarmouth Castle*, the *Yarmouth* continued a lopsided service for a while but missed several sailings while being upgraded. Finally, in April of 1966, she was laid up and subsequently sold to the Hellenic International Lines. She continued under the Panamanian flag in the Caribbean area, but now the already much renamed ship was renamed again. From *Yarmouth* she had gone to *Yarmouth Castle*, to *Queen of Nassau*, back to *Yarmouth Castle* and back to *Yarmouth*. In 1967 she went to Colombia and took on the name *San Andres* and, finally, the following year, *Elisabeth A.* About this time she left the Caribbean for good and headed for the eastern Mediterranean. Current editions of *Lloyd's Register* list her owners as Portside Shipping (Cyprus) with home port of Famagusta. What befell her during the Turkish invasion of Cyprus in the summer of 1974 is unknown. But Captain Brown of the *Bahama Star* and presently a Port of Miami harbor pilot—in 1969 the youngest man to achieve such a prestigious job—contends that the *Yarmouth*, 48 years old as of this writing, having served in the Aegean, may well be laid up now at Salamis Bay, Greece, with several other antique liners. In any event, Portside Shipping went into bankruptcy and was dissolved. According to Ambassador William R. Crawford, the ship's registration at Famagusta was cancelled because of nonpayment of fees.

Yarmouth Cruise Lines, Inc., of Miami immediately announced plans to bolster its sagging reputation by stating that they intended to replace the two *Yarmouths* with new, high-speed, passenger ships built to conform to all safety requirements. Though United States maritime unions pricked up their ears, Yarmouth Lines emphasized that they would continue to use foreign registered ships. Preliminary design plans and specifications prepared by the New York naval architectural firm of John J. McMullen Associates called for 21-knot, 520-foot, 14,000-ton liners. But in the end, nothing came of them.

Expectedly, this nation's maritime unions were moved by the *Yarmouth Castle* disaster, looking upon it as a way to revive the dying U.S. passenger services by citing this proof of the unreliability of foreign-run ships. The National Maritime Union had placed a conspicuous advertisement in the *New York Times* travel section on Sunday, November 21, 1965, headed: "HOW MANY *YARMOUTH CASTLES?*" and it urged prospective cruise passengers to write to their congressmen. The unions hoped that by strengthening the requirements of SOLAS, it still might make it acceptable for American

Johanna Hewlett Brown shown at Shipley School examining ten-year-old *Yarmouth Castle* brochure. She traveled on the boat in June 1965, when at age 7 she had the mumps.

owners to go back to using U.S. registry and not espouse foreign flags. They were correct, of course, in their assumption that the stricter United States requirements had encouraged a flight from the flag originally, but now, since strict regulations were to apply to foreigners as well, they hoped that the flags of convenience, which had contrived to keep the old firetraps sailing, would no longer prove so convenient.

A decade has now passed and, although foreign ships calling at American ports are far better equipped and manned, unfortunately the decline of the American flag passenger ship could not be arrested and is presently complete. With the mighty *United States*, world's finest and fastest liner (also the safest) in permanent lay-up status at Norfolk since her withdrawal from service in 1970, the U.S. East Coast has but two passenger vessels in operation under American colors. They are the 1971 *New Shoreham* of Warren, Rhode Island, a 125-foot, 60-passenger mini-liner which operates in New England and the Canadian Maritimes in the summer, and in Florida and the Bahamas in winter, and the somewhat larger 1975 rival mini-cruiser *American Eagle* of Haddam, Connecticut, which accommodates a similar number of passengers. In spring and fall both make annual transfers north and south via the Atlantic Intracoastal Waterway.

Today, the *Yarmouth Castle* and her 87 victims remain untroubled in the ocean depths while balmy breezes ruffle the blue Caribbean waters more than a third of a mile above. Except for those closely identified with the disaster, and who suffered grievous personal losses of family or friends which they will never get over, and survivors who are still haunted by that night of terror, within this decade the ill-fated liner has been all but forgotten. *Herald* writer Greve recently interviewed many of them in the Miami area and found this all too true. Loss of life has always been the prime mover to safety improvements in all forms of transportation, but, as with the stolen horse, we rush too late to secure the barn door for that particular animal. Yet, trite as the observation may seem, the *Yarmouth Castle's* company did not die entirely in vain. Gone now are the floating firetraps from American waters, present operators of cruise ships carrying American passengers have demonstrable responsibility.

Virginia's much admired First District Congressman Thomas N. Downing of Newport News, chairman, Subcommittee on Merchant Marine, Merchant Marine and Fisheries in the U.S. House of Representatives, is justifiably proud of his role in support of Public Law 89-777, which contrived to banish such unseaworthy craft as the *Yarmouth Castle* from the American scene.

The loss of the 90 persons in the fire on the *Yarmouth Castle*, followed by two more deaths five months later when the *Viking Princess* burned, contrived to give Congress the support it needed to enact the legislation passed on November 6, 1966. Describing the law and its effects, Congressman Downing stated:

Public Law 89-777 is the basic safety legislation which has been enacted since the loss of the *Yarmouth Castle*, in order to protect our citizens who take foreign-flag passenger vessels from United States' ports. The provisions of law set forth in Public Law 89-777 have been amended on more than one occasion since then, and generally protect our citizens in three basic respects:

(a) The American citizen is warned before he takes a cruise on what I would consider a substandard vessel, as all passengers must be notified, and all advertising must clearly state the safety standards with which the vessel complies. This has generally forced the owners of vessels which fail to comply with modern safety standards to upgrade their vessels or remove them from U.S. trade routes.

(b) It is now much safer for the American citizen while aboard such vessels, as a passenger vessel generally may not depart from our ports with U.S. citizens if it does not comply with certain safety standards. These standards are much higher than those of the ill-fated *Yarmouth Castle*.

(c) The American citizen can now effectively sue, should misfortune occur, as the owners of passenger vessels are required to maintain adequate assets or insurance so that they will be financially responsible to pay judgments for death or injury. This requirement has generally increased the insurance costs to operators of vessels not complying with modern safety standards so as to make the vessels' continued operation economically unfeasible without an upgrading of safety standards.

Congressman Downing praised the U.S. Coast Guard for its present vigorous enforcement of these new standards, concluding, modestly, "I am pleased to have played a small part in the enactment of this landmark legislation."

So has greater protection at sea been gained from time immemorial. The required use of the newly-invented steam whistle, and the establishment of Maury's separate east- and west-bound lanes for transatlantic steamers, came out of the loss by collision in fog-shrouded seas of the liner *Arctic* in 1854. The "unsinkable" *Titanic* in 1912 brought about the concept of lifeboats for all on board, and the subsequent establishment of the International Ice Patrol to report North Atlantic icebergs. Criminal overloading of passengers stopped with the capsizing of the top-heavy *Eastland* in Chicago in 1915. And the 1934 *Morro Castle* concluded what the 1904 excursion boat *General Slocum* had begun, namely eliminating the employment of virtually all combustible materials by American shipbuilders.

Many other improvements, both great and small, have come in the wake of catastrophe. Following the death of all 92 persons on board Flight 514 of a Trans World Airways Boeing 727 when it crashed into a Blue Ridge mountaintop in northern Virginia on December 1, 1974, *Time* magazine reported in its December 23 issue that an electronic device of proven benefit, entitled a ground proximity warning system, might have saved the plane. It further reported that the device should become mandatory equipment for all U.S. airlines. At the official National Transportation Board Safety inquiry held in Washington in late January, 1975, the major stress of testimony was laid on human failure, by reason of demonstrated lack of complete understanding between ground controllers at Dulles Airport and those in the cockpit of the ill-fated plane. However, the proximity warning instrument, which indicates forcefully when a plane is on a collision course with an obstruction in time for it to pull up and avert it, obviously has great advantages and is to be in universal use, *Time* reports, by December 1, 1975. Apparently, though, it has taken virtually an identical number of lives as were lost on the *Yarmouth Castle* to induce the Federal Aviation Administration to accede to the long-urged request of the advisory National Transportation Board. That is, it requires aircraft to be equipped with this safety measure costing presently in the neighborhood of $10,000. Without it, however, it might well be argued that the ill-fated 727 was no more airworthy than the fire-prone *Yarmouth Castle* had been fit to put to sea. Hopefully, there will be a continuing course upward in the never-ending quest for safety—whether it be at sea, on land, or in the air.

Expectedly, we shall never forget the *Yarmouth Castle*. And we will remain eternally grateful that ten years ago our mumps-infected child was returned home safely on board the weary old ship. How tragic, though, that 90 people never made it back.

The general cargo freighter *Finncastle*, shown here at anchor at Newport News, December 4, 1965, is a sister ship of the heroic *Finnpulp*, which, three weeks before, had assisted in rescuing people from the ill-fated cruise ship *Yarmouth Castle* off Nassau. Looking the ship over from the end of a Chesapeake and Ohio Railway pier is then seven-year-old Johanna H. Brown who had been a passenger on the soon to be incinerated *Yarmouth Castle* six months earlier.

Index

Index

Italicized numerals indicate pages on which photographs of subjects appear.